the airbnb story

How to Disrupt an Industry, Make Billions of Dollars ... and Plenty of Enemies

Leigh Gallagher

1 3 5 7 9 10 8 6 4 2

Virgin Books, an imprint of Ebury Publishing,
20 Vauxhall Bridge Road,
London SW1V 2SA

Virgin Books is part of the Penguin Random House group of companies
whose addresses can be found at global.penguinrandomhouse.com

Penguin
Random House
UK

First published in the United Kingdom by Virgin Books in 2017
This edition published in the United Kingdom by Virgin Books in 2018

www.penguin.co.uk

A CIP catalogue record for this book is available from the British Library

ISBN 9780753545591

Printed and bound in Great Britain by Clays Ltd, St Ives PLC

Penguin Random House is committed to a sustainable future for
our business, our readers and our planet. This book is made
from Forest Stewardship Council® certified paper.

MIX
Paper from
responsible sources
FSC® C018179
FSC
www.fsc.org

For Gil, Zeb, Anna, Noa, and Ava,
the ultimate home sharers

the airbnb story

Contents

Introduction   ix

1. The Hustle   1
2. Building a Company   34
3. Airbnb Nation   58
4. The Bad and the Ugly   80
5. Air Rage   105
6. Hospitality, Disrupted   138
7. Learning to Lead   161
8. What's Next?   190

Epilogue   211
Acknowledgments   215
Notes   218
Index   229

Introduction

BRIAN CHESKY AND I were sitting across from each other in the velvet, high-backed, regal-feeling chairs of the lobby bar of the Fairmont San Francisco hotel.

It was early November 2015, and we were there so that I could talk to him about the idea of writing a book about his company, the "home-sharing" platform Airbnb, to use the phrase the company has been so successful at popularizing. There was some irony in the fact that we were at a hotel, and not just any hotel: this was the exact venue that hosted the international design conference in 2007 that had maxed out San Francisco's hotel supply and had given Chesky and his cofounder Joe Gebbia their goofy idea to rent out air mattresses on the floor of their three-bedroom apartment in the South of Market district.

Indeed, it was fewer than thirty feet from where we were sitting where Chesky had walked up to one of the designers he'd most revered to tell him about this new business idea, only to have him immediately dismiss it as ridiculous ("I hope that's not the only idea you're working on" were his words). That comment would mark the start of a long stretch of painful rejection and ridicule. But it also marked the start of Airbnb, the company that Chesky now commands, a juggernaut today with a $30 billion private-market valuation, some one hundred forty million "guest arrivals," to use the company's term for tracking the travelers who book on its platform, and an inventory that is three million listings strong. (A note on metrics: the phrase "guest arrivals" refers to the number of people who have arrived at an Airbnb listing for a new trip, a term the company uses to be consistent with international tourism standards; this book will henceforth refer to this number as either "guest arrivals" or "guests.") At this point, Chesky frequents hotels only really for speaking engagements, and he had come to this one to address the Fortune Global Forum, my place of employ's annual gathering of CEOs from around the world. Chesky's speaking slot was in between former U.S. secretary of defense Leon Panetta and Jamie Dimon, CEO of JPMorgan Chase.

Chesky and I had regrouped afterward in the lounge to talk about the project I was proposing. I thought Chesky would be open to my idea, and he was — but not without some reservations. "The problem with a book," he says, clearly having given it some thought, "is that it's a fixed imprint of a company at a particular moment in time." I wasn't sure where he was going, so I asked him to elaborate. "I'm thirty-four," he continued. "Our company is young. We're going to go on to do many more things from here." His point was that it was still early in the game. Whatever I would publish in 2017 about Airbnb, he said, would very quickly be outdated, yet that's what readers would remember. The media, he pointed out, were already behind: "Where everyone thinks Airbnb is today," he said, "is where we were two years ago."

The thought reflected Chesky's ambition as much as it reflected his pragmatism. But he said he was open to cooperating for the book, and he trusted me to get it right. The meeting was ten minutes long. It was a good day: the night before, after a protracted fight, Airbnb had successfully beat back a ballot initiative in San Francisco to dramatically curb its operations. Chesky was soon leaving for Paris for the Airbnb Open, the company's annual celebration of its "hosts" — those people who deliver the product upon which the Airbnb platform is based. As we left the lounge, he talked excitedly about what the company had planned: on one single evening, hundreds of Parisian hosts were scheduled to open their homes to the entire group for a series of coordinated dinners all across the City of Lights. "It's going to be one of the world's largest simultaneous dinner parties," he said excitedly.

And with that, the thirty-four-year-old billionaire left the room.

The first time I heard about Airbnb was in 2008. At the time, I was in charge of the section of *Fortune* magazine that covered the quirkier side of business, and we'd gotten word about a couple of scrappy entrepreneurs who were gaining some attention during the 2008 presidential election season for hawking collectors'-edition boxes of fictitious breakfast cereals called Obama O's and Cap'n McCain's. They were recent Rhode Island School of Design grads trying to build word of mouth for their newly formed start-up, AirBed & Breakfast, which let people rent out sleeping quarters in their homes to other people who needed a place to stay. I thought the business idea itself was nothing new, but the cereal gimmick was plucky and had gotten some national attention, so we ginned up a short piece on it to run in *Fortune.* I didn't give it more than a passing thought.

Over the next year or two, though, the company started to gain buzz, edging onto the radar of our tech-reporting team. Someone brought it up internally as a company to watch. Wait a minute, I thought. *Those* guys? I was not involved with *Fortune*'s tech coverage, which meant that I didn't always know what I was talking about when it came to the companies coming out of Silicon Valley. But I also felt that distance gave me a healthy arms'-length perspective on the self-important euphoria that seemed to waft out of the region. As the keeper of *Fortune*'s "40 under 40" list, I was also used to breathless pitches from companies claiming they would change the world in one year's time, only to be significantly humbled the next. I sometimes took a certain amount of pleasure in pointing out when I thought certain ideas were overblown and overhyped. This new company, I thought, was one of them.

I made a mental list of all the other companies that already existed that offered the ability to rent someone's home or space in it: Home Away.com, VRBO.com, Couchsurfing.com, BedandBreakfast.com. I wondered how this new company could be so different. What is it about these tech start-ups, I remember grousing to a colleague, that think they can take an old, unoriginal idea; gloss it up with a slick, minimalist, design-friendly website; and re-release it back onto the marketplace as something new?

But this company was going to be different from all those others, and in a short time that would become clear. Soon, Airbnb had become a "thing." You could rent someone's home for a night, but people had also started to upload quirkier spaces: a treehouse, a houseboat, a castle, a tepee. Millennials in particular were drawn to this new way to travel that was both affordable and adventurous; you could stay in people's homes in neighborhoods off the conventional tourism grid, connecting with like-minded souls, for much less than the cost of a hotel. Listings and bookings started to catch fire. As early as 2011, Airbnb raised a mega $112 million from backers, was valued by investors at more than a billion dollars, and had booked one million overnight stays on its platform. Over the next few years, it would leave those figures in the dust: one million bookings turned into five, ten, fifty, and then one hundred forty million "guest arrivals" by the end of 2016 — some seventy million of which had occurred in just the past twelve months. Its valuation jumped to $10 billion, to $25 billion, and to $30 billion, where it sits as of this writing. Yet the company still has low awareness and low penetration in the housing market. Analysts predict it will get many times larger than it is today.

It's hard to look at any phenomenon with that kind of growth without trying to understand just why it took off. Part of it was economic: coming as it did right out of the Great Recession, it offered a way for everyday people to make money off of their homes and a much more affordable way to travel. Its first adopters were millennials, the swelling demographic that were coming into their own as apartment-dwellers, but, curiously, the average age of a host in the United States is forty-three. As incomes started to slow in recent years and housing prices in cities began to climb, anyone could monetize their home via Airbnb, even if they didn't own it. The average U.S. host made around $6,000 a year in 2015, but many make a lot more than that (like "home sharing," the terms "host" and "guest" favor Airbnb but have been widely adopted as standard, so I use them here without irony). Travelers loved it, too, for both the prices and the unique experiences it afforded them. Studies have shown that while many people still haven't used Airbnb, when they do try it, they often become regular users.

But Airbnb tapped into something greater than low prices and an abundance of available inventory. It offered an experience that was special and different. Even its imperfections fed into a growing desire for a travel experience that felt a little smaller-scale and more "artisanal" than staying at a standard hotel. It also opened up access to different kinds of neighborhoods than traditional tourist zones, so you could have an experience that felt more local, an advantage Airbnb heavily pushes. These elements were particularly powerful for millennials, who have exhibited a growing dissatisfaction with big brands and a greater sense of adventure, and who grew up so accustomed to digital-only interactions that venturing into the home of someone they'd connected with online wasn't much of a stretch. Many of the rest of us found these characteristics appealing, too.

But this newfound opportunity to stay in other people's homes also fed a greater need — one for an experience that offered more of a human connection. Staying in an Airbnb or hosting someone in your home is a highly intimate exchange; even if the person who lives there isn't there, he or she has prepared an experience for you and gone out of the way for you. Stepping hesitantly into someone's private space, in a corner of a city you wouldn't typically have access to, really can deliver a feeling, however slight, of having connected with another person. If the resident is there, those conditions can often be stronger. (One of the company's early slogans, which it still uses today, was "travel like a human.")

Of course, things can go wrong, and they have. But every time they don't — which is most of the time — yields a little vote of confidence in our fellow humanity. And this has come at a time when our society has become more disconnected than ever, with record numbers of people living alone, spending more time isolated in our cars, spread out in suburban homes, lost in our work, or simply wandering around with our heads down and earbuds sealed in.

Airbnb has a saying for this: it calls it "belonging anywhere," the company's mission, which it champions relentlessly. It says its platform enables a "transformative" experience called the "belong anywhere transformation journey." The company's over-the-top idealism is easy to dismiss, but the experience that it offers does address something that has been lost as we have grown more distant from one another. Staying in a unique, authentic space that's been prepared for you by a real person — even if it's a property-management company, which Airbnb has more of these days, especially in traditional vacation destinations — touches upon something we may not have been aware was missing.

Of course, not everyone feels this way, and Airbnb's growth hasn't come without its complications. In many cities and municipalities around the world, the fundamental activity enabled by Airbnb — individuals' renting out some or all of their homes to other individuals for a short period of time — is illegal. The laws vary from city to city and from country to country, but as Airbnb grew, so did the opposition from critics who started using those laws to try to curtail this massive disrupter at their door. The fight has brought together an odd coalition of liberal politicians, the real estate lobby, labor unions, and the hotel industry, where any mention of Airbnb has now become a third rail. Condo associations and residents in many cities, meanwhile, have protested the parade of transient visitors Airbnb has suddenly created in their buildings and the changes they have brought to their neighborhoods. Among other things, these opponents say that Airbnb is teeming with professional real estate operators who have hoarded housing units to turn them into full-time use on Airbnb. They claim this has kept housing off the market and worsened an affordable-housing crisis in many markets. In a handful of cities, including New York and San Francisco, they are legislating to curb the company's growth. And the bigger Airbnb gets, the louder and tougher the fight.

Over the years, Airbnb has also dealt with all the unintended consequences of putting strangers together, including ransackings, attacks, and lapses in responsibility on the part of its hosts that have led to tragic accidents of the worst possible kind. In recent years the company has had to confront another evil on its site: the presence of racial and other types of discrimination on its platform.

Perhaps this shouldn't have surprised anyone. When you create an open marketplace that lets the public engage with one another, if it's reflected in society, it will be reflected on the platform. The company may have built its brand on the kindness of strangers, but despite what Airbnb would like to believe, not all of humankind is kind.

These kinds of headlines have fed a sort of hysteria in the minds of those whose only experience with the company is what they see in the news. "You'd better write about it before it goes under," warned one person I told about this project. At the peak of the discrimination controversy, I received a stern voice mail from my father: "I hope the reason you're not answering is because you're listening to the report on NPR right now about how Airbnb discriminates against blacks." (Airbnb wasn't doing the discriminating — people on its platform were — but Airbnb demonstrated an inability to see these major issues coming that many felt was worthy of the criticism.)

But at the same time, Airbnb's usage has exploded well beyond the millennial demographic. These days, Airbnb is used by baby boomers, seniors, and so many other people — including celebrities like Gwyneth Paltrow and Beyoncé — that some of its earliest users, those who considered themselves pioneers at the cutting edge of a social experiment, now feel it has gone too "mainstream."

And, like it or not, Airbnb has captured our imaginations. It has become part of the zeitgeist. It has been a punchline on *Saturday Night Live*. It has been written into the plotline of HBO's *Silicon Valley*. It's been the answer to a question on *Jeopardy!* A romantic comedy with mistaken Airbnb host-identity high jinks as its plot device can't be far away. It's been used by marketers to create clever brand extensions: for a few weeks before the latest *Teenage Mutant Ninja Turtles* movie came out, in 2016, a listing showed up on Airbnb for the Turtles' actual "lair," an apartment in Tribeca the movie's producers, Nickelodeon and Paramount Pictures, had converted into a themed hideout. And it can be a showcase for individual creativity: during an epic snowstorm that covered the Northeast in early 2016, a plucky Brooklyn hipster built and listed a "Boutique Winter Igloo for 2" on the site. ("Dripping with ingenuity and alt-lifestyle aura lays this Snowpocalypse's most desirable getaway," he wrote. Airbnb removed the listing because it wasn't up to code, but gave him a fifty-dollar coupon for his creativity.)

The basic idea behind what Airbnb is doing is not new at all. Chesky likes to point out that the only person who didn't tell him Airbnb was a horrible idea in the beginning was his grandfather, who, when he heard what his grandson was up to, just nodded and said, "Oh, of course. That's how we used to travel."

And it's true: whether as tenants, boarders, au pairs, or otherwise, many people will tell you they stayed in some kind of "home-sharing" situation long before there was an Airbnb or even an Internet. Many well-known people in history were their time's equivalent of Airbnb users. From early October through November 22, 1963, Lee Harvey Oswald paid eight dollars a week for a spare room at a residence in the Oak Cliff section of Dallas (the house is now a museum and is available for tours). Isadore "Issy" Sharp, founder and chairman of the Four Seasons Hotel chain, has said he got his first taste of hospitality when his parents took in tenants while he was growing up in the Jewish ghetto of Toronto. Warren Buffett, too, says that for many years his family often had travelers coming through their house as guests — including George McGovern when he was campaigning for president. There is actually a Wikipedia page for "homeshare," but Airbnb isn't even cited as a reference.

My significant other, raised by a single mother in New York City, grew up accustomed to having a series of boarders in the family's second bedroom. Decades later, he'd make a practice of it himself, filling his three-story house in Brooklyn with two or more semester-long student tenants at a time. I soon came to know Lucien, the IT expert from the Netherlands who occupied the downstairs bedroom, and

Ariane, the French film student in the upstairs spare, as well as their shared food in the fridge and weird European toiletries in the bathrooms. All that extra space could be put to work, my partner would say — and he genuinely liked having global student types around for interesting conversation and a broader perspective.

And then of course, there is the more modern era of short-term vacation rentals, which has been with us for decades, whether through big players like HomeAway or VRBO or niche sites like Bedand Breakfast.com, or, before that, advertisements on Craigslist or classified ads. "One of the signature elements of the sharing economy is that the ideas themselves are not new," says Arun Sundararajan, professor at New York University and author of the book *The Sharing Economy: The End of Employment and the Rise of Crowd-Based Capitalism.*

What is new, though, and what Airbnb specifically has done, is to toss aside the barriers and build an easy, friendly, accessible platform inviting anyone to do it. Unlike on previous websites, Airbnb listings were designed to showcase home renters' personalities; the company invested in individual professional photography services to make sure the spaces would look lush and inviting; and searching, messaging, and payment were all self-contained, seamless, and friction-free. (Many people suggest that Airbnb is not a technology company, since it traffics in homes and spaces, but it has one of the most sophisticated back-end engineering infrastructures in Silicon Valley.) The company built a series of tools to reinforce trust, like bilateral reviews that could be completed only by paying customers who'd completed a stay, and a verified ID system. And one of the biggest but least discussed reasons it was so different is that Airbnb was urban. Before it, most home-rental companies focused on second homes or listings in traditional vacation or resort destinations. For all the attention paid to treehouses and houseboats on its site, most Airbnb listings are studios and one- and two-bedroom apartments, which is what makes it so appealing to so many travelers — and so threatening to hotel companies. Airbnb invited everyday people — even if your only claim to real estate was a rented studio apartment — to profit from their space, and that had a transformative impact on both those renting and those traveling. It was urban, it was easy, and it was "millennial"; and in online marketplace businesses, scale begets scale, so once it reached a certain size, its dominance was hard to unseat.

If Airbnb has disrupted hotels, travel, space, and trust, it's also disrupted conventional management theory. One of the unique aspects of the company's rise is the sheer lack of corporate experience that its founders had when they started out — and the sped-up time frame in which Chesky, Gebbia, and Nathan Blecharczyk (whom Chesky and Gebbia pulled in after that first weekend as their third and technical cofounder) had to learn to become leaders. Very quickly this became a grown-up company with grown-up valuations and expectations — and grown-up problems. Yet, unlike previous companies that grew to this size only to have the founding team split up or "professional" management come in, Airbnb's three leaders are still together, very much at the helm of the rocket ship they built.

The evolution has been the most striking for Chesky, now thirty-five, the company's CEO. A complete outsider — he lacked not only any knowledge about business but even the tech skills to build anything beyond a basic website — he had to quickly evolve from not knowing what angel investors and slide decks were to steering a $30 billion company with more than 2,500 employees.

But while Chesky gets the lion's share of the credit, Airbnb would never have existed without the combination of all three founders. Gebbia, also thirty-five, is a design disrupter with bold ideas who displayed a knack for entrepreneurialism dating back to his early childhood. Blecharczyk, thirty-three, is a preternaturally gifted engineer who made a million dollars building and selling software online while still in high school and who single-handedly built the backbone and infrastructure responsible for much of Airbnb's success. The three of them are different in almost every imaginable way, and as Chesky has scaled as the company's leader, Gebbia and Blecharczyk have in recent years forged their own paths and settled into leadership roles suited to their own strengths.

As this book went to press, the company was readying a major announcement that Chesky promised would be the most significant move in Airbnb's young life and would mark the beginning of a dramatic repositioning: an ambitious push beyond accommodations and into "the rest of the trip" with a series of new products, tools, and experiences. Instead of just booking a stay in a home, Airbnb now aims to be a platform for unique, hyperlocal activities like training with ultramarathoners in Kenya, or trimming bonsai trees with like-minded enthusiasts in the city where you live. It wants to provide restaurant reservations, ground transportation, and soon, something involving flights. It is a bold move and a huge new line of business for such a young company—especially one whose core business is still almost doubling every year.

Indeed, Airbnb is growing and changing so fast that after this book is sent to the printer and is published, and then after that, more big change will come. Only toward the end of the process of reporting this book did I begin to understand what Chesky meant when I sat down with him that day at the Fairmont. When I later learned more about the push into these new businesses, I joked to Chesky that Airbnb's plain-vanilla business of offering accommodations started to seem "old." He looked at me very seriously, gestured toward the slide deck he had just showed me, and said, "I hope that soon *this* will be the 'old' Airbnb."

For these three founders, creating and growing Airbnb hasn't been easy, and it hasn't come without huge bumps in the road. And there will be plenty more of those: the legal battles are far from over, and there will be more bad stories and more examples of horrible human behavior. The founders face some big tests in the future as they expand into a new business—and as they ready the company for an eventual IPO. So far, the company has been able to walk that very delicate balance in scaling growth while preserving its "mission," largely because it has had its choice of investors and has chosen only those who share its longer-term horizon. But as it heads toward a debut in the public markets, the company will be forced to reconcile how it can still maintain its original sense of purpose while managing pressure from large institutional investors whom it will not be able to hand-select.

Whatever happens, Airbnb has already had a huge and lasting impact. It has set records in how quickly it scaled, and has disrupted the notion of what it takes to lead a $30 billion company. It has redefined how we look at the space around us and how we view strangers. It has changed how we travel, opening up a new market for "alternative accommodations" that is drawing interest from dozens of upstarts as well as the biggest hotel companies. And now, Airbnb is aiming to change how we experience new places and how we live our lives at home. It has done all this against all odds, after so many people said no, and as well-funded traditional forces of industry have thrown all their might against it. And all because three guys with little experience had a strange, cheeky idea. The tale of how Chesky, Gebbia, and Blecharczyk came this far is one for the ages. It also should serve as an inspirational account to anyone with a bold idea who's told it will never work.

This is their story.

The Hustle

> There's something I need to tell you.
> We're going to start a company one day, and
> they're going to write a book about it.
>
> — JOE GEBBIA

THE BASIC STORY OF how Airbnb came to be is already lore in Silicon Valley and beyond: in October 2007, two unemployed art school grads living in a three-bedroom apartment in San Francisco, needing to make rent, decided on a lark to rent out some air mattresses during a big design conference that came to town and overcrowded the city's hotels. In certain circles this tale has already attained the same mythic stature as some of the legendary founding stories that came before it: when Bill Bowerman poured liquid urethane into his wife's waffle iron, birthing the Nike waffle-sole sneaker; or when Bill Hewlett and Dave Packard built an audio oscillator in Packard's now-famous garage.

In truth, the Airbnb story begins a few years before then, three thousand miles away in Providence, Rhode Island, in a studio on the campus of the Rhode Island School of Design in the summer of 2004. Brian Chesky and Joe Gebbia, two students — Gebbia was in the fourth year of a five-year dual degree in industrial and graphic design, and Chesky had just graduated — were part of a RISD-sponsored research project with the Conair Corporation, the company best known for its hair dryers and other personal-care products.

Companies would often partner with RISD for access to its industrial-design students. Under this particular program, Conair had
hired the school, which assigned a group of students to essentially
work solely on designing products for the company over the course of
six weeks. Most of the work would take place on the RISD campus,
but the company would own the rights to the products, and the students would get real work experience and a stipend. At the end of the
session, they would present their ideas to Conair executives.

The students worked in teams of two, and Chesky and Gebbia decided to team up. They already knew each other well, having first met
through a shared interest in sports. Chesky ran the RISD ice hockey
team, and Gebbia had started the basketball team. To say sports was
an afterthought among the RISD student body was an understatement, but, determined to bolster their teams' images, the two co-con-
spired on an ambitious marketing plan: they raised funding, created
a schedule, designed new uniforms, and cooked up other creative
flourishes — including the liberal use of cheeky bathroom humor —
to give the teams a sense of irreverence. They succeeded; the RISD
games became popular events among the student body and even
drew neighboring Brown University students and the city's colorful
then-mayor, Buddy Cianci, who agreed to be an "honorary coach" of
the hockey team. "I think it was one of the hardest marketing challenges you could ever face," Gebbia later told *Fast Company*. "How
do you get art school students to a sporting event on a Friday night?"

But for all their antics, the Conair internship marked the first time
Chesky and Gebbia had worked together on a design project. The
team of students would travel to Conair's offices in Stamford, Con-
necticut, once a week by bus for briefings with the company's marketing team, then retreat to the RISD shops to work on their designs.
Gebbia and Chesky worked hard on their ideas, often staying up all
night in the studio. They let their creativity run wild, but it wasn't until it came time to present their ideas that they realized just how wild.
While the rest of the teams came back with different designs for hair
dryers, Chesky and Gebbia came back with a different vision for the
company, pitching out-of-the-box products like a shirt made of soap

that washed off. "The look on their faces said everything," says Gebbia of the Conair executives. The marketing manager running the project told Chesky he had drunk too much coffee. "But I didn't have any coffee," Chesky says. For both of them, it was an epiphany, not about hair dryers, but about what they could come up with when they put their heads together. "We kept building on each other's ideas," says Chesky. "Joe and I, when we get together, ideas typically get bigger, not smaller." Gebbia felt the same way: "I got a taste of, 'OK, when [Brian and I] get in the same room together and we work on an idea, we can do things differently than everybody else.'"

Gebbia already had a sense of this. The previous month had brought Chesky's graduation ceremony. It had been a memorable event: Chesky had been chosen by the student body to be the commencement speaker, and he delivered a performance, approaching the stage to the tune of Michael Jackson's "Billie Jean," tearing off his robe to reveal a white jacket, and grooving, Jackson-style, in front of the crowd before taking the podium. A few days after that, Gebbia had invited his good friend and kindred spirit out for a slice of pizza. Their time together on campus was soon coming to an end, and Gebbia had a premonition he had to get off his chest. "There's something I need to tell you," he said. "We're going to start a company one day, and they're going to write a book about it."

Chesky appreciated the sentiment. ("He looked at me and he kind of laughed it off," Gebbia says.) But despite what they later would call their "Casablanca moment," Chesky knew he needed to move on with his life and find a respectable job. After all, wasn't that the whole point? Growing up in upstate New York, Chesky was the son of two social workers who'd worked hard to be able to give their children the freedom to pursue whatever passions and hobbies they chose. His mother, Deb, now a fund-raiser for Rensselaer Polytechnic Institute, and his father, Bob Chesky, who retired in 2015 after working for the state of New York for forty years, were supportive of their son's interest in art; his high school art teacher had told them she thought he was going to be famous as an artist one day. And his parents were thrilled when he'd been admitted to RISD. But they were wary of the job prospects their son would have with a degree in art. ("We were afraid he was going to be a starving artist," Deb Chesky says.) Not wanting to disappoint them, Chesky had switched majors halfway through his time at RISD, from illustration to industrial design, precisely because it would open up a much larger job market. So Chesky and Gebbia said goodbye, and while they were reunited briefly for the Conair program, Chesky eventually moved to Los Angeles to start his new life as an industrial designer.

Before shipping him off, Chesky's parents bought him a suit and a car, a Honda Civic that they arranged would be dropped off at the airport when he landed. (Deb Chesky coordinated the logistics of all this, at one point finalizing the delivery on the phone with the car dealer from the dressing room at Macy's while her son tried on suits. She explained to the dealer that she was buying the car for her son, who was moving to Hollywood. "He said, 'He's not going to be an actor, is he?' And I was, like, 'No,'" she says. "'It's just as bad — he's going to be a designer.'")

Once in Los Angeles, Chesky moved in with some friends from RISD and started working at the industrial-design firm 3DID. For the first few months he liked the work, designing real products for companies like ESPN and Mattel. But soon it started to become evident that the job wasn't what he'd hoped it would be. He dreamed of becoming the next Jony Ive or Yves Béhar, famous designers who'd reimagined companies like Apple and the consumer-technology firm Jawbone, but he found his daily work to be uninspiring, mostly rote execution. "It was not silly stuff, but it was so obviously not in the promise of RISD," he says. The renowned institution had filled him with a spirit of change-the-world idealism: almost any problem in the world could be solved by creative design, he was told; if you could conceive of something, you could design it; and it was possible to design the very world you wanted to live in. As a designer, you could *change* the world. "But when I got to LA, it was kind of a giant reality check," he later said. "'OK, here's the real world. It's not what you thought it was.'"

He hadn't taken to Los Angeles, either. "I spent an hour and a half each way [to work] in a car, an empty car," he recalls. He felt disillusioned — and that he'd made the wrong choice. "I felt my life was, like, I was in a car, and I could see the road disappearing into the horizon in front of me, and I could see the same view in the rearview mirror," he later told Sarah Lacy, the technology journalist and founder of *PandoDaily*, in a fireside chat in 2013. "It was, like, 'Oh, this is all I'll end up doing. I guess it wasn't like they said it would be at RISD.'"

Meanwhile, Gebbia had finished up at RISD and eventually moved to San Francisco, where he was working as a graphic designer for Chronicle Books and living in a three-bedroom apartment on Rausch Street in the city's South of Market district. He'd also tried his hand at entrepreneurialism, attempting to launch a line of seat cushions he'd designed at RISD. Conceived for art school students as a comfortable seat when sitting through famously lengthy critiques, or "crits," they were cheekily called CritBuns and designed in the shape of rear ends. They had won a prestigious award at RISD, with the prize being that the school would pay for the development of the product and give it as a gift to every member of the graduating class. Gebbia had hustled to find a manufacturer and a mold maker in order to produce eight hundred CritBuns within four weeks so they'd be ready by graduation day; the next day, he turned the enterprise into a company. (Gebbia had showed a knack for merging entrepreneurialism and art at an early age: in the third grade growing up in Atlanta, he sold drawings of Teenage Mutant Ninja Turtles to his classmates for two dollars each until their parents told the teachers he had to stop.)

The two talked frequently, Gebbia updating Chesky on CritBuns and the two also brainstorming ideas for any products they might be able to cook up together for 3DID. Always, Gebbia would end their conversations with a plea for Chesky to consider moving to San Francisco so they could start a company together. Chesky was mostly reluctant, always for the same reason: no health insurance, no move. One day, a package arrived in the mail at work from Gebbia, and Chesky opened it to find a pair of commercially produced CritBuns. Gebbia had succeeded at launching them out onto the marketplace, landing a big order at the Museum of Modern Art Design Store, a designer's holy grail. He had really done it, Chesky remembers saying to himself. ("It was a subtle nudge," Gebbia says. "It was a reminder: Don't forget. We could potentially be creating things too.")

It was enough to get Chesky to start looking around for jobs in San Francisco. In early 2007, he heard about a job opening at Method, then a fast-growing home-products company with a focus on sustainability and award-winning packaging. Chesky thought this could be his answer: it would get him to San Francisco, and it was a design-oriented company whose values were much more in line with his own. He went far in the interview process: he went through multiple rounds of interviews, completed a design challenge, and presented in front of a panel of five executives, getting more and more excited about the opportunity at every step. But in the end, he didn't get the job; it went to another candidate. He was crestfallen.

But the interviews had gotten him up to San Francisco a few times, and he instantly loved the city. Its energy and the creative, entrepreneurial types he encountered through Gebbia's circles reminded him of the spirit he'd felt back at RISD. (Gebbia had become the primary leaseholder on the Rausch Street apartment and had fashioned it to be a sort of designers' collective, carefully interviewing and "curating" like-minded roommates.) He and Gebbia started thinking more seriously about what kind of company they could start. By now Chesky had quit his job — much to the chagrin of his parents — and began creating a different plan for himself. He'd been asked to teach industrial design at California State University at Long Beach and had started getting involved in the Los Angeles design community. He thought he could remain based there and commute to San Francisco for a few days each week to work with Gebbia.

That September, both of Gebbia's roommates suddenly moved out after his landlord raised the rent, and Gebbia went into a much harder sell mode trying to get Chesky to move to San Francisco and take one of the rooms. Gebbia had already filled one of the rooms, and Chesky would be a perfect fit for the other. But Chesky was reluctant. He couldn't afford it, and the two of them would need to cover rent for all three bedrooms for a month, because the third roommate couldn't move in until November. Chesky started pitching Gebbia on — of all things — letting him rent his sofa three days a week so he could commute and essentially live in both places. Gebbia thought that was utterly ridiculous. With the deadline looming and no roommates in sight, Gebbia finally decided he would have to give up the apartment. But the morning he was due to call the landlord, Chesky called him and said he was in; he would take one of the bedrooms.

Chesky said a quick goodbye to his life in Los Angeles — he broke up with his girlfriend, delivered the news to his housemates, left his apartment and most of his possessions, and set off for San Francisco in his Honda late on a Tuesday night. Driving up the coast in the dark, he could barely see the road in front of him, yet all he kept thinking was that it was nothing like the empty road he'd kept seeing in his head for so long when he felt trapped in his job. This was not that road. This road, to San Francisco, looked only like possibility.

"Like Craigslist and Couchsurfing.com, but Classier"

As the mythologized version of the story goes, when Chesky arrived at the Rausch Street apartment, Gebbia informed him he was on the brink of losing the place, that the rent had gone up to $1,150, and that it was due within the week. Chesky had $1,000 in his bank account. In truth, they'd known for weeks about the higher rent — plus the fact that they'd have to cover the extra empty room in addition to their own — and they had been brainstorming various schemes to come up with the funds even while Chesky was still in Los Angeles. One idea centered around the International Council of Societies of Industrial Design/Industrial Designers Society of America (ICSID/IDSA) World Congress, the biannual confab for the design community, scheduled for San Francisco in late October. It would draw a few thousand designers to their city, and they knew hotel capacity would be tight and rates would be high.

They thought, why not create a bed-and-breakfast for the conference out of the empty space in their apartment? RISD, after all, had taught them that creativity can solve problems, and Gebbia happened to have three air mattresses in his closet from a camping trip he'd taken. The place was a spacious three-bedroom, so there would be the living room, kitchen, and a full bedroom all for the taking. They could sell a cheap place to stay, and even offer breakfast — and they could advertise their place on the design blogs they knew all the attendees would be reading.

They refined this idea for weeks, and the more they talked about it, the more they realized it was so weird that it just might work — and with a looming deadline to pay the rent, they had little to lose. They started drawing wireframes, or skeleton outlines, and mockups for the website that would advertise their concept. Once Chesky moved in, they hired a freelancer who knew HTML to put together a rudimentary website using their designs, calling the service AirBed & Breakfast. The final product featured a robust website announcing the service ("Two designers create a new way to connect at this year's IDSA conference"), an explanation of how it worked, and included a listing for three airbeds in their apartment for eighty dollars apiece (amenities listed included a roof deck, a "design library," "motivational posters," and 3-D typography). "It's like Craigslist & Couch surfing.com, but classier," proclaimed one "endorsement."

They e-mailed design blogs and the conference organizers and asked them to help promote their website, which they did; the conference organizers thought it was a funny, oddball idea, and the design blogs were more than happy to help support two of their own. Chesky and Gebbia thought that, with any luck, they'd get a couple of hippie backpacker types and would make enough money to pay rent. Within a few days they had booked three guests: Kat, a thirtysomething designer based in Boston; Michael, a father of five in his forties from Utah; and Amol Surve, a native of Mumbai who'd just graduated from Arizona State University's master's program in industrial design.

Their guests weren't hippies at all; they were professional designers on a budget who needed just what Chesky and Gebbia were offering. True, it required a big leap of faith on their part: Surve, the first guest to book, thought the idea was strange, but, he says, "I was desperate to go to the conference," and when he came across the website, he says he knew it was created by like-minded people. "You could tell that the concept was designed by designers for designers." After Googling what an airbed was — new to the United States, he had never heard of one before — he submitted a request on a form on the website asking to stay at the "original" AirBed & Breakfast. When he didn't hear back, he tracked down Gebbia's information and called him on his cell phone. ("He was completely surprised," Surve says. "They had no idea that someone would stay with them.") Surve made plans to stay for five nights at eighty dollars per night. "It was a hack on both our sides," he says. "I was trying to hack and go to the conference, and they were trying to hack and make rent. It was, like, a perfect match."

"I Was Both in the Living Room and in the Slide Deck at the Same Time"

After landing at the airport and following the BART directions his hosts had provided, Surve arrived at the door of the apartment and was welcomed by Gebbia. "This guy opens the door, he's wearing an aviator hat and some big trendy glasses, and I was, like, 'Yep, that's a designer right there,'" Surve recalls. Gebbia asked him to remove his shoes, gave Surve a tour around the place, and showed him to his room, which contained an air mattress, a pillow, and a welcome package that included a BART pass, city maps, and spare change to pass out to homeless people. ("They were so detail-oriented," Surve says. "They said, 'Is there something else we could have added to this package?' I said, 'No, this is already too much.'")

After dropping off his things, Surve sat down on the living-room couch and opened his laptop to familiarize himself with the conference program. Gebbia and Chesky were hard at work at the table, putting together a PowerPoint for their new concept. Surve leaned over and took a peek and spotted a slide about his being their first guest. "It was ironic," he says. "I was both in the living room and in the slide deck at the same time." They began peppering him with questions for feedback and invited him to join them in a pitch session they were participating in that night — a PechaKucha, a kind of poetry slam–meets–PowerPoint presentation in which designers pitch ideas to other designers. Gebbia and Chesky had their presentation; now, they could present their end user, too.

The other guests soon arrived at the apartment, Kat and Amol sharing a room and Michael claiming the kitchen. By the time they all set out for the conference together the next day, Chesky and Gebbia were in major hustle mode to promote their new idea. They dodged the registration fee by telling the organizers they were bloggers. They tooled around the conference together, Chesky with a camera slung around his neck so as to best resemble a blogger, and excitedly talked up their new service. "He would pitch anyone and everyone," says Surve, whom they used as a prop. "Ask him how great it is!" Chesky would say, pushing Surve forward. Surve confirmed how much fun he was having and how it wasn't just a place to stay. ("My product stuck up for us!" Chesky said recently, reflecting on this. "He was the most unbelievable advocate.") People were mostly amused. No one took them seriously. During a happy hour in the lounge of the Fairmont Hotel, Chesky managed to edge into a crowd surrounding a well-known designer he'd looked up to for years. He introduced himself and told him about their new concept. The designer was not impressed. "Brian," he said, "I hope that's not the only thing you're working on." It was the first of many reality checks. ("I remember that so well — like, it's seared in my brain," Chesky said.)

Outside the conference, Chesky and Gebbia showed Surve around their city: they took him to their favorite taco place, to the San Francisco Ferry Building, and to Stanford's design school. They served their guests breakfasts of untoasted Pop-Tarts and orange juice. In a short few days, the five of them became comfortable enough around each other in the apartment that at one point Chesky remembers talking to Michael as he was lying on his air mattress on the kitchen floor in his underwear. All told, they made $1,000 from the weekend.

But even with that, they didn't have the feeling their idea would be *huge*. It was just too weird. It was something they had come up with to help pay the rent, to keep them afloat, and, if anything, to buy them a little more time to think of their *really* big idea.

They turned their attention back toward brainstorming the company they would start for real. They brought in one of Joe's previous roommates, Nathan Blecharczyk, a gifted engineer from Boston who was between gigs. The son of an electrical engineer, Blecharczyk had taught himself to code at age twelve with a book he found on his father's bookshelf. By age fourteen, it had become an "intense passion" and he had started doing work for paying customers who'd found him online. By the time he finished high school, he had made close to $1 million building and selling marketing software. That had paid for his Harvard computer science degree, but Blecharczyk had spent most of 2007 at a failing education start-up and was thinking of leaving his job. Gebbia had just left Chronicle Books and was still working on a new start-up he'd conceived after CritBuns — Ecolect .net, a sustainable-materials marketplace for the design community. The three of them hunkered down to brainstorm, veering from one idea to another. At one point they landed briefly on a concept for a roommate-matching website they imagined as a Craigslist-meets-Facebook for roommates. "We thought, no one would do this AirBed & Breakfast thing, but people need roommates," says Chesky. But after four weeks of designing and refining the idea, they typed "room mates.com" into a browser and were crushed to discover that the idea and website already existed. They went back to the drawing board.

Chesky went home to Niskayuna, New York, for Christmas that year, discouraged. When his friends and family asked him what he was doing, he told them he was an entrepreneur. "No, you're unemployed," his mother corrected him. ("No, I'm an entrepreneur!" he would protest. "No, you're unemployed," would again come the answer.) His parents aside, "entrepreneur" wasn't really a word people knew in Niskayuna. "What are you 'entrepreneur'-ing?" his friends would ask. With nothing truly significant to tell them about, he found himself time and time again coming back to AirBed & Breakfast. Gebbia, at home in Atlanta, found himself doing the same thing. They were getting used to talking up AirBed & Breakfast. And then they started wondering — was *this* the idea?

AirBed & Breakfast "Lite"

Chesky and Gebbia returned from the holidays revved up about trying to make a go of AirBed & Breakfast. As they had discussed it, they had refined the concept: it could be a resource for finding rooms during sold-out conferences across the country. They knew that such gatherings can easily max out a hotel's supply, creating just the kind of demand that led them to book their first three guests in San Francisco. And they had the perfect idea for where to launch it: South by Southwest, or "Southby," as it's known, the Austin-based tech, music, and film-festival confab that had become the preeminent technology-industry gathering in the United States.

But they knew they needed to convince Blecharczyk; they couldn't do it without him. They called him up and said they had something they were really excited about and asked him to dinner, where they pitched the idea to him. He was reluctant. He liked the idea, and he knew from his time living with Gebbia, when they'd help each other out on side projects on nights and weekends, that they shared a similar work ethic. He felt the three of them would make a good team, but as he listened to his designer friends' more grandiose vision, he became apprehensive about the amount of work they were describing. Most of it would fall on him, the only engineer of the three of them, and it would need to be done in just a few weeks in order to get up and running in time for South by Southwest. "I think my response was supportive, but cautious," Blecharczyk recalls. Sensing his reservations, Chesky and Gebbia left the dinner, regrouped, and came back a week later to repitch the idea to him. But as they were in the elevator on the way to see Blecharczyk, Gebbia suddenly realized their vision was still too ambitious. "Nate's going to freak out," he said, shaking his head. "We have to scale it back." They quickly agreed on a retooled alternative, something they called AirBed & Breakfast Lite, a scoped-down version of the concept with fewer features and fewer technical hurdles that would be executable in a few weeks. ("Same great product, half the code," Gebbia says.) They had a few drinks, and Blecharczyk agreed; they would make a run at it.

In those very early days, Chesky felt strongly that the service should be free. "I was a little nervous about starting up a corporation," he says. They had wanted AirBed & Breakfast to become a movement, and he had an idealistic view that everything would be shared freely. "I was extremely progressive in the sense that I initially thought maybe Airbnb should be a free website, like Couchsurfing. Like, no money." Gebbia and Blecharczyk convinced him otherwise, and Chesky says he eventually came around. "I was, like, 'Yeah, you're right. This should be monetized. There should definitely be a business model.'"

They decided that at South by Southwest, they would introduce Airbedandbreakfast.com as an entirely new site, to try to get another round of press. (It's a tactic Chesky has since advised to other entrepreneurs: "If you launch and no one notices, you can keep launching. We kept launching, and people kept writing about it. We thought we'd just keep launching until we got customers.") They spruced up the site, billing it as lodging for sold-out conferences ("Finally, an alternative to expensive hotels," the site read), and notified some tech blogs. But almost nothing happened. "It wasn't really a big moment for traction," Blecharczyk says. That was an understatement: they got only two paying customers — one of whom was Chesky.

Even the person Chesky stayed with — Tiendung Le, a PhD student at the University of Texas in Austin — was someone the founders had recruited off of Craigslist to list on AirBed & Breakfast. When Chesky arrived, he was impressed with the way Le had spruced up the air mattress in his living room, even putting a mint on the pillow. For his part, Le recalls Chesky spending a lot of time out on the balcony, either on the phone or "deep in thought." Le made him an espresso every morning (which he says Chesky drank "in two seconds") and drove him to the festival, during which time Chesky described his vision for the company and his fervent hope to meet Mark Zuckerberg, who was speaking at the conference.

Despite pulling in zero outside business, the South by Southwest launch actually served a few purposes. By using the website himself, Chesky identified some kinks in the payment process. He'd forgotten to go to the ATM not once but twice, so for two nights he was in the awkward position of staying in the home of a stranger who had no reason to believe he'd actually pay. And Le felt that after a day or two of becoming friends, it felt awkward to ask for the money at all. The three founders realized they'd need to build a more sophisticated payment system. Additionally, after the event was over, they heard from a few potential customers who said they were traveling to other places, but not for a conference. Was it still possible to use AirBed & Breakfast? The founders said no.

The Godfounder

At South by Southwest, Chesky and Gebbia also made a key connection. Their third roommate at Rausch Street, Phil Reyneri, was an employee at a start-up called Justin.tv, and he, too, was there in Austin along with his CEO, a twenty-five-year-old entrepreneur named Michael Seibel. Chesky had decided to stay an extra night, and Seibel let him crash in his hotel room. Chesky told Seibel about their idea, and he liked it. "I was, like, 'Yeah, that makes sense,'" Seibel recalls. He had used Couchsurfing.com, and while he didn't foresee AirBed & Breakfast's becoming a multi-billion-dollar juggernaut upon hearing the idea, he didn't think it was out of left field either; they were, after all, themselves crammed into a small hotel room during a conference. "We were sitting in the home of the problem," Seibel says.

Seibel is now an established entrepreneurial adviser with two major successes under his belt: he and his cofounders sold Twitch (which is what Justin.tv eventually became) to Amazon for $970 million and Socialcam, a video app, to Autodesk for $60 million. But back then he was twenty-five, had only recently become a first-time

CEO, and didn't have much experience. "I wasn't someone people pitched," he says. Chesky and Gebbia were the first founders who had ever asked him for advice. But he had just gone through Y Combinator, the prestigious start-up accelerator program cofounded by the entrepreneur and venture capitalist Paul Graham (Seibel is now CEO of the Y Combinator program). Seibel told them he'd help give them counsel, and as they began to devise something more tangible, he could maybe introduce them to some angels. Chesky had no idea what he was talking about ("I'm, like, 'Oh my god, this guy believes in *angels*. What the hell?'" he says now). Seibel explained to Chesky that he was referring to angel investors, people who over dinner might write him a check for $20,000. Chesky thought that sounded even weirder. "No, no, you give them a pitch, a slide deck," Seibel pressed. Chesky didn't know what a slide deck was either, but he sensed that Seibel was someone he should listen to.

After South by Southwest, with their website traffic having flatlined, the founders retreated to San Francisco. They were dejected, but Chesky and Gebbia already had an idea for their next attempt: it was an election year, and the Democratic National Convention was going to be held in August in Denver; they could try again. But Blecharczyk's initial cautiousness had shifted to outright skepticism. He had been working on another idea he was much more excited about, a social-advertising network for Facebook. He still liked AirBed & Breakfast, but he was very practical about accepting their results at South by Southwest, and he wouldn't fully commit until Chesky and Gebbia had a better strategy. "Joe and Brian really wanted to move forward, but I was quite hesitant until we understood how we'd make the product better and achieve a better outcome," he says. So for the next few months Blecharczyk spent most of his time on his own start-up while Chesky and Gebbia kept moving forward refining their idea and product, bringing updates week by week to Seibel, who'd offer feedback and suggestions. "He [Seibel] just kept us in check," Gebbia says. "Whenever we went off the guardrails, he'd be, like, 'Guys, what are you doing? Back this way.'" They called him their "godfounder."

But without Blecharczyk's full attention, many of Seibel's suggestions weren't being implemented. Chesky and Gebbia didn't want to let on to Seibel that Blecharczyk wasn't fully on board, because Seibel had started introducing them to investors, and a start-up without an engineering founder would stand no chance. As far as Seibel knew, Blecharczyk was working full-time on Airbedandbreakfast .com. Gebbia and Chesky assumed it was realistically more like a few hours a day, but they didn't dare tell Seibel. In truth, Blecharczyk was spending no more than an hour every few days on it. "We only started grasping later how checked out Nate was," Chesky says. "He would do less and less work, and the contact would be less and less frequent."

Then, in May, Blecharczyk dropped a bomb: he was moving back to Boston to commit to his girlfriend (now wife), who was in medical school. "That was probably out of left field for Joe and Brian," Blecharczyk concedes. "There was a sense at that point that maybe the team was falling apart." It was. The next month, Chesky and Gebbia started looking for another cofounder. They posted ads for a "cofounder and CTO" at San Francisco's Moscone Center during Apple's Worldwide Developers Conference. Blecharczyk says he wasn't too threatened by that. "For all the same reasons I was skeptical, I thought someone on the street would be more skeptical," he says. "I wasn't particularly concerned that someone else was going to emerge overnight."

But Chesky and Gebbia kept refining their vision, kept collecting feedback from Seibel, and kept talking with Blecharczyk over the phone, and it was actually during this time that a new and much broader vision for AirBed & Breakfast crystallized: instead of targeting sold-out conferences, it would be a website where booking a room in someone's home would be as easy as booking a hotel. It was in essence the same version of Airbnb that exists today. But it meant they had to build a sophisticated payment system that could handle transactions without taking the customer away from the site; and it meant they would need a review system and a much more robust website in general.

This was a much more ambitious vision, but it was also exactly what Blecharczyk needed to hear. He had also decided to throw in the towel on his advertising idea, because he realized the concept needed more than engineering expertise, and he didn't have cofounders. So he recommitted to AirBed & Breakfast, agreeing to work on the concept from Boston.

Meanwhile, Chesky and Gebbia had started meeting with the "angels" Seibel had mentioned — or at least trying to. (By this point, the group decided that Chesky would be CEO. "It wasn't really a major conversation," Chesky recalls. "There was a moment when one of us had to put the title on." The three cofounders have very different skill sets; it had become clear that Chesky was the natural leader among them. "I knew a lot less than Joe and Nate," he says. "They had been involved in start-ups and I had not. So I think I was always trying to make myself very useful, and that transitioned to starting to build a company.") The investor outreach would soon become a lesson in rejection. Of seven investors Seibel had connected them to, most didn't write back. And the ones who did all said some version of no: it was not their area of focus; they hadn't had luck in the travel category; the potential market didn't seem large enough; they were committed to other projects; they were out of town; they were unavailable; they wished him well:

Brian good to meet you — while this sounds interesting it is not something we would do here — not in our area of focus, do wish you best of luck.

Unfortunately don't think that it's the right opportunity for [firm] from an investment perspective . . . the potential market opportunity did not seem large enough for our required model.

Thanks for the follow up. I was unavailable to get on the call today as I'll be out of town through end of day Thursday. I really like the progress you guys have made, but between issues outstanding with ABB and my current time commitments to other projects . . . I'm not going to be able to proceed with an investment at this point. My biggest remaining concerns are:

— significant ramp up in traction post the DNC and RNC
— technical staffing
— investment syndicate

Brian

We decided yesterday to not take this to the next level

We've always struggled with travel as a category

We recognize its one of the top e-commerce categories but for some reason, we've not been able to get excited about travel related businesses

The few meetings Chesky and Gebbia did set up were mostly disastrous. Investors thought the idea of renting out space to strangers was totally weird and unbelievably risky. They were put off by Chesky and Gebbia's art school background; they thought they lacked technical DNA (at the time, investors were still looking for the next Google, that is, two PhDs from Stanford). One investor they met with at the University Café in Palo Alto simply got up with no warning and walked out halfway through the meeting, leaving his half-full smoothie on the table. Gebbia and Chesky took a photo of the smoothie.

It should be said that at this point the founders were looking for someone to buy 10 percent of their company for $150,000, valuing the company at $1.5 million. Under certain scenarios, that $150,000 could have been worth a few billion dollars today. But at the time, it was a radioactive idea. "No one wanted to touch this," Chesky says.

"Just Keep Launching"

Undaunted, the three cofounders kept refining their product, so by the time the DNC in Denver approached, they had finessed a way to facilitate payments on the site, they had a review system up and running, and they had come up with a new marketing slogan: "Stay with a local when traveling." Excitement about the DNC, too, was heating up: Barack Obama's nomination for the presidency had led to a frenzy of media coverage and a surge of interest in the convention. The DNC organizers decided to move the location of Obama's acceptance speech from the Pepsi Center to Invesco Field, which held some eighty thousand people. Local articles started appearing suggesting that Denver had only twenty-seven thousand hotel rooms and forecasting a massive housing shortage. "The hysteria was perfect for us," Chesky later told an audience at the Urban Land Institute. This could be their moment.

Chesky, Gebbia, and Blecharczyk launched their site — now for the third time — on August 11, 2008, a few weeks before the convention. Through persistence and connections, they had managed to secure a feature on the prominent tech blog TechCrunch. ("AirBed and Breakfast Takes Pad Crashing to a Whole New Level" was the headline; writer Erick Schonfeld wrote that the "combination of the AeroBed and the Internet has now made everybody into an innkeeper.") The story succeeded in building awareness, but it drove so much traffic that Airbedandbreakfast.com crashed. Chesky and Gebbia happened to have another meeting with an angel investor, Mike Maples, that day, and since their site was now live, they decided to skip the slide deck and just show Maples the real thing. But when they tried to open the site, they realized it had crashed — and they hadn't brought their slide deck. "It was mostly us staring at each other for an hour," Chesky later said. Maples did not invest.

The founders had another problem leading up to the DNC, which was supply: no one wanted to list his or her home if no one else was going to book it; and with few homes listed, no one would use the site. They weren't going to be able to get off the ground, let alone trigger any kind of "network effect," where the more people use something, the more valuable it becomes — leading even more people to use it. Their preliminary outreach showed them people either didn't want to rent their homes or thought they were being asked to participate in some kind of weird social experiment.

Chesky may not always have known what angels or slide decks were, but he and his cofounders always had a very good instinct for using the media, and, much like that first October weekend, they knew that success or failure lay in their ability to drum up news coverage. They also knew that the political news media were desperate for any new wrinkle they could find. Thinking creatively, the founders pitched to the smallest local blogs they could find, on the principle that the smaller they were, the more likely they were to pay any attention to them. They were able to get a few stories on microblogs, which started a domino effect: the smaller-blog stories were then picked up by bigger blogs, which were then seen and covered by local newspapers like the *Denver Post*, which in turn triggered a call from the local broadcast stations. And those stories were then seen and covered by the national media: Politico, the *New York Daily News*, the *New York Times*, and others.

The press strategy worked, and things began to happen: eight hundred people listed their rooms, and eighty guests booked. It was nail-biting at times. The founders were using a PayPal account to handle all payments, but when PayPal saw the huge spike in activity, it deemed it suspicious and froze their account. Blecharczyk spent hours on the phone with PayPal customer service in India, while Chesky and Gebbia frantically pleaded with annoyed customers to be patient, they would get paid (they did, by the end of the weekend). But overall, the founders were elated. "As far as I was concerned, we were the Beatles," Chesky told Lacy in their fireside chat.

But once again, the success would be short-lived. Despite the bookings and the media coverage, as soon as the convention was over, traffic crashed. "We realized if only there were political conventions every week, we'd be huge," Chesky said. Instead, they were back at square one. Chesky would later put it in medical terms: they were losing their patient.

"I Don't Remember Mark Zuckerberg Assembling Cereal Boxes"

Back at home in San Francisco, with Blecharczyk back in Boston, Chesky and Gebbia were launched, out of money, in debt, and without traffic. Desperate and nearly out of options, they resuscitated an idea they'd had before the DNC, which was to ship their "hosts" free breakfast that they could then in turn give to their paying guests. After all, breakfast was half of the name and a big part of the concept. They had landed on cereal — and, with the convention on their minds, they'd come up with a fictitious brand called Obama O's. They'd designed a cereal box, added slogans — "The breakfast of change" and "Hope in every bowl" — and added a Republican version, Cap'n McCain's, "A maverick in every bite." An illustrator designed the box, and Jonathan Mann, a jingle writer who was an early host on the site, drummed up a jingle for each. (These are both available with a quick web search and are highly worth listening to. The Obama lyrics are as follows.)

> *Oh-my-god it's Obama O's*
> *Mommy, can I have some please?*
> *There's a really cool cereal that you oughta know*
> *Everybody's talking about Obama O's*
> *Just one bite and you will understand*
> *Cause every single O sings "Yes, we can!"*
> *Oh-my-god it's Obama O's*
> *Mommy can I have some please?*

Back in the kitchen after the convention, Gebbia and Chesky started getting excited about resurrecting the cereal idea. If they could produce one hundred thousand boxes and sell them for two dollars each, they reasoned, they'd be able to fund the company; Chesky even rationalized that it would be just as if the "angels" they had talked to had given them money. By this point, they had filled up baseball-card binders with credit cards to the tune of $20,000 in debt each. Blecharczyk thought this was crazy, at first thinking they were playing some kind of prank on him (which they had been known to do). He told them they could do it, but he wanted no part of it and made them promise not to spend any money on the idea. "We'd each been out of jobs for almost a year," Blecharczyk says. "They were on their own."

Chesky and Gebbia retreated into a mode they were familiar with — the creative hustle — and found a RISD alum in Berkeley who had a printing shop. He wasn't willing to make one hundred thousand boxes, but he said he'd print them five hundred boxes of each for free if they'd give him a cut of the sales. That smaller scale would crush their economic model, but they decided to recast the idea as "limited edition" boxes; they'd number the boxes, pitch them as collectors' editions, and charge forty dollars per box.

They scoured San Francisco's supermarkets to find which sold the cheapest cereal and filled up shopping cart after shopping cart until they had a thousand boxes of one-dollar cereal, loaded them into Gebbia's red Jeep, and hauled them home. Back in the kitchen, with a thousand flat boxes and a hot-glue gun, they got to work, hand-folding the boxes and sealing them shut with the glue. "It was like doing giant origami on my kitchen table," Chesky recalled during the Lacy interview. He burned his hands. He thought to himself that he couldn't remember Mark Zuckerberg hot-gluing anything or burning his hands assembling cereal boxes to launch Facebook. Maybe, he thought, this wasn't a good sign.

But they finished the boxes, and, in their last-ditch attempt at stirring up attention for their failing company, alerted the press. Tech reporters got bombarded with pitches, they reasoned, but they probably didn't get cereal shipped to their desks all that often. Maybe they'd respond; and if they displayed the boxes on their desks or on bookcases in the newsroom, all the other reporters would also see it. The gimmick worked: the press ate it up, and the boxes started moving. Obama O's sold out in three days, after which people started reselling them on eBay and Craigslist for as much as $350 per box. (Cap'n McCain's never sold out.)

The founders paid off their debt, but they still had no traffic on their original idea, which had nothing to do with cereal, and they had no sense of how to develop more traffic. It was a grim time. (During one phone conversation, Deb Chesky asked her son, "So wait — are you a cereal company now?" Even worse than the question was that Chesky didn't know how to answer it.) They had made less than

$5,000 from their core business and somewhere between $20,000 and $30,000 selling cereal. Blecharczyk, deeply skeptical of the cereal plan from the start, decided enough was enough. Back in Boston, he started consulting again and got engaged.

In effect, Chesky and Gebbia were back at square one, in their apartment with no money. Chesky had lost twenty pounds over the course of the year. Out of money and out of food, for the next few months they lived off of dry Cap'n McCain's; even milk was too expensive. (And yet even during these difficult times, Chesky was still strategizing. At one point Deb Chesky remembers urging her son to go buy some milk. "No, we're just going to struggle through," she says he told him. "It'll be a better story someday.")

One night in November 2008, Chesky and Gebbia were having dinner with Seibel, who suggested that they consider applying to Y Combinator. Chesky took umbrage at the suggestion. Y Combinator was for prelaunch companies. AirBed & Breakfast had already launched — they had customers! They had been written up on Tech-Crunch! But Seibel delivered the truth that, deep down, they all knew: "Look at you," he said. "You guys are dying. Do Y Combinator." The application deadline had passed, but Seibel sent a message to Graham, who said he'd consider them if they got their application in by midnight. They called Blecharczyk in Boston, waking him up at 1 a.m. to ask if they could put his name on the application with them. He hardly remembers agreeing, but he did.

They applied, got an interview, and somehow convinced Blecharczyk to come back to San Francisco for it. Y Combinator's application process is famously brutal; interviews are just ten minutes flat, consisting of Graham and his partners asking rapid-fire questions; no presentations are allowed. After several hours of prepping and mock-interviewing one another, the founders were ready to leave for the interview. On the way out, Gebbia went to grab a box of Obama O's and Cap'n McCain's to put them in his bag, but Chesky and Blecharczyk stopped him. "Are you out of your mind?" Blecharczyk asked him. "Leave the cereal at home." (Says Gebbia, "I felt very outnumbered in that moment.") They piled into Gebbia's Jeep and drove down to Mountain View, where Y Combinator's headquarters were located.

The interview didn't go well. After the founders explained the idea, Graham's first question was "People are actually doing this? Why? What's *wrong* with them?" Chesky felt Graham was impressed that they knew so much about their market and customers, but it seemed like he dismissed the idea itself entirely. (Graham and others often point out that at this time the idea for the company was still that the person renting out the space would be present; the founders hadn't yet conceived of their users renting out their entire home or apartment.) As they started to pack up to leave, Gebbia pulled out the cereal boxes; against Blecharczyk's wishes, he'd sneaked them into his bag. He walked over to where Graham was talking with his partners and handed him one. Graham thanked him, awkwardly — he thought they had bought some cereal for him as a weird or bizarre gift. The founders told him, no, they had made and sold the cereal boxes — it was, in fact, how they'd funded the company. They told him the story behind the Obama O's. Graham sat back and listened. "Wow," he mused. "You guys are like cockroaches. You just won't die."

The founders were told to expect a call from Graham very shortly if they were accepted. But the rules were strict: if they got an offer, they needed to accept on the spot; otherwise Graham would go down the list and offer the slot to the next person. In the Jeep on the way back to San Francisco, Chesky saw Graham's number pop up on his cell phone. He picked it up, with Gebbia and Blecharczyk eagerly listening in. Just as Graham started to say, "I'd love to . . . ," the call dropped. They were on a stretch of I-280 between Silicon Valley and San Francisco where it was well known that there was no cell signal. "I'm, like, NOOOO!" Chesky later recalled. "Me and Joe are freaking out, and Joe is, like, 'Go, go, go!'" They weaved frantically through traffic to try to get a signal. "I'm, like, 'Oh my God, I just ruined it,'" says Chesky.

It wasn't until they were back in San Francisco that Graham called again and got through — and offered them the spot. Chesky feigned that he had to "check" with his cofounders, put him on mute to ask if they would accept — they were, of course, totally out of options — and told Graham they were in. Graham would later tell Chesky it was the cereal that clinched it. "If you can convince people to pay forty dollars for a four-dollar box of cereal, you can probably convince people to sleep in other people's airbeds," he said. "Maybe you can do it."

The founders would get the $20,000 in seed funding that came with admission, in return for a 6 percent stake in the company, and they would enroll in the next three-month term, which would begin in January. They were due to report for a welcome dinner on Tuesday, January 6, 2009. After what Chesky would later refer to as an "intervention," Blecharczyk finally agreed to relocate to San Francisco for three months and moved back into the Rausch Street apartment. The band was back together. They had been given another chance.

"What Are You Still Doing Here?"

Founded in 2005 by Paul Graham and three copartners, Y Combinator very quickly became one of the most prestigious launchpads in Silicon Valley, a "quasi startup factory, university, and venture capital fund rolled into one," as *Fortune* called it. It wasn't easy to get in, but start-ups it deemed worthy got seed funding of $5,000 plus another $5,000 per founder and a priceless wealth of knowledge, connections, operational assistance, and more offered by Graham and his copartners. Between their expertise and that of the program's influential network of alumni, advisers, and investors, "YC" provided hands-on guidance for everything from incorporating and lawyering to hiring, building a business plan, selling to acquirers, and mediating disputes between founders. It was a full-on start-up school, as well known for the access it provided — through dinners, speakers, and the high degree of hand-holding provided by its leaders — as for its specific way of doing things. Its motto, "Make something people want," originally attributed to Paul Buchheit, the creator of Gmail and now a Y Combinator partner, is one of many YC principles that often run counter to conventional MBA wisdom. Chesky would later say that although he went to RISD, he graduated from the school of Y Combinator. Graham himself has become a Silicon Valley folk hero, a prolific thinker and writer on entrepreneurialism known as much for his wisdom as for his tough-love approach.

These days, YC takes on more than a hundred companies each season, but in January 2009, AirBed & Breakfast was one of just sixteen start-ups participating. It was the depths of the Great Recession, and venture funding had dried up; a few months earlier, Sequoia Capital had held a meeting where partners famously presented a slide deck entitled "RIP Good Times." Anyone who was accepted to YC that year was offered the chance to defer and wait for a better investing climate. But the cofounders of AirBed & Breakfast couldn't defer. They were at the end of their rope.

Partially because of the funding conditions, Graham told the entire group to focus on one thing: being profitable by "Demo Day," the twice-yearly event where the newest classes of entrepreneurs present their business plans to investors. Demo Day was set for March; "profitable" was defined by Graham as "Ramen profitable" — raising enough for the entrepreneurs to afford to feed themselves, even if on cheap store-bought noodle mixes. They had three months.

Going in, Chesky, Gebbia, and Blecharczyk had made a pact with one another that for three months they'd give it their all. They'd wake up at 8 a.m. and work until midnight, seven days a week. For once, they would be 100 percent focused; none of them would work on any other side projects. And they decided that if on the last day they didn't get funding, they would go their separate ways. After Graham's introductory lecture, they made their own version of the hockey-stick revenue chart he had showed them and taped it to their bathroom mirror so it was the first thing they saw when they woke up and the last thing they saw before they went to bed. They would update it every week.

There was an almost infinite amount to learn, but the three of them did their best to soak it all up. Very early on, Graham would teach them two important lessons. First, he asked them how many users they had, and they told him not many at all — only a hundred, if that, they said. He told them not to worry, that it's much, much better to have one hundred users who love you than one million users who "sort of like you." It's a tenet that flies in the face of conventional Silicon Valley wisdom, which prioritizes scale and growth above all else, but it sank in, and it gave them hope. Next, he asked them about these users. Where were they, exactly? The founders told them they were mainly in New York City. Graham paused, then repeated back to them what they had just told him: "So, you're in Mountain View, and your users are in New York?" he asked. They looked at each other, then back at him. "Yeah," they said.

"What are you still doing here?" Graham said to them. "Go to New York! *Go to your users.*"

So to their users they went. For the next three months, Gebbia and Chesky flew to New York every weekend. While Blecharczyk stayed behind coding, they went door-to-door, trudging through the snow and meeting or bunking with every user they could. They learned a lot from talking to their customers, but they learned more by simply parking themselves in their living rooms and observing them as they used their product online. Chesky and Gebbia quickly identified two pain points: people had trouble pricing their properties, and photos were a huge problem area. Users didn't take very good ones, and back in 2009 many people still didn't know how to upload them properly. As a result, homes that looked inviting in person looked tired and dingy on the site. So they decided to offer to send professional photographers to each host's home at no charge. But they had no money, so Chesky borrowed a camera from a RISD friend and did it himself, often knocking on the door as the "photographer" to the same hosts he'd visited the day before as the CEO.

Chesky was also a one-man payment system, often taking a checkbook ledger out of his backpack and writing individual paper checks to the hosts they visited. Any customer-service calls went to Gebbia, who took them on his cell phone. They went door-to-door signing people up for the website, hosting meet-ups and approaching people wherever they could to tell them about this great new service that would let them monetize their apartment. They'd take any feedback they received each week and bring it back to Blecharczyk, and week by week they'd make improvements and tweaks to the site.

They also went to Washington, D.C., where they had a small group of users, and made a fast play in late January to pull together another plucky launch around another major event: the inauguration of Barack Obama. They started a website called crashtheinauguration .com and combined the press tactics that had worked so well at the DNC in Denver with their new microtargeting approach of visiting hosts door-to-door, holding meet-ups, cajoling people into listing, and generally rousing the community to life. They ended up getting 700 D.C. residents to list their spaces, and 150 bookings.

Among other things, these experiences also opened their eyes to the narrow view they'd been taking of their business. To qualify for AirBed & Breakfast, the rules required that hosts had to rent out air mattresses, even if they had an actual bed to spare. (Chesky remembers suggesting to one user who wanted to rent out a real bed that he blow up an air mattress and put it on top of the bed so it would qualify.) Another host, a musician who was about to go on tour, asked if he could rent out his full apartment, but Chesky and Gebbia said no; if he wasn't there, how could he provide breakfast? That musician was David Rozenblatt, who was the touring drummer for Barry Manilow, and he forever changed AirBed & Breakfast's business: His request led the cofounders to see that their business could have much bigger potential. They eliminated the breakfast requirement and added the option to rent an entire residence. (Giving a talk at Y Combinator's Startup School, Chesky later recalled Rozenblatt calling him while he was backstage, complaining to Chesky through muted chants of "Barr-y! Barr-y!" that he couldn't log on to his account.) Graham had noted the limitations of the company's early model, too, and somewhere around this time, he suggested they remove "airbed" from the name to broaden its market potential. They bought the domain Airbanb, but it looked too much like "AirBand," so they chose "Airbnb" instead.

During one of those trips to New York, they met with the esteemed venture capitalist Fred Wilson, cofounder of Union Square Ventures. Paul Graham had thought that if any investor were to see the potential in Airbnb, it would be Wilson, who had been early to invest in many of the Web 2.0 start-ups. But after meeting with them, Wilson passed; he and his team liked the founders, but they didn't see the idea as having a huge market. "We couldn't wrap our heads around air mattresses on living room floors as the next hotel room and did not chase the deal," he later wrote on a blog post.

All the while, the cofounders were still model students of Y Combinator, Chesky and Gebbia flying back every week and learning everything they could. They'd arrive to Y Combinator events early even as they were trailing their luggage fresh off the plane from New York. The three of them constantly pestered Graham to meet with them. "We got office hours with Paul Graham every single week, even though he doesn't have time to do office hours," Chesky recalls. "We just showed up before everyone else and stayed after everyone else. We were more shameless than other people, and we were more curious." Graham agrees this was an accurate portrayal: "I certainly talked to them an awful lot," he says. He also noted that, having seen several hundred start-ups come through the program, he'd observed an interesting pattern: the most successful companies always end up being the ones that participated most eagerly. "It's not that the most successful thought they were too good for this," he said. "It's always the crappy companies."

As Demo Day approached, the founders started getting signs of traction — what Graham called "wiggles of hope." Bookings had started to climb, edging up to twenty per day; the sessions with users in New York and the guerilla marketing were paying off, and they could see it in the numbers. The bookings, and the fees to Airbnb, were coming in. A few weeks later they became "Ramen profitable"; they had hit the revenue target — $1,000 in revenue per week — that they'd been aiming for on the chart on their bathroom mirror every day for three months. They celebrated with a champagne toast on the roof of the Rausch Street building.

The Rocket Ship Takes Off

The cofounders had just one other big problem to solve: they needed funding. Investors were always coming by Y Combinator to pay regards to Graham and his partners and to see what was cooking; one day in April 2009, Greg McAdoo, a partner at Sequoia, the vaunted venture-capital firm that had funded Google, Apple, Oracle, and many more, came for a visit. McAdoo and his partners had come to believe the bleak economic climate probably made it a smart time to invest, and he asked Graham what kind of founders he thought were good at getting companies off the ground in down economic times. Graham said founders with "intellectual toughness." McAdoo asked him if any of the founders in the current class exhibited that trait, and Graham said there was an interesting three-person founding team with a unique idea for renting out homes that he might want to talk to. As it turned out, McAdoo happened to have just spent a year and a half doing a deep analysis of the vacation-rental business and knew a great deal about it. He said he'd love to meet them.

McAdoo found Chesky, Gebbia, and Blecharczyk sitting at a long bench huddled over a laptop. They got to talking, and McAdoo asked them if they knew that the vacation-rental industry was a $40 billion industry, as Sequoia had found. Chesky told him he hadn't even thought about putting the words "vacation" and "rental" together when describing their company; the last time he'd even heard that phrase was when his parents rented houses in the summer when he was a kid. "We hadn't connected those dots," he says. But the conversation led to a series of meetings, much to the surprise of the stunned founders, who couldn't believe that after having been summarily dismissed by every investor they'd pitched, one of the most prestigious firms in the venture-capital world was now interested. But interested McAdoo was. He was impressed by their philosophy of building a community of hosts and guests, as well as the way they had designed social mechanisms to address trust issues. These concepts, he said, were "so far out of the thought process of the traditional vacation-rental business, yet it was very clear to me that they solve some if not all of the challenges of bringing together hosts and guests at scale."

Around the same time, the founders had also been talking with Youniversity Ventures, an early-stage fund founded by Jawed Karim, the cofounder of YouTube; Kevin Hartz, the cofounder of Xoom and Eventbrite, now at Founders Fund; and Keith Rabois, a former top executive at PayPal, LinkedIn, and Square, now at Khosla Ventures. The three had been drawn to the idea because it seemed radical but harked back to the age before hotels, when people opened up their homes. "This was almost a reversion to a very standard practice," says Hartz. And they liked the founders, who "seemed like this ideally balanced founding team."

A few weeks later, the Airbnb founders had a term sheet from Sequoia for $585,000. Youniversity invested $30,000, for a total of $615,000. The investments valued the company at $2.4 million.

It's hard to overstate how significant this was. "The moment Sequoia funded us, the rocket ship took off," says Chesky. "There was no turning back." Even more significant than the money was the legitimization. The fact that after so many outright dismissals and rejections Silicon Valley's most prestigious firm had committed to Airbnb was validation that the trio had been onto something all along. It was a huge injection of confidence. "That was by far the most important [thing]," Chesky says now. "The biggest enemy of a start-up is your own confidence and your own resolve. We were told for a long time that this was terrible. Then we were told we were exciting." There would be plenty of pain and hardship still to come, but at least at this critical point they had been proved right. They had been given a chance. (It would be significant for Sequoia, too: that $585,000 investment is, as of this writing, worth roughly $4.5 billion.)

A few other things fell into place. Blecharczyk had told his fiancée, Elizabeth Morey, he'd be back in three months to start their life together in Boston. But on the same day Chesky, Gebbia, and Blecharczyk got their term sheet, Morey learned she'd been matched at Stanford's Lucile Packard Children's Hospital for her medical residency.

Blecharczyk could make a go of the start-up, and Morey would move out to San Francisco.

Over the next few months, the groundwork they had laid in New York continued to pay off. By August, their twenty to thirty bookings a day had hit seventy bookings a day. They started to get attention for quirkier listings, like treehouses, igloos, and tepees. With the Sequoia funding, they started paying themselves an annual salary — $60,000 each, which felt almost gluttonous after their days of milkless bowls of cereal. Chesky's mother and father started, ever so slightly, to relax.

None of them would ever forget how painful the struggle had been. "If you are successful, it will be the hardest thing you ever do," Blecharczyk told YC's Startup School in 2013. Chesky says he has now told the founding story hundreds of times, but there was a time when he didn't think he'd ever tell it a second time. When I first met him, in 2012, I asked him to describe the lowest moment in his career. He said it was starting Airbnb. "It was exciting and in hindsight it's nostalgic and romantic, but at the time it wasn't at all. It was actually very scary."

Chesky continues to maintain that the idea itself is not that crazy, and there was little special about him and Gebbia that made them come up with it. "We weren't visionaries," he says. "We're ordinary guys. We thought, 'There have to be other ordinary people like us with a little extra space that want to make a little money.'"

Some of Airbnb's earliest advisers say there was indeed a lot that was special about them. "People talk about 'minimum viable team,'" Michael Seibel says now. "That was an amazing team." He also points out that they were extremely serious about their business. "You have to understand the number of people you talk to about doing a business versus the number of people who actually did it," he says. "They did it." When they didn't understand something, he says, they went and learned it. If you told them to look something up to learn more, they looked it up. "They didn't spend a lot of time 'imagineering' things," Seibel says. "They launched."

A few years later, the venture capitalist Fred Wilson wrote a rare-for-the-industry mea-culpa blog post describing how passing on Airbnb was a mistake. "We made the classic mistake that all investors make," he wrote. "We focused too much on what they were doing at the time and not enough on what they could do, would do, and did do." Wilson's firm now keeps a box of Obama O's in its conference room as a daily reminder of the one that got away.

2

Building a Company

It's like jumping off a cliff and assembling
the airplane on the way down.

— BRIAN CHESKY, quoting Reid Hoffman,
  partner, Greylock Partners

THEY HAD MADE IT.

While they had come very close, they hadn't died; they had not had
to part ways and each return to their own projects. Airbnb had found
an audience, and it had started to grow; they had liftoff.

In Silicon Valley start-up terms, Chesky, Gebbia, and Blecharczyk
had achieved what's known as "product/market fit," a holy grail,
proof-of-life milestone that a start-up hits when its concept has both
found a good market — one with lots of real, potential customers
— and demonstrated that it has created a product that can satisfy
that market. Popularization of the term is often credited to Marc Andreessen, the celebrated technology entrepreneur–turned–venture
capitalist–turned–philosopher-guru to legions of start-up founders in Silicon Valley. Thousands of start-ups fail trying to get to this
point. Product/market fit is a key first achievement; without it, there
is no company. Another way of saying this is Y Combinator's mantra
that the company has to "make something people want." Whatever
you call it, Chesky, Gebbia, and Blecharczyk had reached that critical
juncture back in April 2009 when their "wiggles of hope" had graduated into a full-fledged revenue stream. They had a product that

people wanted. And it was growing: by August 2009, their $1,000 a week in revenue had become $10,000, and the weekly volume of bookings on Airbnb totaled almost $100,000.

Now came the hard part. The focus had to shift to the longer term: they needed a plan, a road map, a strategy. They needed employees. They needed a culture. They had the product; now they needed to build the company that would *make* that product.

But it was still just the three of them, working eighteen hours a day, seven days a week, together and doing pretty much everything else together. "We may as well all have gotten jumpsuits," Chesky later said during a talk about culture with Sequoia partner and Airbnb board member Alfred Lin for the Stanford University course, "How to Start a Startup." They'd started thinking about their most pressing need — hiring their first engineer — as early as the Y Combinator days, but now it had become crucial. Blecharczyk was still doing all the technical work himself.

But they had also started imagining the kind of company they wanted to build, and had come to the conclusion that getting the right people in the door would have a dramatic long-term impact. Such decisions were not something to be taken lightly. Chesky had read several books about corporate culture and felt that he and his colleagues needed to be careful about whom they would bring in. "I think hiring your first engineer is like bringing in DNA to your company," he told the Stanford students. In other words, they weren't looking for someone to build the next few features; if all went well, this person would end up bringing in hundreds of people like him or her. So getting the first hire right really mattered.

They made a list of companies whose cultures they wanted to emulate. Now possessing the ability to access high-level introductions through the Sequoia network — Greg McAdoo had become a close adviser, and they all were having breakfast once or twice a week together at Rocco's, a neighborhood spot around the corner — Chesky, Gebbia, and Blecharczyk were able to reach out to companies like Zappos, whose culture of friendliness and "zaniness" they particularly admired, as well as Starbucks, Apple, Nike, and others. During one breakfast meeting, they asked McAdoo for an introduction to Zappos CEO Tony Hsieh, whom McAdoo knew since Zappos was a Sequoia portfolio company. McAdoo fired off a quick e-mail introduction as he was on his way to his car, and the next day when he called Chesky was surprised to learn that the founders were already on the ground in Las Vegas, touring Zappos's headquarters.

One thing the founders noticed was that all the companies they admired had a strong mission and a set of defined "core values," a somewhat overused term for the general principles that guide an organization's internal conduct as well as its relationship with its customers, shareholders, and other stakeholders. Core values are a bit of a "thing" in Silicon Valley. But they are seen by organizational-behavior experts as being critical in helping a company define the kind of people it wants to bring in, and they are especially helpful when shaped during a company's formative days.

Chesky, Gebbia, and Blecharczyk decided to compose their core values before they hired anyone. They came up with ten traits, including "Hard-working Olympic animal," "Builds family spirit," and "Passionate about Airbnb." (These would later be replaced with a set of six new core values in 2013, and then whittled down and refined again in 2016.) Then they started seeing people — many, many people. After months of vetting résumés and interviewing candidates, they settled on a fellow Y Combinator alum, Nick Grandy, who'd founded a search-oriented start-up that hadn't gotten off the ground. He believed in the Airbnb product and saw that it was working and being used by people, and he was drawn by the chance to grow it. After a series of interviews, he started in the late summer of 2009 as an engineer, setting up shop in the living room of Rausch Street. The number of employees slowly grew from there, and the founders added a few more engineers and their first customer-service people within a few months. "There was a quiet hum," Grandy said of the apartment setup when he got there. "I joined right at this time that they had done a lot of the hard work of finding product/market fit . . . right at the beginning of a steep growth curve that was an amazing roller-coaster ride."

The interviewing process was intense even by the standards of Silicon Valley engineering recruiting. Joe Zadeh, a bioengineering PhD from Caltech who started in May 2010 as the third engineer and is now VP of product, remembers a months-long process that involved two phone screens and in-person meetings with engineers numbers 1 and 2 before he could even meet with Blecharczyk. Then came a meeting with Gebbia and Chesky together, and after that he was brought back two additional times for a series of one-on-one meetings with every person in the office at the time ("I think some of them were summer interns — it was hard to know," Zadeh says). All told, he went through about fifteen hours of interviewing, after which point he was given a timed three-hour take-home coding challenge.

Zadeh says he knew he was looking at a singular opportunity. He loved the energy and excitement he felt stepping into the Rausch Street apartment — "You could cut it with a knife," he says — and he calls his meeting with Chesky and Gebbia "probably the most fun interview I've ever had" (among other things, they talked about their favorite superpowers). There were also what Zadeh saw as a series of strange coincidences that told him he should join the company. He'd first heard of it only weeks earlier when a few friends texted him about a new service called Airbnb they had been using. A few days later, he was interviewing with another company in Silicon Valley when the employee tasked with driving him to the Caltrain station after the interview spent the whole ride raving about how great Airbnb was. Back at his apartment that night, he went on Airbnb.com, and the first thing he saw was a Frank Lloyd Wright house bookable for $300 per night in Wisconsin. Living in Los Angeles during graduate school, Zadeh had taken an interest in architecture and in Wright, and now this odd website he'd logged on to from this strange company he'd been hearing so much about was offering the chance to stay in one of Wright's homes. The next day, when he happened upon a posting on Hacker News by Blecharczyk saying Airbnb was looking for engineers, he e-mailed him. "There was basically a neon sign that said, 'You have to join this company,'" Zadeh says.

By the summer of 2010, there were twenty-five people, give or take, working out of the Rausch Street apartment. The bedrooms had become meeting rooms, and the founders had taken to doing interviews in stairwells, in the bathroom, and on the roof. Partially to make room and partially to sample their product, Chesky moved out, living on Airbnb for what turned into a year.

Hacking Growth

During this phase, the company was adding more and more users, but it was still largely unknown, so building awareness was still a huge challenge. The founders were still doing everything they could to generate growth. Many of the company's new listings and users were coming from PR and word of mouth, as well as from the frequent trips Gebbia and Chesky would take around big conventions to try to "turn on" new markets with events, host meet-ups, and other guerilla-marketing tactics.

But they had another secret weapon in Blecharczyk, who was making clever use of new tools and technologies available to implement several "growth hacks." He'd created technology to interface with Google's AdWords advertising service, for example, to allow Airbnb to more efficiently target potential users in specific cities. He also cooked up a clever tool by building a back door into Craigslist. In 2009, Craigslist was one of the few sites that had massive scale — it had amassed tens of millions of users — yet it was easily penetrable by marketers and clever entrepreneurs looking to tap in. Blecharczyk created a one-click integration tool whereby Airbnb users could click a button embedded in an e-mail sent to them and instantly rebroadcast their listings on Craigslist. Their listing would be viewable by Craigslist's millions of viewers, but the tool brought the actual bookings back to Airbnb. Many in the engineering community tipped their hats to Airbnb for the sheer ingenuity of the feat, calling it a "remarkable integration" — especially since Craigslist didn't have a public API, or application programming interface, an official set of rules and guidelines for one piece of software to work with another. "This was something that frankly nobody else had," Blecharczyk says. "But because of our know-how, we were able to do it." They experimented with Craigslist in ways that drew criticism, too, at one point hiring contractors who set up automated targeted e-mails to Craigslist users who'd listed their homes on the site for rent, soliciting them to try Airbnb instead. (The company says leveraging Craigslist was common back in those days but it wasn't aware the contractors were engaging in the spamming, which didn't result in meaningful business, and that when they found out they shut it down.) And, of course, when they went to South by Southwest back in 2008, they had lured their first host, Tiendung Le, off of Craigslist to host Chesky on AirBed & Breakfast instead.

The growth hacks became less meaningful over time, as real momentum grew. But it's hard to overestimate the significance of the ability to find these "free ways to grow," as Blecharczyk calls them; had the founders not implemented them, the company might not have mushroomed the way it did.

So how, exactly, does Airbnb work? The company's business model is much like eBay's; it connects buyers and sellers and takes a commission, what's known as the "service fee," politely described on the website as the fee "charged for all reservations to help Airbnb run smoothly and offer 24/7 customer support." This is the company's revenue. For travelers, fees range from 6 percent to 12 percent; the higher the subtotal, the lower the fee. Hosts pay a 3 percent booking fee to cover the costs of payment transfer.

So if a traveler books a listing for $100 per night and its fee is 12 percent, Airbnb adds $12 on top of that, the traveler pays $112 (in addition to any other fees, including cleaning charges levied by the host), and Airbnb keeps the $12 as well as 3 percent of the $100 fee from the host (so the host collects $97). Airbnb charges travelers at the time a reservation is made, but holds funds until twenty-four hours after check-in before releasing it to hosts to make sure everything was as the travelers expected. Hosts can get their money via direct deposit, PayPal, or prepaid debit card (until only very recently, customers could also elect an old-fashioned check in the mail).

Airbnb is a two-sided marketplace, serving one market in travelers and potential travelers, and another in people who rent out space in their homes. But it's lopsided: the traveler side — the demand side — is naturally much bigger; there are many more people who travel, and it's much easier to scale that side by getting people interested in an inexpensive, interesting place to stay than to find people who want to go through the trouble of opening up their own homes to guests. "It's the most difficult supply game I've ever seen anyone play," says Arun Sundararajan, author of *The Sharing Economy*. So while the company has notched more than one hundred million guests, it has just three million listings as of this writing, not all of which may be active on any given day. Anytime Airbnb enters into a new market, it has to grow both sides, but the supply, or host side, is inevitably harder to grow. This is why almost all of the fee structure lies on the guest side. The 3 percent host-booking fee basically covers payment processing only; if anything, Airbnb subsidizes hosts with not just the fee but also its free-professional-photography policy and many other forms of coddling, from mailing out free mugs to featuring stories about some of the hosts on its website to flying certain hosts to its occasional launch events and annual conventions.

Airbnb's business is fundamentally about leveraging a network effect: the more people who list on Airbnb, the more inherently attractive the platform becomes to anyone who wants to travel, because there are more choices; and the more people who travel, the more appealing it becomes for people to list on it, because there are more customers. In Airbnb's case, because its product is travel and the very act of using it involves moving from point A to point B, it is a global network effect enabled by fast and cheap cross-pollination: when a traveler from France uses Airbnb in New York, he or she is more likely to go back to France and consider hosting, or to talk up the company to his or her friends, sparking awareness and ultimately leading to more listing activity in that market. These two points are often continents away from each other, yet new markets are seeded quickly, cheaply, and organically, without staffers or teams ever having to set foot in them. This is a big difference between Airbnb and, say, Uber, which has to physically launch each new market with a heavy investment of fresh marketing, employees, and other resources. The vast majority of Airbnb's growth, both travelers and listings, has come through these travel patterns and this global network effect.

You can look at Airbnb's size and scale in a number of ways. The easiest is those 140 million "guest arrivals" since its inception. Its 3 million active listings — 80 percent of which are outside North America — makes Airbnb the largest provider of accommodations in the world, bigger than any hotel chain. (With its acquisition of Starwood, Marriott International has the largest inventory of any hotel company, with 1.1 million rooms.) Airbnb is not like a hotel, though — its number of listings changes on any given day and swells around large events, and a large number of them go vacant each night, depending on home renters' schedules and frequency preferences. So the sheer number of listings does not correlate with occupancy or transaction volume, though it indicates breadth and scale. The company operates in 191 countries — everywhere but Iran, Syria, and North Korea, as it likes to point out — and in 34,000 cities. Two of the things Airbnb's investors like most are its efficiency and its growth. Because it can expand in such a low-cost manner, it has spent less than $300 million total over eight years, according to estimates; its sharing economy peer Uber was said to have lost $1.2 billion in the first half of 2016 alone. And, eight years in, Airbnb is still growing like a weed. As of this writing, the company was said to be adding 1.4 million users a week, and those 140 million "guest arrivals" were projected to grow to 160 million by early 2017. Investors were expecting the company to see $1.6 billion in revenue and to become cash-flow positive in 2016.

The Steve Jobs Three-Click Rule

One question frequently posed about Airbnb is why it took off when so many other similar sites already existed — Couchsurfing.com, Home Away.com, VRBO.com, even Craigslist itself. Why did Airbnb succeed in popularizing short-term rentals while others did not?

Much of the explanation lies in the product itself. "Product" is a vague and all-encompassing term in the tech world for everything after the idea: it's the actual website or app; the way it looks, the way it works, the things it can do, the engineering that powers it, and the way you use it and interact with it (the "user experience"). The very first Airbnb product was simply the oddball idea and a WordPress website, but when it came time to get ready for the third launch, at the DNC in Denver, the founders had expanded their vision, going from a simple platform for housing supply for sold-out conferences to a website where you could book a room in someone's home as easily as you could book a hotel room. But from the start, Chesky and Gebbia were emphatic about certain things regarding the website and the experience: specifically, it had to be frictionless, it had to be easy. The listings had to look beautiful. And, based on the famous three-click rule from Steve Jobs, a design hero of Chesky and Gebbia's — when Jobs conceived the iPod, he wanted it to never be more than just three clicks away from a song — the founders wanted their users to never be more than three clicks away from a booking.

In fact, what so many investors had seen as a red flag during those early pitch meetings — that Chesky and Gebbia were designers from RISD who lacked technical background — turned out to be one of their biggest assets. To them, design was not just about an object, or in their case a website; it was about how something worked — from the product to the interface to the experience. Later, this approach would infiltrate every aspect of their business, including the way they built the culture, conceived the offices, structured the company, and ran board meetings. But in those early days, it was mainly about the look, simplicity, and overall experience of the website. In tech terms, that's what they "optimized" for.

The focus on design, along with the fact that it traffics in homes, rooms, and travel, sometimes feeds a perception that Airbnb isn't a technology company, but the depth of the technical challenge the platform presented from the outset was significant. There were many elements that the site needed to handle: payment, customer service, and reviews, each a significant engineering undertaking, each taking time to build and refine — and for a very long time, there was only Blecharczyk to do it.

The most complicated part of getting all this right was payments. To reach their goal of booking a room on the site as easily as booking a hotel, the founders knew they needed a seamless, sophisticated online payment mechanism — and, unlike hotels', theirs needed to handle not just taking payment in but also remitting 97 percent of it back to individual hosts. In the run-up to their launch at the DNC, Blecharczyk turned to Amazon to build this mechanism; thanks to the web retailer's new cloud-payments service, it had the ability to collect money from one person and remit it to another without giving Airbnb any of the responsibility of being a bank. It was brand new at the time and therefore not that well documented in the engineering world, so it took Blecharczyk a month to get it working.

But when he showed Chesky and Gebbia, they were underwhelmed: they thought the user experience was terrible — it took too many steps, and there was too much Amazon branding involved. They scrapped it and decided to try becoming the middleman; they would collect money, hold it in their bank account, and then remit it to the customer. That presented its own complications: if they were caught in the middle of a fraudulent, late, or contested transaction, they would be responsible for the chargeback, the make-good amount refunded to the customer. They had steered clear of this approach for that very reason. But they decided this would be the easiest, most seamless experience for the user, so they had to figure out a way to make it work. In time for the DNC, Blecharczyk replaced the Amazon effort with the solution that relied upon PayPal, but he ultimately built an end-to-end payments system that was able to handle the complexities of global markets and currencies and could remit payments to individuals hundreds of thousands of times a day. Airbnb's payments system has evolved over time, and while its sophistication may barely register among travelers who use it, it is considered a feat among engineers.

Given that the company was putting strangers together at night in people's homes, a robust customer-service mechanism was critical. Customer service — the company now calls it Customer Experience — today makes up the largest single group of employees at the company, but up through most of 2009, Gebbia was still handling all incoming calls from his cell phone. So also on Blecharczyk's to-do list was building up a sufficient 24/7 customer-service platform through the site, which would ultimately serve as a "front desk" for the hundreds of thousands of guests staying at Airbnb properties on any given night.

Another challenge was search, or building out a mechanism that would match guests seeking a place to stay with those offering accommodations. That might seem as simple as finding someone with a listing available in a certain location for the selected dates a guest requests. Yet figuring out how to get the right listings in front of the right people was and remains a complicated process. Every listing is unique, not just in its look, feel, location, and price but also in its availability, its host, and its host's set of rules and preferences. And what's great for one person might be terrible for another. It is a two-sided, super-personalized matching problem, yet the founders knew that for the site to succeed, it had to deliver product that both the guest *and* the host would not just like but like so much that both would use the platform again and would tell their friends.

In the early days of Airbnb, the search capabilities were pretty straightforward, returning the highest-quality set of listings that met certain basic filters — number of travelers, dates, amenities — within a certain geographic area. But over time, the company's algorithms grew more advanced, able to factor in things like quality, hosts' behavior patterns, and booking preferences. For example, Airbnb can tell by its users' past behavior that some hosts like to book months ahead of time, while others are more comfortable with eleventh-hour planning; it tries its best to match a last-minute booker with a host who has shown a willingness to accept those kinds of reservations, to reduce the chances of a guest trying to book and being rejected.

Over time, the technology powering Airbnb's search and match would become much more sophisticated. The company now has four hundred engineers and a machine-learning engine that is marching ever closer to Airbnb's holy grail: the nimbleness to extract from perhaps ten thousand available listings for certain dates in, say, Paris, only the five or six that each particular user would like most.

Airbnb continued to iterate on product throughout 2010 and 2011, launching new features like wish lists, which let users create aspirational, Pinterest-style lists of the spaces they most coveted and to publicly view well-known celebrities who'd created theirs, and the ability to link a user's Airbnb account to his or her Facebook account. After the company saw that professionally photographed listings generated two to three times as many bookings as the market average, in late 2011 it expanded the photography program from one thousand shoots per month to five thousand, which fed a surge in bookings.

Airbnb's ability to scale all of this quickly was greatly helped by the fact that it was born in the newfound era of cloud computing. Instead of having to own and build out expensive, resource-intensive servers, warehouses, and data centers, it could store all of its online infrastructure in the cloud; it could rent features and tools from providers that were also in the cloud; and it could essentially outsource all of its computing power. It migrated all these functions to Amazon Web Services, the subsidiary of the online retail giant that has since grown to dominate the market for third-party cloud computing for businesses. Without having to spend any time or energy figuring out how to maintain and run a complicated infrastructure, the Airbnb engineering team could work only on building a robust site and solving the problems unique to its core business. Had the company been founded earlier, that might not have been the case.

But while Airbnb had the benefit of these new innovations, these tools were new and young themselves, and they didn't always work as well as they do today. On any given day, just keeping the site working consistently was sometimes a challenge, because glitches would pop up or "random things would happen," says Blecharczyk. For the first eighteen months and even beyond, a good part of his job would be simply keeping the platform up and running. He set his phone to alert him whenever the site went down with a pop-up that read "Airbeds deflate!" When it went back up, the pop-up read "Airbeds fluffed!" "I was getting pinged by this thing all the time, every other day or so, often in the middle of the night," he says.

Nevertheless, all of this back-end sophistication enabled the company's growth. Ever since the first round of funding from Sequoia, the biggest challenge had been not creating the growth but keeping up with it. In 2010, the company grew nights booked by 800 percent, according to TechCrunch. By November of that year, Airbnb had booked seven hundred thousand nights — 80 percent of which had occurred in the previous six months. The team had by that point moved to new headquarters on Tenth Street in San Francisco.

The company had also started attracting the attention of some high-profile investors who had previously passed. In spring 2010, the founders scored a meeting with someone they'd been trying to land for a while: Reid Hoffman, the cofounder of LinkedIn and partner at venture capital firm Greylock Partners. Hoffman had originally been pitched the idea as a Couchsurfing model, and wasn't interested. "The first person who told me about them pitched the business badly," he says, adding that that person was "a little bit of a doofus when it came to these businesses." But Jeremy Stoppelman, the cofounder of Yelp and an early Airbnb angel investor, told Hoffman it was an exciting idea and said he really needed to meet with its founders.

Ten days later, the Airbnb founders drove down to the Greylock offices on Sand Hill Road in Menlo Park — the mecca for venture capital — to meet with Hoffman. Within a few minutes, Hoffman says, it became clear to him that the concept was not Couchsurfing at all; it was eBay for space, which he saw as an infinitely bigger and far more original idea. He stopped them midway and told them there was no need to keep pitching. "I said, 'Look, I'm going to make you an offer to invest for sure,'" he says. "'So let's still go through your pitch, but let's make it an actual work session. Let's talk about what the challenges are, and let's work through the pitch.'" In November, the company announced its series-A round of funding: $7.2 million in a round led by Greylock Partners. (Hoffman says he learned a lesson from having passed earlier: when a "doofus" pitches a business badly, don't presume it's accurate. "Wait for the good pitch that's reliable," he says.)

One of the things Hoffman liked most was not just the idea but also the chutzpah and hustle the founders had demonstrated — skills, Hoffman says, that are especially critical for entrepreneurs who are starting online-marketplace businesses. "Different kinds of businesses require founders with different primary strengths," he says. "And one of the strengths for marketplace founders is a willingness to think out of the box and be scrappy." Some of the things the Airbnb founders had already done — doing unscalable things in order to later scale — were, Hoffman says, classic marketplace-founder behaviors. "If it were a network or gaming company, that might not have mattered much," Hoffman says. "But in marketplaces, that's really key, and that was in their founding story." The challenge of making rent, the Obama O's, the not dying — "That was the reason I immediately went to, 'I'm going to immediately invest,'" he says.

Two months later, Airbnb announced it had hit one million nights booked. Just four months after that, it doubled again, to two million. But its biggest news was still to come: after months of rumors in tech circles, in mid-July 2011, Airbnb confirmed it had secured a new round of $112 million in funding, led by Andreessen Horowitz. The firm had passed earlier, but had done an about-face. The round also included other key investors like DST Global and General Catalyst Partners, and pegged the company's valuation at $1.2 billion, officially turning it into what's known as a "unicorn," a private company worth at least $1 billion — though the term wouldn't be coined until two years later. The tech website AllThingsD called the amount raised "astonishing" given that Airbnb's first round totaled just $7.8 million.

More than anything else, the fund-raising round was a sign not just that the company had arrived but also that many thought it had the potential to be much bigger. The size and scale of the funding, along with the names of the investors, reverberated around the Valley. The news infused a palpable fear among the investing world of missing out on the next big idea. "Airbnb has become the sleeper hit of the startup world," TechCrunch wrote. During a video interview in May 2011, Chesky marveled that the company had yet to have any kind of problem with a guest's safety. "So, no arrests, no murders, no rapes — you haven't had your Craigslist moment yet," the interviewer, Sarah Lacy, then at TechCrunch, pointed out. "We've had 1.6 million nights booked, no one's been hurt, there's been no reports of any major problems," Chesky boasted. Lacy pressed him: it had to be coming, though, right? "I've driven cars for shorter periods of time, and I've been in three car accidents," Chesky said, "so I'm gonna say it's safer than a car, I have no idea." His comments seemed almost to be tempting fate, his words having a foreshadowing ring to them even as he said them.

The founders had made it past almost unfathomable obstacles to get to where they were. No one had believed in them. Through hot glue and icy investors and heart-pounding nights and panicked parents, they had beaten the massive obstructions in their way. But now they were entering the big leagues. And they were about to face some big-league problems.

A Few "Punches Right in the Face"

During the first Internet boom, a trio of brothers in Germany — Marc, Alexander, and Oliver Samwer — started making a living taking the ideas of the most successful U.S. tech start-ups and cloning them abroad. Their Berlin-based venture capital firm had funded the launch of clones of eBay, Zappos, and Amazon. In 2007 they started another firm, Rocket Internet, to apply this same strategy to the new crop of Internet start-ups. Their playbook was always the same: start copycat websites in Europe early, while the originals were still focused primarily on the United States and before they had the bandwidth and capital for overseas expansion; spend lavishly to grow them almost overnight to dominate the market; and then sell the idea back to the original company, which would by that point pay a huge premium to reclaim "ownership" of its own brand overseas.

In 2010 the three had focused on Groupon, to great success — Groupon ended up buying the clone for a reported $170 million

—and in 2011 they turned their attention to Airbnb. They started a company called Wimdu and its Chinese subsidiary, Airizu, raised $90 million, and within a few months had hired four hundred employees, opened more than a dozen offices, and claimed ten thousand listings. According to Airbnb, it started to hear from members of its platform in Europe about Wimdu's aggressive tactics, which included poaching listings from Airbnb's nascent business there and soliciting hosts to switch to Wimdu. "It was an all-out ground war," says Sequoia's Alfred Lin. When Airbnb first heard about the activity, it sent out an e-mail to its community, warning its users not to engage with these "scam artists."

Airbnb was at a serious disadvantage. It comprised only forty people at the time, and they knew they needed to claim the European market, and fast—Airbnb couldn't call itself a travel company and not be available all over the world, particularly in Europe. ("It would be like a cell phone without a signal—there would be no reason to exist," Chesky said during an interview with Reid Hoffman at Hoffman's Stanford University class "Technology-Enabled Blitzscaling.") Sure enough, soon the Samwer brothers made a proposition to Airbnb to sell it Wimdu. It prompted a major moment of soul-searching for Airbnb. By now having access to the top minds in Silicon Valley, as Chesky recounted to Hoffman's students, he asked for advice from a growing panel of high-octane advisers: Mark Zuckerberg, Andrew Mason, Paul Graham, and Hoffman. Everyone had a different opinion: Mason, he said, having just gone through the experience, told him Wimdu had the potential to kill Airbnb. Zuckerberg, Chesky said, advised him not to buy, because whoever had the best product would win. In the end, the advice Chesky took came from Paul Graham, who told him that the difference between Airbnb and Wimdu was that Airbnb owners were missionaries, and Wimdu owners were mercenaries. Missionaries, he told him, usually win.

In what Chesky would later call a "bet the company" moment, the cofounders decided not to buy Wimdu, mainly for the reason Graham mentioned: Chesky didn't want to absorb four hundred new employees who he felt were mercenaries and whom Airbnb had had no say in hiring. They also decided that since the Samwer brothers likely had no interest in running the company long-term — their whole business model revolved around selling companies, not running them — the best revenge was to force them to actually run the giant company they'd just built. "You had the baby, now you've got to raise the child, and you're stuck with it," as he told Hoffman.

But while saying no might have been the right thing for the company's values and culture, the pressure was now on to reclaim the European market. Airbnb immediately acquired another German company, Accoleo — an imitator but not an extortionist — and started an international sprint in terms of hiring and training country managers and tasking them with opening and growing in their local markets. Within the next three months, Airbnb had opened ten offices and hired hundreds of people overseas. (Wimdu is still operating and boasts ten million nights booked.)

Overall, it was a close call and a big lesson. But in terms of a crisis, it was nothing like what happened a few weeks later.

For years, one of the biggest reasons investors had hesitations about Airbnb was the safety issue; in many, many people's minds, the biggest reason the very idea of letting strangers sleep in their homes was asinine was that it was simply asking for trouble. But from the start, the Airbnb founders maintained that the tools they had designed — personal profiles and photos for guests and hosts, plus the robust two-sided review and reputation system — would help guard against safety concerns. And, by 2011, since nothing bad had happened yet, they felt confident that they were doing everything right.

On June 29, 2011, as has been well documented, a woman named EJ published a wrenching post on her blog about how Airbnb renters had trashed her home earlier that month. It wasn't just trashed; it was violently destroyed. The tenants had torn through everything EJ owned, turning her apartment and her world inside out. They broke through a locked closet door and stole her camera, iPod, computer, her grandmother's jewelry, her birth certificate, and her Social Security card. They found coupons and shopped online. They burned her things in her fireplace without opening the flue, so ash covered every surface. They cut tags off of pillows and doused powdered bleach over her furniture, counters, desk, and printer. Her clothes and towels were left in a wet, mildewed pile on the closet floor. Her bathroom sink was caked in a "crusty yellow substance." All the while, the person or account who'd rented the apartment — an Airbnb user named "Dj Pattrson" — was sending EJ friendly e-mails about how much he or she loved the "beautiful apartment bathed in sunlight," especially the "little loft area" upstairs.

It was an extreme version of what could go wrong, well beyond anyone's imagination. And the victim could not have been more sympathetic: a freelancer who was trying to make ends meet, she wrote movingly how she had made her home into her "own private retreat, my sunny, bright, cozy loft that I would melt into on those rare occasions when I wasn't traveling," and how it reflected "a home life that was all mine, a place that was peaceful, and safe." She wrote about her decision to rent it out: "It seemed silly to let a perfectly good apartment sit empty while I traveled, when there were so many visitors to San Francisco in need of a place to stay, who wanted to experience a city as I preferred to: in a local's home, outside the tourist bubble of a hotel." She was not new to home sharing, having rented her place through Craigslist several times when she lived in New York, with "exceptional results." She had recently tried Airbnb as a traveler and loved it. In short, if Airbnb could have drawn up a poster-child user, one who embodied all the values the company was trying to engender among its community members, they couldn't have done better than EJ.

In her post, she was remarkably level-headed about Airbnb's role, even giving the company the benefit of the doubt. "I do believe that maybe 97% of airbnb.com's users are good and honest people," she wrote. "Unfortunately I got the other 3%. Someone was bound to eventually, I suppose, and there will be others." But she asked what, exactly, she had received for her fee to Airbnb. Craigslist was free, she wrote, but it warned her over and over again that her use of the site was at her own risk and encouraged her to communicate with potential houseguests. Airbnb tightly controls the exchange of personal contact information until a reservation is paid for. The implication, she wrote, was that Airbnb had already done the research for her and that that was what her fee went toward. But the system had massively failed.

EJ wrote that the perpetrators had stolen something that couldn't be replaced — her "spirit." She wrote of staying with friends, suffering through panic attacks, and spending afternoons scouring pawnshops looking for her stolen belongings.

EJ had e-mailed the company's "urgent@airbnb" emergency line, but she didn't hear back until the next day and only after she'd gotten in touch with a friend who had done some work for the company. Immediately after customer service learned of her situation, they were empathetic and proactive; as EJ wrote in her first post: "I would be remiss if I didn't pause here to emphasize that the customer service team at airbnb.com has been wonderful, giving this crime their full attention. They have called often, expressing empathy, support, and genuine concern for my welfare. They have offered to help me recover emotionally and financially, and are working with SFPD to track down these criminals."

Few people knew about the story for almost a month. But then EJ's post was picked up by Hacker News, and it went viral. Internally, Airbnb was reeling. It had never been through a crisis like this before, and it wasn't prepared for it. Chesky, Gebbia, and Blecharczyk, the executive team, and the company's entire customer-service department, including a dozen or so who had flown in from remote posts, were there almost 24/7 in the coming weeks — they pulled in air mattresses, but no one laughed at the irony — and the founders had their entire team of advisers weighing in, too. Their newest investors, Andreessen Horowitz, split their duties into two shifts at one point, Jeff Jordan, general partner and new Airbnb board member, handling days and Marc Andreessen taking over for nights. (The megaround of funding had just been announced, and many felt it was the attention around the publicity of the news that caused EJ's story to get picked up and go viral.)

Yet everyone had a different opinion on how to handle the crisis. Some argued that taking any responsibility would just open the door to more complaints; others said the company should admit that it dropped the ball; still others said they should just retreat and stay completely quiet.

On July 27, Chesky released the company's first public response and attempted to reassure the community that someone was in custody, that Airbnb held safety as its highest priority, and that it had been in close contact with EJ and authorities to "make this right." He outlined some of the safety improvements the company would begin instituting.

The letter made things worse.

EJ wrote another post contradicting Chesky's claims: she said that the customer-service team that had been so helpful suddenly disappeared after she'd written publicly about the attack, and said a cofounder, but not Chesky, called her shortly after and told her they had knowledge about the person in custody but couldn't share information. She said this cofounder — it was Blecharczyk — expressed concern about the negative impact her blog post could have and asked that she take it down. She said the company had not done anything to secure her safety or to compensate her for expenses in doing so. She ended the post suggesting that anyone who wanted to help should keep their money and use it to book a real hotel the next time they traveled. Meanwhile, another Airbnb user came forward with an equally horrific story about how crystal-meth users had similarly trashed his apartment a few months earlier.

The bad situation was getting worse. And despite having access to the best advisers, Chesky was still getting a lot of conflicting advice. Almost everyone was focused on the impact on the company, and afraid of doing or saying anything that would exacerbate the situation. Advisers were telling Chesky not to bother EJ, that she said she wanted to be left alone. Lawyers urged him to be very careful about what he said. But being cautious and quiet was exactly what was making things worse. At one point, Chesky finally realized he needed to stop listening to these advisers. "I had this really dark moment where I wouldn't say I stopped caring, but my priorities completely changed," he says. He realized he needed to stop managing for the outcome and manage instead in accordance with his and the company's values. He felt he needed to apologize, and in a big way.

On Monday, August 1, Chesky posted a strongly worded letter. "We have really screwed things up," he wrote. "Earlier this week, I wrote a blog post trying to explain the situation, but it didn't reflect my true feelings. So here we go." He said that the company had mishandled the crisis and the importance of always upholding your values. He said Airbnb had let EJ down and that they should have responded faster, with more sensitivity and more decisive action. He announced a $50,000 guarantee protecting hosts against damage, effective retroactively as well. (A few months later, Airbnb increased the guarantee to $1 million.) He announced a twenty-four-hour customer hotline — something EJ had said they should have had in place — and said they were doubling customer support.

All of this went against the advice Chesky was receiving. "People were, like, 'We need to discuss this, we need to do testing,'" he said, "and I said, 'No, we're doing this.'" The one piece of advice he did take: Marc Andreessen, who gave the letter a close read at midnight, told Chesky to add his personal e-mail address to the letter of apology, and he added a zero, changing the guarantee from $5,000 to $50,000. (The San Francisco Police Department subsequently confirmed that it had made an arrest. Airbnb says there was a settlement in the case but declined to comment more than that.)

Chesky's primary takeaway from this experience: stop making decisions by consensus. "A consensus decision in a moment of crisis is very often going to be the middle of the road, and they're usually the worst decisions," he says. "Usually in a crisis you have to go left or right." From then on, "add a zero" became a euphemism for taking one's thinking to the next level. He would later call the experience a "rebirth" for the company.

Chesky has said these challenges were like sudden blows that came when he was least expecting them. "It's like you're walking down the street and someone just punches you in the side of the face, and you never saw them coming," he told Reid Hoffman during their Stanford talk.

As part of Airbnb's rebirth, the founders made a few key hires. If the experience with EJ had taught them anything, it was that they needed a communications pro. They found Kim Rubey, a veteran of Democratic politics who'd decamped for eBay and then Yahoo. She had crisis, consumer, and government experience, which seemed like the right combination. She interviewed with all three founders and put together a hundred-day plan. After she accepted, they told her that, by the way, they'd be launching in ten new markets in Europe in a few weeks. "It was, like, 'Oh, we forgot to tell you . . . ,'" she says.

And Chesky made a key executive hire in Belinda Johnson, the former deputy general counsel of Yahoo. Johnson had gone to the search giant with its acquisition of Broadcast.com, where she'd been general counsel, helping navigate the nascent days of radio streaming, copyright infringement, and privacy issues, all in the earliest days of the Internet. She had left Yahoo and was looking for her next opportunity, which she was hoping would be an earlier-stage, consumer-facing business, and she'd been following Airbnb in the news. "I was excited about what I was reading," she says. She started in the fall of 2011 at the new San Francisco headquarters the company had recently moved into, on Rhode Island Street.

Surviving Versus Firefighting

Airbnb's three founders had started to scale, but they were also learning some big lessons on their way to becoming a billion-dollar company. Before, in the days when Chesky, Blecharczyk, and Gebbia were trying so desperately to get the idea off the ground, the focus was simply on surviving. "Before product/market fit, thinking long-term seemed preposterous," Chesky later said. "When you're dying, you're not thinking, 'What do I want to be when I grow up?' You're thinking, 'How do I not die?'"

In retrospect, those milkless-cereal days were more straightforward. Now, they had crises and competitors. Make-or-break decisions happened in an instant. Everyone was starting to think more about the long-term goals, but there were still minute-to-minute decisions to deal with, because the company hadn't built out simple foundational work.

As Reid Hoffman once said to Chesky, it was like "jumping off a cliff and assembling the airplane on the way down." In a short period of time, the founders had to hire lots of people — by late 2011, it had roughly 150 people in the office and another 150 overseas — and then figure out what management even meant. They had to design and build a culture and needed things like road maps — not just for the next day or the next two weeks but for the next three months, so their new employees would know what to work on. On the customer side, there were now millions of people staying at Airbnbs and on some days not enough customer support to service them.

People often ask Chesky about the founding days, but he says that to think about the company only in those terms glosses over stages 2 through 5, which are much, much harder; he describes them as "firefighting." This phase can be a lonely place — there are plenty of books on starting a company, he says, and plenty on managing people in large organizations, but there aren't a lot of books on the stages that are in between.

In Airbnb's case, the hypergrowth phase would last for a really long time. Chesky told me in early 2012 that it was finally at that point when he started to develop a rhythm and was able to think more long-term. The company wouldn't exit hypergrowth for quite a long time — it is still in it — but more key executive hires would come, as would a move in 2013 into huge new headquarters. Airbnb had gone from being called the "eBay for space" in Silicon Valley elevator-pitch parlance to becoming a standard that other start-ups were modeled after: Boatbound pitched itself as the Airbnb of boats, dukana was to be the Airbnb of equipment, and DogVacay was the Airbnb for dogs.

These days, Airbnb is a juggernaut. There are more than 2,500 employees, including 400 engineers and a customer-service department that's bigger. And that's just inside the company. There is also the most important constituency in the Airbnb story, and it lies outside the four walls of its headquarters: the hosts and the travelers; in other words, the millions of people who turned Airbnb from a company into a movement.

3

Airbnb Nation

Uber is transactional; Airbnb is humanity.

— ELISA SCHREIBER, Greylock Partners

THE FORMATION AND GROWTH of Airbnb the company is an entrepreneurial saga for the ages. The struggle the founders faced to get it off the ground, the technology, product, and culture they built, and the way it swiftly became a high-performing growth machine make up a tale of surprising corporate agility. That they did it all within just a matter of a few years, with little prior experience, is striking.

But to study only what happens within the four walls of the company itself would be to miss almost the entire "story" of Airbnb. Airbnb — the company — is those 2,500 or so people, mostly in San Francisco. Airbnb — the movement — is millions of people on the ground, everywhere.

Many millions of people have used an Airbnb. Its business is seasonal, but the company hit a new nightly peak during the summer of 2016, when 1.8 million people were staying on Airbnb-procured accommodations in a single night. Yet even with those numbers, the company's penetration is still low: many people still haven't heard of it at all, and when you mention the concept to them, it still sounds just as bizarre as it sounded to the first few investors who wouldn't touch it.

Many people I brought it up to over the course of reporting this book recoiled when I mentioned the idea. For some of them, there's an "ew" factor. "I would *never* do that," says one friend of a friend. "What if you end up on someone's dirty sheets?" The reaction of a driver hired by a major morning news show to pick me up and take me to the studio one morning was typical. He hadn't heard of it, but after I explained the idea, he shook his head and said he would simply never do it. First, he said, this is exactly how you spread bedbugs. Plus, he pointed out, if you open your doors to strangers, you have no idea whom you're letting in your home: "You could have a killer on the loose!" He's right. You could. Plenty of things did go wrong: There was the EJ situation, of course, and more bad incidents to come. But any study of the Airbnb phenomenon has to first look at the need it identified and the hole it has filled. Because you don't get to millions and millions of customers without, as Y Combinator's Paul Graham would say, making something people want.

In Airbnb's first few years, it had a reputation for being a website where millennials went for cheap options and stayed in someone's living room or in a spare bedroom. But over time, it evolved. If there were three phases of Airbnb, they could be very loosely categorized as the couch-surfing phase of the very early days; the igloo-and-castle phase, when the growth started to take off and the company became known for all the odd, quirky, get-a-load-of-this spaces; and the Gwyneth Paltrow phase, when its user base and inventory had expanded to such a degree that the actress spent a vacation in January 2016 at an $8,000-per-night Airbnb listing in Punta Mita, Mexico, and then returned a few months later to book a villa on the Cote d'Azur for $10,000 per night. The significance of the Paltrow phase was twofold: first, that Airbnb had become a legitimate option for the pickiest, most sophisticated of travelers, and, second, that it had become so large a platform that it basically had something for everyone.

Today the scope of Airbnb's inventory reflects the diversity in the world's housing market. Its three million listings are all unique, and the range of properties and experiences available is hard to imagine.

You can pay $20 to sleep on an air mattress blown up in someone's kitchen, or you can pay tens of thousands per week for a villa in Mexico like Paltrow's. On a recent day, the options in New York ranged from $64 a night for a basement apartment in Jamaica, Queens, to $3,711 for a five-story townhouse on East Tenth Street. In Paris, $24 would have scored you a room with a twin bed and a washbasin in the southwestern suburb of Fontenay-aux-Roses, but lay down $8,956 and you could have spent the night in a triplex apartment in the Sixteenth Arrondissement with a private garden facing the Eiffel Tower and "VIP hotel services."

The breadth and whimsy of the options offered makes scrolling through Airbnb's listings an exercise in escapism. There are almost three thousand castles on the site, like the Château de Barnay in Burgundy, France, or the medieval fortress in Galway where travelers sleep in the turret. There are scores of windmills and houseboats. There are hundreds of treehouses, and they are some of the most popular listings on the site: the most "wish-listed" property is a series of three rooms suspended in the treetops of a woodsy neighborhood in Atlanta, connected by rope bridges and draped in twinkly lights. The most popular listing is the Mushroom Dome, a rustic geodesic dome cabin in Aptos, California, that has five stars and more than nine hundred reviews and books up to six months in advance. Says Reid Hoffman, "If I were giving advice to someone, I would say give serious thought to building a nice treehouse. They have waiting lists for months." Other listings include horse ranches, retro trailers, shipping containers, wagons, yurts, and buses, like the one located in a vegetarian community in Sweden (house rules: "We appreciate that you do not eat or bring meat to the bus"). There are one hundred lighthouses.

Over time, Airbnb started to assume a place in the cultural conversation: during the 2016 presidential election, *The New Yorker* ran a humor piece listing Airbnb customer reviews of the candidates. "During the 2000 race between Al Gore and George W. Bush, the question of the day was: who would you rather have a beer with?" the spoof read. "In the 2016 primary season, it's: who would you rather rent your home to on Airbnb?" Companies started using Airbnb as a marketing platform, creating specially themed listings around their brands: in the summer of 2016, pegged to the release of the movie *Finding Dory,* Pixar listed a night on a chic floating raft in the Great Barrier Reef designed to bring winners as close as possible to the natural habitat of Dory and Nemo.

Of course, not everyone wants to stay on a raft or be suspended in the trees (the Aptos geodesic dome has a composting toilet, so you have to throw your toilet paper in the garbage), or even sleep in the turret of a fifteenth-century castle. If anything, the more fanciful listings may serve more as image boosters, fodder for an endless stream of Airbnb-friendly news stories like "18 Fairytale Airbnb Castles That'll Make Your Dreams Come True."

The vast majority of the listings are more utilitarian. They are all over the map, both literally — only a quarter of Airbnb's business is in the United States — and figuratively, coming in every size, shape, price point, and level of host interaction. You can stay in someone's home that is excessively personalized, with all their trinkets, books, and bathroom products, or you can choose one that looks much more like a modern minimalist hotel room. You can stay while the host is on the premises, you can have the full place to yourself, or you can choose a situation that falls somewhere in between, like a guest cottage where the owner lives full-time in the main house or an in-law suite with a separate entrance. The level of interaction with the host can be zero, or it can be over the top; some hosts make dinner for their guests and, of course, breakfast (the hosts of a thatched cottage in the countryside of Salisbury, England, for instance, offer both a full English breakfast in their kitchen or the option of having a basket of home-baked pastries and jam delivered to the door of the upstairs suite they rent out).

"It's Anticommodity"

Exactly why Airbnb has caught on in the way it has is due to a combination of factors. A big one is price. The company was formed in the depths of the Great Recession, in 2008, and while listings run the gamut, by and large they are usually a lot cheaper than staying in a standard hotel. One of the most truly disruptive things about Airbnb is that you can now find a simple place to stay in New York City for under one hundred dollars per night.

The other reasons are less tangible but arguably even more important. Part of Airbnb's success is that it tapped into a dissatisfaction with the mass commodification of large-scale hotel chains. Even the hotel companies recognize this. "Twenty years ago when you listened to what travelers wanted, they wanted a clean room and not to be surprised," Arne Sorenson, CEO of Marriott International, explained in an onstage interview about disruption at the American Magazine Media Conference in early 2016. "That fed our brand's strategy: OK, let's make sure it all looks similar." Now, he says, what the traveler wants has changed: "If I'm waking up in Cairo, I want to know I'm in Cairo. I don't want to wake up in a room that looks like a room in Cleveland."

Much in the same way we now want homespun, small-batch artisanal everything — from bread to pickles to cocktail ice — many travelers, and especially millennial travelers, want the same kind of imperfect authenticity from their travel experiences. That could mean staying with a retiree who likes the company, or having a chic Soho loft all to yourself that you have to find through a back entrance off a side street. It could be opting for a room in a Craftsman tucked away in the hills of Los Angeles's Silver Lake that comes with access to a sunny private garden. Whatever form it takes, it's something that's different, real, and unique. It's making travel excessively personal when it had become impersonal. "It's anticommodity," says Greylock's Reid Hoffman. "It's uniqueness. It's humanization."

Just as disruptive as the spaces themselves is the option Airbnb gives travelers to stay outside the main hotel and tourism districts and within corners and crevices of cities they don't typically get to see. This is a big marketing hook for Airbnb, and it's a smart one: hotels in big cities are often centralized to the commercial zones. The ability to stay on a tree-lined block in brownstone Brooklyn or a newly surfacing residential neighborhood in Prague is a novel concept and, for many travelers, is more desirable. And while this experience has always been possible on sites like Craigslist or through classified ads or local messaging boards, Airbnb ripped the market open; put it on an accessible, fast, user-friendly platform; and drew millions to it. So it became both acceptable, since millions of people were using it, and desirable, since it was populated with all that growing and beautifully photographed inventory.

I think of my own experience traveling recently to Washington, D.C. I love nice hotels, and once a year, thanks to the grace of corporate negotiated rates, I get to stay at the Four Seasons in Georgetown, one of my favorite hotels in what I truly believe is one of the most beautiful neighborhoods in America. In the spring of 2016, I decided to try Airbnb instead, and booked a hundred-year-old carriage house with a landscaped garden tucked behind a townhouse and down a narrow stone alleyway in the neighborhood's historic residential section. It was less than a mile away from the Four Seasons but deep inside a neighborhood I wouldn't have otherwise ventured into. I still love the Four Seasons Georgetown, and this same example also serves as a reminder of what hotels offer that Airbnb doesn't (the cable went out during a rainstorm). But it also demonstrates why Airbnb is so disruptive. It's less commodified, more unique. It's less about the big avenues and wide arterial roads and the commercial zones where the hotels are often located, and more about the parts of the city reserved for the people who live there. It's about, as Airbnb would later promote, experiencing a place like a local rather than as a tourist. And while that's not always right for everyone — and that very aspect of it can have plenty of consequences on those who live in those quiet residential neighborhoods, a phenomenon we'll explore later — there are a whole lot of people who prefer to see the world in this way. On a subsequent to Washington, D.C., I returned to that listing.

A Logo, a Rebrand, a Mission

Sometime in 2013, Airbnb started thinking about reorienting its entire mission and center of gravity to better articulate the elements that made using its platform so unique. In a process led by Douglas Atkin, the company's global head of community who'd joined earlier that year, it had come to focus these aspects around a single idea, the notion of "belonging." Atkin, an expert on the relationship between consumers and brands and author of the book *The Culting of Brands*, had come to the idea after months of intense focus groups with some five hundred members of Airbnb's user base all around the world, and by mid-2014 the company had settled on an entire repositioning around this concept. Airbnb had a new mission statement: to make people around the world feel like they could "belong anywhere." It had a new color: magenta. And it had a new logo to symbolize this: a cute, squiggly little shape that was the result of months of conceiving and refining that it called the "Bélo." It had been named by the company's new chief marketing officer, Jonathan Mildenhall, who'd recently joined from Coca-Cola. Mildenhall also convinced the founders to expand "belong anywhere" from an internal mission statement to the company's official tagline.

In July 2014, the company introduced the rebrand, as well as an attendant redesign of its mobile app and website, in a big launch event at its headquarters. Chesky introduced the concept in a cerebral, high-minded essay on Airbnb's website: A long time ago, he wrote, cities used to be villages. But as mass production and industrialization came along, that personal feeling was replaced by "mass-produced and impersonal travel experiences," and along the way, "people stopped trusting each other." Airbnb, he wrote, would stand for something much bigger than travel; it would stand for community and relationships and using technology for the purpose of bringing people together. Airbnb would be the one place people could go to meet the "universal human yearning to belong." The Bélo itself was carefully conceived to resemble a heart, a location pin, and the "A" in Airbnb. It was designed to be simple, so that anyone could draw it; rather than protect it with lawyers and trademarks, the company invited people to draw their own versions of the logo — which, it was announced, would stand for four things: people, places, love, and Airbnb.

To say Airbnb can be idealistic at times is an understatement, and while its customers seemed to embrace the concept, the media were more skeptical. TechCrunch called "Belong anywhere" a "hippy-dippy concept," while others wondered whether it was really warm and fuzzy "belonging" that drove people to Airbnb or whether they just wanted a cheap and cool place to stay. And as soon as it launched, media outlets lampooned the Bélo, not for its idealism so much as for its shape, which they said looked alternately like breasts, buttocks, and both male and female genitalia all at once. Within twenty-four hours the sexual interpretations of the logo had been curated and posted on a Tumblr blog. "Nothing says temporary home like the vagina-butt-uterus abstraction that Airbnb chose as its new logo," tweeted Katie Benner of the *New York Times*.

I, too, remember being highly skeptical — not of the logo but of the "belonging" concept upon first hearing about it. I thought it meant spending time with the person who lived in the space you rented. In the few times I had used Airbnb, I definitely hadn't met or seen my host and didn't want to; I mainly wanted to save money.

But "belonging" in the Airbnb-rebrand context didn't have to be about having tea and cookies with the person who lives in the space you rent. It was much broader: it meant venturing into neighborhoods that you might not otherwise be able to see, staying in neighborhoods and places as a traveler you wouldn't normally be able to, bunking in someone else's space, and having an experience that person "hosted" for you, regardless of whether you ever laid eyes on him or her. A few months after my spring 2016 trip to Georgetown, when I booked a place through Airbnb in Philadelphia during the Democratic National Convention, I warily pushed open the door to an apartment in a run-down walk-up in Rittenhouse Square to find an inviting studio with high ceilings; huge, heavy doors; walls lined with books; cozy, minimalist decor; and a string of twinkly lights hanging over the fireplace. I liked everything about "Jen's" place, from her book collection, which mirrored mine, to the towels she'd fluffed and folded, to the handwritten card she left for me. (It helped that Jen and I had the same aesthetic taste, but then that's precisely why I picked her listing.)

"When you stay in an Airbnb, even if the host isn't there, it's personal," says NYU's Arun Sundararajan. "It's intimate. There's this connection that you have with this person, with their art, with their choice of linens, with their wedding pictures. And that evokes in us a sense of something that we have lost."

Whatever the press thought of the rebrand, Airbnb's users seemed to "get" it — over the next few months, more than eighty thousand people went online and designed their own versions of the logo, a rate of consumer-brand engagement that would be considered off the charts by larger brands. (Airbnb even embraced the hubbub around the logo. Douglas Atkin, who spearheaded the journey to "belonging," later referred to it as "equal-opportunity genitalia.")

By this point, the company's user base had also evolved. While Airbnb's first adapters were cash-strapped millennials looking for a good deal, its demographics started to broaden. Millennials are still the company's core — they are the ones most likely to use the term as a verb, as in "I'll be able to go to Coachella after all — I'll just Airbnb" (the translation being that cost isn't an impediment; they will find a way to be there). But the company's user base has fanned out as it has matured. The average age of a guest is thirty-five; a third are over the age of forty. The average age of a host is forty-three, but those over sixty are the company's fastest-growing host demographic.

These days, Airbnb users are just as likely to be people like Sheila Riordan, fifty-five, a marketing and client-services manager and founder of cmonletstravel.com, a service that plans unique travel itineraries, who lives with her husband and three children in Alpharetta, Georgia. In 2013, Riordan had a business trip to London and was planning to bring her husband and eleven-year-old son with her, but she waited too long to book a hotel, and by the time she tried, even the Holiday Inn Express was $600 a night. So she tried

Airbnb instead, renting the apartment of a woman who lived across the Thames for around $100 per night. Riordan's husband was reluctant — "He loves his American bathrooms," she says — but the space was charming and fit all of them and was a bargain relative to the city's hotels.

Not too long after that, Riordan took her eighteen-year-old daughter to Paris and Amsterdam and used Airbnb. In Paris, they rented a studio on the Left Bank that was "nothing fancy," but it was a nice building in a nice neighborhood, with double doors that opened out onto a view of a patio garden below. In Amsterdam, they stayed in an apartment between two canals ten steps from the Anne Frank House. The homes had their quirks — the apartment of their Paris host, Ahmed, featured an 18 x 24 portrait of himself with his mother over the bed — but they loved it. "It makes the trip more interesting," she says. Back home in Alpharetta — a conventional suburb characterized by culs-de-sac and spacious, similar-looking homes — many in her circle think she's crazy. "They say to me, 'You're so daring.' They want to come home to the air-conditioned Hilton. I would much rather come home and sit in the garden with the host, who can tell us the best places to go in town."

The Super-Users

The company's most hardcore users are a small subgroup of people who choose to live full-time on Airbnb rentals, nomadic globetrotters who migrate from one listing to another. A few years ago, when David Roberts and his wife, Elaine Kuok, relocated to New York City from Bangkok (Kuok is an artist, Roberts is a documentary filmmaker and former academic physicist), they decided to live in a different neighborhood, one month at a time, using Airbnb.

Their story gained attention after they were featured in the press, but in fact it's becoming a trend. TechCrunch labeled this phenomenon the "rise of the hipster nomad" in an article penned by Prerna Gupta, an entrepreneur who, with her husband, opted out of the

Silicon Valley rat race to wander the globe. They got rid of most of their things, put the rest in storage, and spent much of 2014 living for weeks or months at a time in Costa Rica, Panama, El Salvador, Switzerland, Sri Lanka, India, and Crete.

Kevin Lynch, a creative director for an ad agency, moved to Shanghai from Chicago with his wife and daughter four years ago. When his company asked him to assume responsibility for the Hong Kong market as well, instead of renting an apartment for his trips there and settling into what he calls the "expat bubble," he decided to sample his way through the city on Airbnb. He's stayed in more than 136 different listings so far and says the ability to constantly seek out new, unfamiliar environments let him tap into an "explorer" mind-set. "I believe the better you know a place, the less you notice it," he says.

None of these "hipster nomads" can really compare with Michael and Debbie Campbell, a retired couple from Seattle who in 2013 packed up their belongings, put everything that didn't fit into two suitcases into a storage unit, rented out their townhouse, and "retired" to Europe, where they have lived almost exclusively on Airbnb for the past four years. As of the fall of 2016, they had stayed at a total of 125 listings in fifty-six countries. They spent months plotting everything out before making the decision, but doing the math, they realized that if they kept their costs in check, they could essentially "live" on Airbnb for the same amount of money it would cost them to live in Seattle.

To make it work, the Campbells — Michael is seventy-one, and Debbie is sixty — are frugal and meticulous about what they spend. Their nightly budget is ninety dollars, though they will go above that in cities that are more expensive, like Jerusalem, and make up for it in, say, Bulgaria or Moldova. They eat almost every meal at home and keep up the same rituals they'd have if they were still living in Seattle, like playing Scrabble or dominoes after dinner. So when they hunt for listings, they look for a big dining-room table, a well-equipped kitchen, and good Wi-Fi. They rent a full apartment or a home rather than a room in a home, but they almost always stay in places where the host will greet them. Their average stay is nine days;

they book three to four weeks ahead of time; and they often ask for discounts, but nothing too extreme and only because they are militant about staying on their budget: spending 20 percent more than you'd planned when you're on a two-week vacation is one thing, but do it for 365 nights and, as Michael points out, "there goes your nest egg. We're not on vacation," he says. "We're just living our daily lives, in other people's homes."

The Campbells have made lots of friends along the way, including their host in Madrid who took their Christmas-card photo; the host in Cyprus who gave them a walking tour of Nicosia and helped them through the checkpoint; and Vassili, the host in Athens who served them a Greek barbecue and took Michael with him to a World Cup–qualifying soccer match, speeding to the stadium together on the back of Vassili's motorcycle.

In the summer of 2015, the Campbells sold their home in Seattle officially. They know their Airbnb global approach is not for everyone, and they're not sure how long they'll continue, but they have no plans to stop. As Michael said in an onstage talk the couple were invited to give at the 2015 Airbnb Open, "We're not rich, but we're comfortable, we're lifelong learners, we're healthy, and we're curious." They chronicle their adventures at seniornomads.com.

They seem to have struck a chord: A *New York Times* article on the Campbells was among the paper's most e-mailed articles that week; after it ran, they heard from lots of people in their age group whose adult children had encouraged them to try it out. The Campbells' oldest son and his family decided to follow in their footsteps: he and his wife pulled their two kids out of school for a year and took a year off themselves to travel around the world. They called themselves the "junior nomads."

Getting the Most out of Hosts

The key to all of this, of course, to the entire Airbnb ecosystem and to the company itself, is the people who deliver the inventory: the hosts. The platform offers a place for travelers to stay in other people's homes or apartments, but without those residences there simply is no company; there is no Airbnb. It's a hefty ask: city by city, getting millions of real people to agree to open up their most personal spaces to strangers and effectively to become citizen hoteliers.

And it's not enough just to get the hosts to sign on and to offer their spaces; Airbnb has to get them to work hard to offer a good experience. The sheer number of listings makes the company the world's biggest provider of accommodations, but it neither owns nor controls any of the inventory it offers, or the behavior of any of the people offering it.

The founders knew this from the earliest days, when convincing people to list their spaces was one of their first struggles. But it wasn't until late 2012, when Chesky read an issue of *Cornell Hospitality Quarterly,* the journal of the esteemed Cornell University School of Hotel Administration, that he started thinking more seriously about the actual experience the company was offering. He decided they needed to transform Airbnb more deeply from a tech company into a hospitality company.

Shortly after that, Chesky read the book *Peak: How Great Companies Get Their Mojo from Maslow.* The book's author was Chip Conley, the founder of the Joie de Vivre boutique hotel chain, which he started in San Francisco in 1987. He grew it to thirty-eight boutique hotels, mostly in California, and then sold a majority stake in 2010. Over time, Conley himself had become something of a guru. In *Peak,* he explained how he had saved his company in the wake of 9/11 and the dot-com bust by applying the psychologist Abraham Maslow's hierarchy of needs — the pyramid of physical and psychological needs humans must have met in order to achieve their full potential, with food and water at the bottom and self-actualization at the top — to corporate and individual transformation. Chesky saw in Conley's writing both business and hotel-industry savvy and perhaps a kindred spirit of idealism (Conley talked about wanting his hotel guests to check out three days later as a "better version of themselves"). He

asked Conley if he would come to Airbnb to give a talk to his employees about hospitality.

After Conley's talk, Chesky made a pitch: he wanted Conley to
come on board full-time in a major executive role to lead the company's hospitality efforts. Conley, who was newly retired at fifty-
two, was reluctant to sign on. But after talking with John Donahoe,
then the CEO of eBay, who was a friend of Conley's and a mentor to
Chesky, Conley agreed to sign on as a consultant: he told Chesky he
had enough time to contribute eight hours a week to Airbnb.

Over dinner the night before he was to start, Chesky convinced
Conley to double his time to fifteen hours a week. That plan, too,
soon went out the window. "Within a few weeks it was, like, 'Oh, this
is more like fifteen hours a *day*,'" Conley recalls. In the fall of 2013,
he joined full-time as head of hospitality and strategy. He says he ultimately took the role because he was fascinated by the challenge of
effectively democratizing hospitality. "How do you take hospitality,
which in many ways had gotten very corporatized, and take it back
to its roots?"

Conley went to work right away, trying to help bring organization
and know-how to Airbnb's host community. He traveled to twenty-
five cities giving talks and hosting tips to help regular apartment-
dwellers channel their inner innkeeper. He set up a centralized
hospitality-education effort, created a set of standards, and started
a blog, a newsletter, and an online community center where hosts
could learn and share best practices. He developed a mentorship program wherein experienced hosts could help bring new hosts on board
and show them the ropes to good hospitality.

Among the tips, rules, and suggestions that are now articulated in
Airbnb's materials: Try to respond to booking queries within twenty-
four hours. Before accepting a guest, try to make sure their idea for
their trip matches your "hosting style"; for example, if someone's
looking for a hands-on host and you're private, it may not be the best
match. Communicate often, and provide detailed directions. Estab-
lish any "house rules" very clearly (if you'd like travelers to take their

shoes off, or not use the backyard, or not smoke or stay away from the computer). Clean every room thoroughly, especially the bathroom and kitchen. Bedding and towels should be fresh. Want to go beyond the basics? Consider picking up travelers at the airport, leaving a welcome note, sprucing up the room with fresh flowers, or providing a treat upon check-in, like a glass of wine or a welcome basket. Do these things, he says, even if you're not present during the stay.

Conley and the hospitality team can, of course, only suggest or encourage hosts to do these things; they can't require it. This is where Airbnb's review system kicks in, the company's two-way rating mechanism that prompts both hosts and guests to review one another after a stay. The blind reputation assessments have become a vital element of the Airbnb ecosystem: they provide a layer of third-party validation for both the host and the guest, and with both parties looking to bolster their reputations for future use within the system, the incentive to review is mutual and engagement is high: more than 70 percent of Airbnb stays are reviewed, and while there is some "grade inflation," it helps keep both parties in check. The system has additional value for Airbnb: it is used as a lever to encourage and to reward good host behavior and to discourage bad behavior.

Early on, the founders learned that they were in possession of a valuable currency: the ability to determine where a host's listing would show up in search rankings. That ability could be used as a powerful reward mechanism to its hosts: those who provided positive experiences for guests and received good reviews would get vaulted to the top of search results, giving them greater exposure and increasing their chances of future bookings. But decline too many requests or respond too slowly or cancel too many reservations or simply appear inhospitable in reviews, and Airbnb can drop a powerful hammer: it can lower your listing in search results or even deactivate your account.

Behave well, though, and Airbnb will shine its love upon you. If you hit a certain series of performance metrics — in the past year, if you have hosted at least ten trips, if you have maintained a 90 percent response rate or higher, if you have received a five-star review at least 80 percent of the time, and if you've canceled a reservation only rarely or in extenuating circumstances, you are automatically elevated to "Superhost" status. That means you get a special logo on your site, your listing will be bumped way up in the rankings, you'll get access to a dedicated customer-support line, and you might even get the chance to preview new products and attend events. The reward-based ecosystem works: these days, Airbnb's platform is populated with two hundred thousand Superhosts, and while not every one of them is perfect, of course, awarding the status is Airbnb's most powerful tool for ratcheting up the service while not actually having any control over the people delivering it.

The "Hosticians"

Airbnb's data reveals that the average host makes around $6,000 a year, but many hosts make much more than that. Evelyn Badia has turned her hosting business into a full-fledged branded enterprise. A charismatic former producer of television commercials, she runs two listings out of her three-story, two-family row house in Park Slope, Brooklyn. Badia, fifty, started hosting when she lost her job in 2010 and now hosts full-time, making a "low six-figure" income by booking her listings about 80 percent of the time; she says she's hosted four hundred people. A few years in, she started a consulting business for hosts, Evelyn Badia Consultations, for which she charges ninety-five dollars per hour. There were other similar services, but she felt they were run by young guys offering tips for monetization and efficiency, and women were not being spoken to: "I was, like, 'Dude, do you realize how many hosts are baby boomers and over forty?'" In 2014, she added a blog and a subscription newsletter, anointing herself a "hostician" and sharing her learnings with others. She also hosts a monthly webinar — Chip Conley has been a guest — sells a house manual for thirty-nine dollars, and runs a Facebook group called The Hosting Journey, which has more than seven hundred members. She has become a quasi-celebrity in the Airbnb hosting community, holding barbecues and events for area hosts and speaking at the 2016 Airbnb Open in Los Angeles. She's thinking of offering a class on the challenges of dating and hosting on Airbnb. (Being single and bringing suitors home while also hosting guests is, she says, "like living with your parents.")

Pol McCann, a fifty-two-year-old Superhost in Sydney, Australia, first used Airbnb as a guest when he and his boyfriend came to New York City on vacation in 2012. They rented a studio apartment in Alphabet City for what McCann says was less than half what they'd pay for a hotel — a price so low that they were able to extend their stay from three nights to twelve. Everything on the trip worked so well that McCann thought he should try listing his own apartment back in Sydney. He spruced it up, took some photos, and listed it, and within twenty-four hours he had his first booking. Within short order, his apartment was booked twenty-eight or twenty-nine days a month. After six months, he had earned enough from renting the apartment that he was able to put down a deposit on a second apartment in the same complex across the street.

Between the two properties, he estimates that he earns $100,000 a year after his costs. In mid-2015, he then put a deposit down on a third apartment, a much bigger one-bedroom that he spent six months renovating. He's done the math and worked it all out: by the time he's ready to retire, in five years, the apartments will be paid off and he'll become a permanent, full-time host.

Jonathan Morgan, forty-one, runs six listings out of three homes in Savannah, Georgia: one entire home that he rents, three rooms in the house where he lives, and two rooms in a vacation house on an island off the coast, to which he shuttles people by boat. He says he started hosting in 2010 — "when there were twelve people in the Airbnb office" — and he's ridden the wave of Airbnb and seen the members of its community grow more sophisticated. In his early days, he says, "nobody knew what to do, what the experience was. 'Are you the psycho killer? Or am I the psycho killer?'" He draws young, tech-savvy travelers and invests in things that appeal to them: twelve fixed-gear bicycles, video-game systems — "anything that will attract our target group, because then our lives are easier." He charges from seventy to ninety-nine dollars per night and accrues some intangible benefits, too: his last two girlfriends have been Airbnb guests he rented to.

Let a Million Pillow-Fluffers Bloom

The growth of the Airbnb host community has also fueled a robust cottage industry of start-ups offering services to support them, everything from linen changing, pillow fluffing, turndown service, key exchanges, property management, minibar services, tax compliance, data analytics, and more. Call them the "pick and shovel" purveyors of the Airbnb gold rush: there are dozens of these start-ups, almost all of them started by Airbnb users themselves who spotted a need, hole, or pain point somewhere in the process. Many of them are raising venture funding. Guesty, a professional management service for hosts, started by Israeli twin brothers, is one of the largest: hosts give Guesty access to their Airbnb accounts, and it handles booking management, all guest communication, calendar updating, and scheduling and coordinating with cleaners and other local service providers, for a fee of 3 percent of the booking charge. San Francisco–based Pillow creates a listing, hires cleaners, handles keys, and employs an algorithm to determine best pricing options. HonorTab brings a minifridge concept to Airbnb. Everbooked was founded by a self-described yield-management geek with expertise in data science who saw the need for dynamic pricing tools for Airbnb hosts.

One of the biggest chores that hosts often need help with, for example, is turning over keys to guests. It can be hard to always arrange to be home when the guest arrives, especially if the host has a full-time job, or is out of town, or when travelers' flights are delayed. Clayton Brown, a Stanford Business School alum living in Vancouver who worked in finance, started using Airbnb in 2012 to list his apartment whenever he traveled on business, and soon identified the key-exchange process as his biggest point of friction. He would arrange for his cleaning service to be at the apartment to let the guest in, but on one occasion a guest's flight was late, the cleaner had gone home, and the guest had to take a taxi to the cleaner's house in the remote suburbs to fetch the key, leading to frustrations all around. "I started thinking, "There has to be a better way, and Airbnb is growing crazy fast, so maybe there's something here,'" Brown says. In 2013 he and a partner started a company that essentially turns local cafés, bars, and gyms into neighborhood key-exchange hubs. Keycafe provides the establishment with a kiosk, and the host pays $12.95 per month (plus a fee of $1.95 per key pickup) for an RFID-enabled key fob. Travelers are remotely assigned a unique access code through the Keycafe app, which they then use to unlock the kiosk. The host gets notified anytime a key is picked up or dropped off, and the local establishments like the arrangement because it brings in foot traffic.

While Keycafe serves customers beyond just Airbnb, including dog walkers and other service professionals, Airbnb and property managers are more than half its business, and the company is one of the stronger Airbnb "bolt-ons": it is an official partner in Airbnb's Host Assist platform, which integrates some of these vendors into its website, and Brown and his business partner have raised almost $3 million, more than most of the other ancillary services. "As Airbnb has become larger and the valuation and sheer scale of the company has grown, it's kind of a known play in the venture space," Brown says.

Airbnb has been gathering hosts informally since the beginning, but in 2014 it formalized these efforts with the launch of Airbnb Open, its first global summit of hosts. That November, some 1,500 hosts from around the world convened upon San Francisco for three days of talks, seminars, dinners, and other forms of Airbnb immersion. They heard inspirational stories from a series of speakers. They heard from Chesky, who in a rare moment was visibly overwhelmed as he took the stage and asked them to stand up if hosting has changed who they are as a person (they stood). They heard from Conley, who told them to save their personalized badges and gift bags, because five or six years from now, "this will be the largest hospitality event around the world."

The next year, in 2015, the Open was much bigger: held in Paris as a nod to the significance of that market — it is the company's largest market in terms of both listings and guests — the event drew five thousand hosts and more than six hundred Airbnb employees to the Grande Halle de la Villette for the three-day gathering. Attendees, who paid their own way, would hear speakers as varied as the Swiss-born philosopher and author Alain de Botton and home-tidying guru Marie Kondo. They'd hear inspiration from Chesky, Gebbia, Blecharczyk, and Conley, as well as updates from the company's head of product, Joe Zadeh, and head of engineering Mike Curtis. They'd get an update on the regulatory battle from the head of legal and business affairs, Belinda Johnson, and public-policy chief Chris Lehane. They would be entertained by Cirque du Soleil. The event was months and months in the works, was a major production, and began as planned; at the end of day one, the crowd disbursed to a thousand simultaneous dinners held at hosts' residences and restaurants all around the City of Lights.

After a rousing day two, on November 13, 2015, that night the co-founders hosted a reunion of the company's first forty employees who were still there, which it billed as the Tenth Street Dinner. Held at an Airbnb listing in the Eighteenth Arrondissement, it was a catered dinner designed to celebrate all that the company had achieved. Chesky had delivered two keynotes that day, and now, surrounded by his friends and family, he felt he could relax and, for once, take a moment to sit back and reflect on all they had accomplished.

But an hour or so into the dinner, just after Gebbia had given a toast, Chesky and others in the room started getting buzzed on their phones. A shooting had been reported at a restaurant a few miles away. At first it seemed like an isolated incident, albeit a troubling one, so they went back to their dinner. But soon news of more attacks came in: explosions were reported at the Stade de France, the city's soccer stadium. Now there were mass shootings in the Tenth Arrondissement; there was a hostage situation at the Bataclan. It was, of course, the horrific, ISIS-coordinated terrorist attack that would kill 130 people and injure almost 400 more. And Airbnb had 645 employees and 5,000 hosts out at dinners scattered throughout the entire city. Many were staying in neighborhoods where the shootings took place. One of their groups was at the stadium.

Chesky got in touch with his head of security and staged a make-shift command center from the upstairs bathroom of the Airbnb listing where the dinner took place. With a lockdown in place all night, they cleared out the furniture and put down as many pillows and blankets as they could. Over the course of the long night, they accounted for every single employee and host; no one had been harmed. The next day, they canceled the rest of the program and worked on flying everyone home. That Sunday, one hundred employees boarded a plane bound for San Francisco.

In November 2014, four months after the company launched "Belong anywhere" as its mission, Chesky went back to Douglas Atkin. He said that he loved "Belong anywhere," and he truly felt it would be the company's mission for the next hundred years. But he still had some pressing questions: What does it actually *mean*? How do you measure it? How does it happen? He sent Atkin back out on another focus-group odyssey to figure it out. When Atkin came back, after talking to another three hundred hosts and guests around the world, he had an answer: belonging anywhere wasn't just a single moment; it was a transformation people experienced when they traveled on Airbnb. The company has codified this as something it calls the "belong anywhere transformation journey," which goes like this: When travelers leave their homes, they feel alone. They reach their Airbnb and they feel accepted and taken care of by their host. They then feel safe to be the same kind of person they are when they're at home. And when that happens, they feel like freer, better, more complete versions of themselves, and their journey is complete.

This is Airbnb-speak, and while it may sound hokey to the rest of us, Chesky and Atkin would say this is a huge reason why Airbnb took off the way that it did. There is a cultlike devotion among Airbnb's truest believers, who embrace this vision. (During his focus-group travels exploring the meaning of Airbnb, Atkin encountered one host in Athens who had painted "Belong anywhere" on his bedroom wall, and another in Korea who had changed her name to a Korean phrase meaning "welcome to my house." But whether or not it is a full-fledged "transformation journey" for the average traveler, Airbnb has enjoyed success that is about something more than just low prices and freely available, quirky spaces. It touches on something bigger and deeper.

The opportunity to show some humanity or to receive some expression of humanity from others, even if you never experience that person outside a few messages, some fluffed towels, and a welcome note, has become rare in our disconnected world. This is another element about Airbnb (and other short-term-rental services) that makes it uniquely different from other aspects of the so-called "sharing economy." At its core, Airbnb involves the most intimate human interactions — visiting people in their homes, sleeping in their beds, using their bathrooms. (Even in the listings that are run by professionals, there is still the semblance of this one-to-one intimacy.) That is of course precisely what makes it polarizing and objectionable to so many people who can never imagine using it. But it's also what makes it unique. This kind of "sharing" — this hyperpersonal opening up of the most intimate and safest aspect of one's life to a stranger — is not present when you hire a person to fix a leak on TaskRabbit, or when you get into someone's air-conditioned black car for a silent ride to the airport with your head in your phone. More than anything else, it is this aspect of Airbnb that distinguishes it from Uber, Lyft, and any other of its sharing-economy peers. Elisa Schreiber, marketing partner at Greylock Partners, an investor in the company, summarized this distinction concisely after we got to talking about it one day. "Uber is transactional," she said. "Airbnb is humanity."

Unfortunately, as we are about to see and as Airbnb has learned, despite its best intentions, that "humanity" can be a frustrating thing. It is not always well meaning, and it is not always good.

4

The Bad and the Ugly

Our product is real life.

— BRIAN CHESKY

OF COURSE, HUMANITY IS NOT always well behaved, and despite Airbnb's idealism-filled promise, there is an obvious question here: How can you smush all these strangers together and not have things go wrong?

After all, there are some very bad actors in the world. And there are seemingly few easier ways to attract them than to offer a service whose core mission is getting someone to hand over the keys to his or her home to a complete and total stranger. So wouldn't these types flock to Airbnb? Some did. In other cases, accidental oversights had unintended, sometimes grave consequences. And while overall these instances are very rare, they are part of the brave new world of large-scale home sharing — and they have had important implications for the company.

There were incidents like EJ's ransacking back in 2011, the company's first major lesson in how to handle extreme violations of the trust it had tried to create, as well as the related PR and crisis-management issues. But the ways in which people can misuse Airbnb are numerous, and the most colorful instances over the years have become media sensations. In 2012, police busted prostitutes using an apartment they found on Airbnb in Stockholm as a brothel. In a well-publicized incident in New York in 2014, Ari Teman thought he rented his Chelsea apartment out to a family that was in town for a wedding, but when he stopped in to pick up his bags before heading out of town, he found what he said was a sex party for overweight people in full swing. A few weeks earlier, start-up executive Rachel Bassini rented her penthouse in New York City's East Village and returned home to find furniture damaged and overturned and everything from used condoms to chewed gum and other detritus — including what seemed to be human feces — on the floors, walls, and furniture.

In the spring of 2015, Mark and Star King, married parents of two young children in Calgary, rented their three-bedroom home in the city's suburban Sage Hill residential neighborhood to a man who said he was in town with a few family members for a wedding. Toward the end of their stay, a neighbor called to tell them the police were at the house. The Kings returned to find the home completely wrecked after what police later called a "drug-induced orgy." It was a level of destruction similar to or worse than what happened to EJ in San Francisco: furniture was broken and stained; Star's artwork had been destroyed; and the house was littered with used condoms, puddles of alcohol and cigarette butts, and piles and piles of trash. There was broken glass on the floor, and food products were bizarrely spread and strewn throughout the house, including barbecue sauce and mayonnaise on the walls and ceiling and chicken legs stuffed in some of Star's shoes. Because there were unknown fluids present, police taped off the house, put up biohazard signs, and returned with white suits and masks. "We wished the home was burnt down to ashes. It would have felt way better," Mark King told the CBC at the time. Neighbors later told them that shortly after the Kings had left, a party bus had pulled up to the home and let out what looked like one hundred people. The home had to be stripped down to the baseboards, the flooring torn out, walls repainted, and the ceiling retextured, a process that took six months (and was paid for by Airbnb's

Host Guarantee). "Most of the contents in the house were not sal-vageable," says Mark King.

These kinds of parties have been going on for years, with their or-ganizers using all kinds of websites, from Craigslist to HomeAway to others, to find spaces to rent. But as Airbnb grew and offered an easy, friendly interface and millions of listings beyond just those in vacation-home markets, it became a very accessible place to fish for venues.

"They Don't Look like Golfers"

In July 2016, the annual PGA Championship tour was coming to the Baltusrol Golf Club, a 121-year-old golf course in Springfield, New Jersey, about twenty miles west of New York City. Barbara Loughlin (not her real name), who lived in a wealthy suburb nearby with her husband and four children, started thinking that maybe they should rent out their home during the event. They were spending most of the summer at their vacation home at the Jersey shore anyway, and what were the odds that a prestigious national event would come and create lodging demand in their sleepy area?

Loughlin had recently been doing research for an upcoming trip to Napa Valley, and had been browsing short-term-rental sites and liked the array of nice-looking properties she was finding, so she had become comfortable with the practice. She took some photos and posted the four-bedroom Victorian with its spacious backyard and a pool, listing it for $2,000 per night ("which is sort of outrageous for our town," Loughlin says. "With the exception of a golfer wanting to stay there, why would anyone want to pay $2,000 to rent our sub-urban home for the night?"). She started getting some queries, but she turned most of them down because they looked suspicious, like the eighteen-year-old who wanted to have his high school graduation party there. But soon she heard from someone named Kay, an event coordinator whose listing name was "Plush." Kay said he was work-ing with an editor for *Golf Digest* magazine who wanted to rent the

Loughlins' house for the weekend and host a "launching party" for fifty to sixty golfers outside in their pool area on Saturday afternoon.

Loughlin thought this sounded appealing: Kay wanted the house for only three nights and was willing to pay the fee of $2,000 per night, and what better-behaved crowd could there be than golfers on a Saturday afternoon? Plush was an odd name, to be sure, but he had a Verified ID account, Airbnb's opt-in method of enhanced identification verification. Even so, Loughlin, the daughter and sister of attorneys, took extra measures: she generated an additional contract and requested the driver's licenses of not just Plush but all six adults whom Kay said would be staying overnight on the property. Kay obliged, sending copies of the licenses; all six names went on the additional contract, it was signed and returned a few days before the weekend of the event, and the booking was made and paid through Airbnb.

Just to be sure, Loughlin then Googled the names on the driver's licenses to make sure they seemed legitimate. They all looked like real people and professionals with profiles on LinkedIn and other sites, but Loughlin thought it seemed odd that there was no reference to golf or *Golf Digest* in any of their online profiles. By then it was the day before the tenants were scheduled to arrive, and she called Kay and said she still didn't quite understand the golf connection. He reassured her that he could provide a link that would explain it. They talked three times that day, and each time she reminded him to send the link, and each time he said he would send it — but no link arrived.

The next day, as planned, Loughlin and her husband drove up from their beach house to meet Kay and his caterer at the house to hand over the keys. Kay called to say he was in Brooklyn meeting with his attorney and running late, but the caterer arrived, gave Loughlin a copy of his driver's license, and assured her it would be a small party and a simple affair. Kay called again and said he was still in the city, tied up at the airport picking up the other renters, so Loughlin gave the caterer the key. Loughlin and her husband drove back to their beach house at the Jersey shore that night.

Loughlin had alerted her neighbors to the golf event, so the next morning when one of them texted her a photo of a furniture-rental-company truck in her driveway, Loughlin replied yes, that made sense and was OK. Everything was happening as planned.

A few hours later, another neighbor called Loughlin. "I don't want to alarm you, and everything's fine," she said. "But the people coming to your house don't look like golfers." She described groups of young people scantily clad in bathing suits. Loughlin called Kay and asked what was going on. He told her the neighbor had probably just seen the setup crew, which hadn't left yet; the golfers had yet to arrive. Somewhat wary, Loughlin took him for his word. But soon the neighbor called back and said more and more people were arriving, all looking the same: women dolled up in bikinis and cover-ups and high heels, men in bathing suits, all roughly between the ages of eighteen and twenty-five.

When Loughlin called Kay back yet again, this time he had a different explanation: he told her that his clients had rented two houses for two different events, and at the last minute they had decided to switch the events. The event at the Loughlin house was now a family party where the main organizer of both events, a man named Jean Manuel Valdez — one of the six names on the lease who'd provided a driver's license — would be proposing to his girlfriend.

At this point Loughlin and her husband sensed something was not right, so they got in the car and headed back from their beach house once again. Along the way, their neighbors continued to text them photos and told them that more and more people were arriving, groups of young men and women who were streaming into their house by the dozens. By the time the Loughlins arrived, every street in their neighborhood was lined with parked cars, and clusters of attendees were approaching the house on foot. When the Loughlins made it to their house, they were greeted at the end of their driveway by professional security guards who were checking people in with wristbands. Hired by the event organizers, the guards had no idea about any party for golfers. There was a second check-in station in the Loughlin's garage, and in the backyard there were three DJs, a cash bar, a barbecue, six large, resort-style cabanas — and somewhere between three hundred and five hundred revelers. "It was insane," says Loughlin.

The Loughlins couldn't enter their property, since doing so would violate the terms of their lease. Because their neighbors had called to complain, though, the police were already on the premises, and they had authority to enter the property, shut down the party, and evacuate the guests, which took two hours. Barbara Loughlin asked for Jean Manuel Valdez and was told he was out getting lunch. "I said, 'I don't think anybody on this lease is on the property,'" Loughlin says. Kay, her main contact, was nowhere to be found, and she never met Valdez. After the last guests were gone, the Loughlins walked through their home with a police officer to assess the damage, which was minimal — a broken candlestick, a damaged wicker chair, and some cracks in the pool decking. Since none of the tenants were there to give the Loughlins their key back, they called a locksmith, who came and changed the locks.

The Loughlins later learned that their home had been used by promoters to host a hip-hop party called In2deep. The bash had been advertised on Instagram and Eventbrite for weeks, selling itself as a "private mansion pool party" with VIP cabana service, "VIP champagne for the first 100 ladies," and DJs spinning hip-hop, dance-hall, and Afrobeats music. "Style it up in a Cabana or Wet it up in the Pool," the ad read. Attendees paid fifteen to twenty-five dollars per ticket and were given the address after payment.

Despite the minimal damage to the property, Loughlin was distraught: she felt she had been defrauded, their vacation had been ruined, and she was mortified at having caused her neighbors so much disruption. She was afraid — she had seen posts on Instagram from some of the attendees (one wrote, "Yesterday was on pace to be something great but you know the white devil wouldn't let the children of God prosper but don't worry we got a few surprises") — and she thought annoyed guests might return to their property for retribution. Mostly, though, Loughlin wanted Plush to be caught and to pay a price: the Loughlins' sense of trust had been violated, and they had been scammed.

The Monday after the event, Loughlin called Airbnb and, after looking for the phone number on the website for what she said was forty-five minutes and being put on hold for another fifteen, relayed her experience to a customer-service manager. The employee she spoke with said she would escalate it to a case specialist who would get back to her within twenty-four hours, and encouraged Loughlin to send in any additional details about her case in the meantime. Three days later, Loughlin hadn't heard from anyone, so she sent an e-mail asking when she could expect to hear back, and she provided more details: a description of what had happened and a Dropbox link to some forty photos of the event that they'd collected from Instagram. She asked if someone from Airbnb could call her.

Five days after that, still not having received a response, she e-mailed Airbnb again, asking what was taking so long. The following day, an Airbnb case manager, Katie C., sent her cheery greetings ("Thank you for reaching out to us, although I'm so sorry it had to be under these circumstances!") and apologized for the delay. Katie suggested that Loughlin take full advantage of the Host Guarantee, Airbnb's reimbursement program for host property damage, explaining in detail the benefit and the process for filing a claim. Loughlin told Katie C. that the damages she was concerned with were not to her property but that rather, she was looking for answers to some urgent questions: she wanted to know whether Airbnb had run a report on the driver's licenses; whether the company had looked to see if these same actors were still on the website renting other properties on Airbnb; and whether the company had gotten to the bottom of how Plush could have had a Verified ID. After her e-mail went unanswered for two days, Loughlin wrote Katie C. again and said it had been two weeks since the incident and they still had not received a response from Airbnb on her questions. She added that a local television reporter had called the Loughlins, wanting to do a story on the incident, the news of which had spread throughout their town.

Two days after that, Katie C. wrote back and said Airbnb couldn't give out personal information but if Loughlin was working with local law enforcement, those officers could e-mail Airbnb's special law-enforcement liaison to make a formal request for information regarding Plush's identity. She again encouraged Loughlin to file a claim for physical damages under the Host Guarantee. She had received the photos, but in order to consider the case for compensation, Airbnb would need the official Host Guarantee claim filled out with an itemized list of damages and receipts. "I understand this is a frustrating incident," she wrote, "and we are doing our best to provide support, such as forwarding you to our Host Guarantee process."

After more back-and-forth, during which Loughlin filed a Host Guarantee claim for $728 and repeated her questions, Katie C. told Loughlin that unfortunately, the company's privacy policy prohibited the disclosure of any information regarding Plush's account, but if Loughlin's local law enforcement wanted to investigate, they could contact Airbnb's law-enforcement liaison, who would cooperate with any investigation. She added that she was committed to doing everything she could to advocate for Loughlin through the Host Guarantee program.

Loughlin had little interest in the heralded Host Guarantee. She wanted Airbnb to help identify Plush and prevent him from defrauding others on the platform. She and her husband wanted to press charges against Plush, but they had no personal information for him, and they didn't think their local police would take up their case the way Katie C. had suggested; it wouldn't be worth their time. Loughlin wanted Airbnb to help. At the very least, she wanted a phone call. "They never spoke to us on the phone," she says.

In the meantime, she realized that around the same time, she had received a request to book her home through VRBO from a Christopher Seelinger, one of the other names from the group of fake driver's licenses. "These guys are just scamming again and again and again, and Airbnb is doing nothing," she says. "They won't even call me back to talk about it."

The circular responses continued. After she filed the Host Guarantee claim, another Airbnb representative named Jordan wrote to Loughlin, saying that he noticed she hadn't used the Resolution Center as she had been instructed in a previous e-mail.

Airbnb refers all disputes between hosts and guests to the Resolution Center, a messaging platform on the website where parties can attempt to resolve conflict on their own by requesting extra payment. If no agreement is reached, the parties can ask Airbnb to step in to resolve the conflict. Loughlin was confused — no one had made any mention of a Resolution Center to her — but she followed Jordan's instructions, filing a lengthy request and asking for $4,328 in damages, itemized in detail as $728 for the physical damages to the property, $350 for some extra landscaping services that were needed, and $3,250 to cover the ten hours of legal counseling she and her husband had received. ("You defrauded us," began the nine-hundred-word statement that she addressed directly to Plush.)

A few weeks later, Katie C. wrote back to let Loughlin know that Airbnb had processed payment of $728. Loughlin was flummoxed: she had requested $4,328, had not heard back from Plush, and had not agreed to any other payout plan. And she still had not received any phone call from Airbnb. She relayed this to Katie C., who wrote back and said she did not understand, since the physical damage expenses totaled $728. "Can you elaborate on how you came to $4,328?" she wrote. Loughlin e-mailed back and again explained that the remainder was for legal bills. She again asked whether Plush had responded and what steps Airbnb had taken "to reach out to him about his fraudulent acts."

Three days later, Katie C. wrote back and said that the guest had not responded, his account had been quarantined, and the Host Guarantee did not cover legal expenses, so they were not included in Airbnb's final offer. She was, however, happy to process additional reimbursement, through the Host Guarantee, for the extra landscaping services Loughlin had mentioned — could she please send an invoice for that?

Loughlin was exasperated. All she wanted was for Airbnb to find Plush and prevent him from acting again and for someone from Airbnb to call her toward that effort, since she had his contact information and had heard from the real owners of some of the other stolen driver's licenses the group used — and instead, she felt trapped in an endless circle of chirpy discussions about the Host Guarantee. In the end, Loughlin elected not to take the reimbursement: in order to receive it, Airbnb requires payees to sign a form that, among other things, relinquishes the company from any future liability related to the booking, which Loughlin refused to do. She felt that the document was "unconscionable" and that Airbnb's policy was protecting Plush, since it wouldn't release his information to her. "Plush could knock on my front door or rent to me again and I would have no idea who he was," she wrote to the company. Airbnb sent several follow-up e-mails asking her to sign, after which point a supervisor contacted her and said the company was able to authorize payment of $271 of the remaining $350 without her signature — and the supervisor said she was also including a $100 coupon toward an upcoming reservation.

Emily Gonzales, who heads Airbnb's Trust and Safety Operations team for North America, says the company's delay in responding to Loughlin was "unacceptable" and that the team was looking into ways to make sure it wouldn't happen again. She said that since Loughlin's legal fees didn't relate to any specific legal action being taken, they could not cover those expenses. She said that the company did cover the damage claims, as was its policy, that it had removed the Plush account permanently and confirmed for Loughlin that it had been removed, and that it had checked and was able to confirm that the "Chris" she had subsequently heard from was not the same Christopher whose name had appeared on one of the fraudulent driver's licenses.

Nick Shapiro, Airbnb's global head of crisis communications, says the company's delay was "absolutely unacceptable." He also points out that the tools the platform provides give hosts multiple opportunities to assess potential guests and to use their own judgment: factors like the number of reviews a potential guest has, whether they have a Verified ID, and the way they communicate during messaging, all of which can help a host evaluate a potential guest and signal potential trouble. Shapiro pointed out that in this case, the guest was new and didn't have any reviews and clearly stated his intent to have a party, which Loughlin consented to. "There is no silver bullet," Shapiro said. "That's why we have a multilayer defense." He added that if a host books a guest and someone else shows up, as happened in Loughlin's case — when Kay did not show up to her home but the caterer did — a host can and should call Airbnb and cancel the reservation on the spot. Loughlin maintains that since Plush had a Verified ID, she felt secure: "They're saying he's a real person." When I relayed this to Gonzales, she said that "what you're describing is something we're working on and improving." The company is developing an enhanced version of Verified ID that it plans to launch in the near future.

A Scary Attack

Another incident came in the summer of 2015, when, as was reported at length in the *New York Times,* a nineteen-year-old from Massachusetts named Jacob Lopez was staying at an Airbnb in Madrid. According to the *Times* account, his host locked Lopez in the apartment and demanded that he submit to a sexual act. He said that the host, a transgender woman, threatened him.

According to the account, Lopez texted his mother in real time, asking her to call for help. His mother called Airbnb, but the employees she spoke with said they couldn't give her the address of the listing in Madrid — they needed the Madrid police to call them directly to request that information — and they also said they could not call the police directly to report the incident; she would have to do that herself. They gave her the phone number for the Madrid police, but when she called, according to the *Times,* she got a voice recording in Spanish that disconnected her.

Meanwhile, the situation inside the apartment had escalated and, as Lopez recounted, he was assaulted. He was ultimately able to talk his way out of the apartment by telling his host that the friends he was meeting nearby knew where he was staying and would try to find him if he didn't show up. (According to the *Times* article, the host denied these charges, said the incident was consensual, and said Lopez was transphobic. The *Times* also said that the Madrid police declined to comment and that the host indicated that the police had already visited her and she expected to be cleared of charges.)

Like the ransacking of EJ's apartment in 2011, the story went viral as soon as it was written about. Lopez appeared on the *Today* show. "If You've Ever Stayed in an Airbnb, You Have to Read This Horrifying Tale" read a headline on Cosmopolitan.com. Airbnb quickly made changes: it updated its policy to grant employees authority to contact law enforcement directly in cases where there is an emergency situation playing out in real time. It also added the option for travelers to set up an emergency contact on their profile who would be authorized to receive any information in case of an emergency; and it made it easier to share itineraries with friends and family, especially from a mobile device.

But this situation raised a question as to why, in 2015, seven years after the company had been started, it wasn't already Airbnb's policy to have employees call law enforcement directly in the middle of an emergency playing out in real time. "We were a little shy about calling law enforcement before," Chesky conceded when I asked him. He said the company had developed its emergency-reaction policy with input from experts who had specifically advised that it's better to not intervene and that victims should ask for help from law enforcement directly, to avoid the chance of escalating a situation the victim may not be ready for. But Chesky said Airbnb personnel hadn't considered the possibility of an incident unfolding in real time. "We missed the nuance" in developing the policy, Chesky said. He also said that when they reviewed the details of the case afterward, the judgment call that was made in the Lopez incident to not refer the case to authorities "didn't pass the smell test."

Airbnb's responses tend to carefully stress that such incidents are rare and often part of a bigger problem. "The issue of sexual assault is a global challenge, but there's nothing more important to us than the safety of our community," read a statement the company issued after the Lopez incident. "That weekend, more than 800,000 people stayed on Airbnb with no incident — including 70,000 in Spain alone — but even one incident is one too many." "No one has a perfect record" is a common refrain — "but that's what we strive for," the statement continued.

But safety is paramount to Airbnb's business; more than "belonging," one could argue, not being hurt and not being vandalized are fundamental in Maslow's hierarchy. And just like entrusting a user to provide good hospitality, safety, too, is a real challenge when the company doesn't own its assets. "Our product is real life," Chesky says. "We don't make the product." Because of that, he says it can't be perfect. "What you end up with isn't a community where nothing ever happens." But he maintains that Airbnb is a "high-trust community" (the "real world on the street," he says, is by comparison a low-trust environment), and when instances do happen, the company always tries to go above and beyond to make things right. In every instance, he says, "I hope we would have done more than you thought we would have done in that situation. I think most of the time, people would say we do."

Airbnb's strongest defense against these headlines is that despite these high-profile incidents, they are rare. The company says that of forty million guests staying on Airbnb in 2015, instances that resulted in more than $1,000 of damage occurred just 0.002 percent of the time. "It's something that we wish was point zero-zero-zero, without any point-twos, but it is an important stat for context," says Shapiro, whose job is to manage the media melee when things do happen. (If that sounds like a stressful role, consider that Shapiro was previously the assistant press secretary to President Obama and the deputy chief of staff for the CIA.) Out of a total of 123 million nights booked as of early 2016, the company says that fewer than a fraction of one percent were problematic at all.

And of course, bad things happen all the time at hotels, too, though statistics on hotel crime and safety are hard to find. Some experts have estimated that a big-city hotel may have a crime per day, typically a theft. According to the U.S. Bureau of Justice Statistics National Crime Victimization Survey, from 2004 to 2008, 0.1 percent of total violent victimizations occurred in a hotel room, and 0.3 percent of property victimizations did.

These statistics don't allow for much comparison. But Jason Clampet, cofounder and editor in chief of the travel-industry news site *Skift*, says that, as a matter of practice, the platform doesn't run stories on bad things that happen on Airbnb precisely because he sees the headlines that come across the wires about equally bad things happening at hotels. But he points out that these incidents can and still do cause Airbnb serious PR damage and can discourage hosts from signing up. "It's one of the challenges when you have a company built on other people's assets."

Designing for Safety

The potential for bad things to happen was also one of the main issues that scared off investors when the company was first getting off the ground. "I pulled the guys aside and I said, 'Guys, someone is going to get raped or murdered in one of these houses, and the blood is going to be on your hands,'" the venture capitalist Chris Sacca recalled saying to Airbnb's founders before passing on the investment, in a recent podcast with the author Tim Ferriss. Sacca says this was back in 2009, when the primary focus of the company was renting out rooms when the host was present, and he says that's what kept him "from getting the nightmare scenario out of my head." (The decision cost his fund hundreds of millions of dollars. "I was completely distracted from the larger opportunity," he later said. "That proved to be an incredibly costly position to take.") And indeed, the EJ crisis in 2011 was a near-fatal experience for the company, a breach of trust that touched on every potential user's worst nightmare and had investors afraid that the new company's nascent user base could lose trust in it completely.

In fact, the few weeks of immersive crisis management during that time — that stretch veteran employees still remember, when teams were sleeping in the office for several days — were pivotal, leading not just to new tools like the Host Guarantee and the 24/7 hotline but also to the creation of the company's Trust and Safety division, a sort of parallel operation to its customer-service team designed to focus exclusively on issues of security, safety, and emergency response.

These days, Trust and Safety is a team of 250 operating out of three big operational centers in Portland, Oregon; Dublin; and Singapore. The department is divided into an operations team, a law-enforcement-liaison team, and a product team. Within that framework, a community-defense team performs proactive work to try to identify suspicious activity in advance, conducting spot checks on reservations and looking for signs that might suggest fraud or bad actors, while a community-response team handles incoming issues. The product team includes data scientists, who create behavioral models to help identify whether a reservation has a higher likelihood of, say, resulting in someone throwing a party or committing a crime (reservations are assigned a credibility score similar to a credit score), and engineers, who use machine learning to develop tools that analyze reservations to help detect risk. There are also crisis-management and victim-advocacy specialists trained to help intervene and de-escalate situations; insurance experts, who analyze claims; and veterans of the banking and cybersecurity worlds, who help detect payment fraud.

When bad things do happen, they're coded from Tier One — issues of payment fraud or stolen credit cards or chargebacks (where in most instances the victim is Airbnb) — through Tier Four, which is any case where a host's or guest's physical safety is at stake. A triage system helps route the right cases to the right people as quickly as possible. Once cases are under way, a law-enforcement engagement team works with any local law-enforcement investigations that happen on the ground, and a policy team shapes standards for responding.

Then there are features built into the product so things don't happen to begin with: the review system the Airbnb founders created from the outset is still one of the most effective tools for reputation assessment (travelers can complete a review only after they have paid for a stay, so it's not possible for someone to gin up a favorable image by asking friends to write several reviews). In the United States, the company runs background checks on all users, but in 2013 it introduced Verified ID, the enhanced verification process that includes a more rigorous proof of identity and confirms a connection between a person's online and off-line identities. Both hosts and guests have the option to only do business with Verified ID guests. And with all interactions, personal information like a phone number and an address isn't visible until a host has accepted a guest and a reservation has been booked, eliminating the chances of two parties going off the site to book.

There's a trust-advisory board, a team of advisers including the former deputy administrator of FEMA, a former assistant secretary for the Department of Homeland Security, a former U.S. Secret Service agent, the head of security for Facebook, a top cybersecurity expert at Google, and an expert in preventing and addressing domestic violence. The board meets once per quarter to talk about ways Airbnb can become better at preventing incidents from happening.

But even with all of this, there is room to improve. "Plush" somehow got through the Verified ID process. Barbara Loughlin should have been quickly called by an Airbnb representative expressing empathy and gently explaining why the company leaves the prosecuting of bad actors to law enforcement. She should not have been put on hold for fifteen minutes when she called the Airbnb emergency help line and it should not have taken her forty-five minutes to find that number on the Airbnb website. Looking for a customer-service or emergency phone number on the Airbnb website can indeed be an exercise in frustration—because, at least as of this writing, it's not there. Shapiro says there are reasons for this: if there is a true life-safety emergency, it's better and safer if the parties call 911 immediately. He points out that the Airbnb number comes up immediately on Google, and the company has teams that monitor Twitter and Facebook for calls of distress. The company has had a phone number on its website in the past, and it says it is building out infrastructure to be able to answer non-urgent calls without wait times, and when it does it will return. But for now all searches for a phone number funnel into the online help center.

Good Actors, Bad Accidents

Bad actors are one thing. What about accidents due to safety issues in the homes themselves — things that no one ever intends to happen? In November 2015, Zak Stone, a writer in Los Angeles, posted a heart-wrenching essay in the online magazine *Medium* about the tragic death of his father at an Airbnb rental in Austin, Texas, where the family had traveled for a vacation together. When his father sat on a rope swing in the home's backyard, the tree limb broke in half and fell on his head, leading to traumatic brain injury that killed him, a horrific and tragic scene that Stone described in graphic detail. In the piece, Stone also revealed another Airbnb-related death: in 2013, a Canadian woman staying in a listing in Taiwan was found dead after a faulty water heater had filled the apartment with carbon monoxide. Danger lurked in both places: The apartment in Taiwan didn't have a carbon-monoxide detector, and in his piece, Stone wrote that his family later found out that the tree in the backyard of the Austin listing had been dead for two years.

From a legal perspective Airbnb claims it is not liable in these kinds of instances, which it makes very clear with a disclaimer on its website: "Please note that Airbnb has no control over the conduct of hosts and disclaims all liability. Failure of hosts to satisfy their responsibilities may result in suspension of activity or removal from the Airbnb website." But who bears the cost when such an accident takes place? Though some allow exceptions for it, most homeowner's insurance policies do not cover commercial activity, and most insurers would consider renting out rooms on Airbnb commercial activity. In Stone's case, the host of the Austin home happened to have a homeowner's insurance policy that covered commercial activity, and the Stone family reached a settlement with the insurance company.

In the Canadian woman's case, Stone reported that Airbnb paid the family $2 million. (Airbnb declines to comment on the case.)

Chesky says these incidents were "heartbreaking" for the company. "I take them very, very personally. I am very idealistic about the notion that you're helping to create this version of the world that's better, and that people are going to be better in it. If something is antithetical to that, let alone a bad experience . . . that just stops you in your tracks." He says the company tries to learn how to be better from every experience. "You have a responsibility to learn to do everything you can so that it's something that will not happen again."

I spoke with Zak Stone about his father's death. "I think the question comes down to what's preventable, and if so, is there anything they could have done to prevent it," he says. "I would argue that it was preventable." He maintains that the host deliberately posted a photo of the swing in order to market the property. Airbnb, he says, has the ability to see something like that and to potentially screen for higher risk. "I would advocate Airbnb taking a much more cautious approach to onboarding new properties," he says. He also points out that he was coming from a perspective of someone who had lots of positive experiences on Airbnb. "I'm twenty-nine, I work in start-ups, and many of my friends are Airbnb landlords who make double their rent on their New York apartments so they can be artists and travel," he says. "But my story is just as important, if not more so, than all the other stories used to sell the platform."

In 2014, Airbnb started offering $1 million in secondary liability coverage to all hosts — meaning that if the host's primary insurer denied a claim, Airbnb's policy would kick in — and one year later, Airbnb made the insurance primary. Airbnb hosts in twenty-plus countries get automatic liability coverage of up to $1 million in the event of a third-party claim of bodily injury or property damage, even if their homeowner's policy does not cover them for commercial activity, and even if they don't have a homeowner's or renter's insurance policy.

Not surprisingly, the issue of the safety of the premises is one of the hotel industry's biggest beefs with Airbnb and with short-term rentals in general. Hotels have to adhere to rigorous safety standards regarding fire prevention, food and health safety, compliance with the Americans with Disabilities Act, and more. Airbnb — and all home-rental sites — have no such requirements. In its section about "responsible hosting," Airbnb recommends that its hosts ensure they have a functioning smoke alarm, carbon-monoxide detector, fire extinguisher, and first-aid kit; that they fix any exposed wires and address any areas where guests might trip or fall; and that they remove any dangerous objects. But relying on the hosts to actually *do* those things is outside the company's control.

Bad accidents can and do happen in hotels, too. For example, in 2013, a *USA Today* investigation found that 8 people had died in hotels and 170 others had been treated for carbon-monoxide poisoning over the previous three years. (A hotel-industry consultant in the article said that relative to the risk, it was too expensive for hotels to equip each room with a carbon-monoxide detector.) An earlier study found that from 1989 to 2004, sixty-eight incidents of carbon monoxide poisoning in U.S. hotels and motels led to 27 deaths and 772 people accidentally poisoned. According to the National Fire Protection Association, hotels and motels averaged 3,520 fires a year from 2009 to 2013, resulting in 9 deaths.

To some degree, we are putting ourselves at risk anytime we enter someone else's home. But at least guests know whom to blame, complain to, or sue when there's an accident at the Sheraton. They are largely on their own in the brave new world of widespread home rentals, where the company providing the product has no control over the product or all the bad things that can happen with it. "It will never not happen," Shapiro says. "We're dealing with people entering a home, and you can't predict people's behaviors. We do as best a job as we can, and I think that shows."

The scale of the Airbnb platform has grown so large that the fact that more things haven't gone wrong may show that perhaps that trust is deserved. Some say we may also be heading toward a new paradigm of adjusted expectations for the brave new world of the sharing economy. "Fundamentally, this model of business isn't going to have the same kind of protection that the hotels or the car-rental companies or the taxi commission provide," says NYU's Arun Sundararajan. "We always make a trade-off, and we'll start to make different trade-offs with the sharing economy."

Some of the people who were victims of some of the worst incidents of breached trust seem to support this argument: Mark King of Calgary, whose home was trashed and had to be rebuilt, called the Kings' experience "one in several million" and said, "It didn't turn me off to the idea of Airbnb." Rachel Bassini, whose penthouse was trashed in 2014, returned to hosting on Airbnb. She has lots of positive reviews.

The Opposite of "Belonging"

Airbnb spent a good long time refining its trust and safety mechanisms, because the company's founders knew at the outset that there were risks to be encountered, and they knew that finding a way to minimize them as much as possible was critical to getting people to use its platform. But they were less prepared for another epidemic of bad behavior: racial discrimination.

In 2011, Michael Luca, an assistant professor of business administration at Harvard Business School, began studying online marketplaces. He had become intrigued with the way they had shifted over time from fairly anonymous platforms — those like eBay, Amazon, and Priceline — to newer, fast-growing, sharing-economy platforms where users' identities played a much greater role. In particular, Luca was interested in the way these later sites made heavy use of personal profiles and photographs about the people behind the transactions in attempting to build trust. While those tools helped serve the admirable goals of trust building and accountability, he suspected they may have an unintended consequence as well: facilitating discrimination. Conducting a field experiment of Airbnb — because it was the largest such platform and because it required users to post large photos — Luca and his team found that nonblack hosts were able to charge roughly 12 percent more than black hosts, even when the properties were equivalent for location and quality — and that black hosts saw a larger price penalty for having a poor location relative to nonblack hosts.

Curiously, the study got little attention when it was published in 2014. When it came out in the press, Airbnb issued a dismissive statement saying that the research was two years old, it was from just one of the thirty-five thousand cities in which the company operates, and that the researchers made "subjective or inaccurate determinations" when compiling the findings. Two years later, Luca and his team published a second study that looked specifically at the booking-acceptance rates of black guests compared with white guests. They created twenty profiles — ten with "distinctively African American names" and ten with "distinctively white names" — leaving all other elements of the profiles identical. They sent 6,400 messages to hosts across five cities inquiring about availability for a specific weekend two months in the future. The results bore out their suspicions: requests from the guests with the African American–sounding names were roughly 16 percent less likely to be accepted than guests with "distinctively white names." The differences persisted when other factors, like ethnicity or gender of the host, price of the property, and whether it was a shared or a full home, were held constant. "Overall, we find widespread discrimination against guests with distinctively African-American names," the researchers wrote.

The researchers focused on Airbnb because it was the "canonical" example of the sharing economy, but they cited previous research that found similar issues on other online lending sites, such as Craigslist.com and elsewhere. "Our result contributes to a small but growing body of literature suggesting that discrimination persists — and we argue may even be exacerbated — in online platforms."

This time, the study got a little more attention. A few months later, the issue would hit full boil when an NPR piece put a face to the issue. In April 2016, a segment focused on the experience of Quirtina Crittenden, an African American business consultant from Chicago. She told the broadcast that she was declined routinely on Airbnb while using her real name, but when she changed it to Tina and switched her photo to a landscape shot, the rejections stopped. She had started a hashtag on Twitter, #AirbnbWhileBlack, which had gotten traction.

Airing during the popular drive-time slot to an audience of millions, Crittenden's story went viral. Multiple stories followed, and tweets poured in with the #AirbnbWhileBlack hashtag, with many more people coming forward with similar stories.

A few weeks later, Gregory Selden, a twenty-five-year-old African American in Washington, D.C., filed a lawsuit against Airbnb, claiming that a host in Philadelphia had denied him accommodations but then accepted him after he applied using two fake profiles of white men. In his suit, he claimed violations of the Civil Rights Act and said Airbnb did not respond to his complaints. He said that when he confronted the host with the results of the fake profiles, the host told him that "people like [him] were simply victimizing [himself]."

A few weeks later, when a black woman tried to book a room in Charlotte, North Carolina, she was approved, but then the host canceled, sending her a message that called her the worst kind of derogatory term multiple times, telling her, "I hate XXX, so I'm going to cancel you," and "This is the South, darling. Find another place to rest your XXX head."

The racial-discrimination controversy had now become full blown. Airbnb reacted swiftly, issuing a statement saying the company was "horrified," and assuring the members of its community that this kind of language and conduct violated its policies and "everything we believe in." The next day, Chesky sent out a strongly worded tweet: "The incident in NC was disturbing and unacceptable. Racism and discrimination have no place on Airbnb. We have permanently banned this host." Chesky repeated publicly in the following weeks as much as possible that Airbnb wanted and needed help and ideas and suggestions for how to make this issue better. The company emphasized that "we don't have all the answers," that it was putting out a call for ideas for any and all suggestions, and that it would reach out to a wide range of experts to get their ideas and advice. Racism is a problem that belongs to all of us, the message was; we need your help, too.

Later that week, two start-ups emerged, called Noirbnb and Innclusive, as lodging platforms directed at people of color.

As the controversy continued to heat up, the company launched a ninety-day top-to-bottom review to figure out how to address the issue, bringing in outside experts like former attorney general Eric Holder and Laura Murphy, former legislative director of the ACLU. A few months later, the company released a thirty-two-page report and announced an extensive set of changes based on the experts' recommendations: The company would soon require anyone seeking to use its platform to sign a "community commitment" pledging to abide by a new nondiscrimination policy. It started a policy called Open Doors that would find any guest who had been discriminated against a similar place to stay on Airbnb or elsewhere, and it could be applied retroactively. It also said it would create a new product team dedicated to combating discrimination and that the team would experiment with reducing the prominence of user photographs and placing more emphasis on reviews. It increased the number of listings available by Instant Book — listings available to be booked without any approval process — from 550,000 to 1 million; said it would implement unconscious-bias training for hosts; and set up a special team of specialists to help with enforcement and handling complaints. "Unfortunately, we have been slow to address these problems, and for this I am sorry," Chesky wrote. "I take responsibility for any pain or frustration this has caused members of our community."

Leaders in the African American community praised the changes; the Congressional Black Caucus called it "a standard that can be modeled throughout the tech industry." Some, like Jamila Jefferson-Jones, associate professor of law at the University of Missouri–Kansas City School of Law, felt the changes didn't go far enough and that the platform should remove photos altogether. She also said the issue raises serious questions as to where the legal line is drawn between a platform and a provider — it hasn't been tested yet in the courts — and that rather than Airbnb's effort to "self-regulate," new laws may be necessary. It would prove difficult to use the courts on the issue, though: Airbnb responded to the Selden suit with a motion forcing him into arbitration — like all customers, he had agreed to binding arbitration when he signed the company's terms-of-service agreement, meaning he had forfeited his right to bring a suit against the company in order to use the service. In early November 2016, a judge ruled that the arbitration policy prevented him from suing.

For his part, Harvard's Luca calls Airbnb's antidiscrimination changes "reactive": "I don't think anybody at Airbnb set out to facilitate discrimination," he says. He says he thinks the company was too focused on growth.

Legally, the issue is murky. Hotels have to abide by civil rights laws, but Airbnb operates a platform, not a provider of public accommodation, with arm's-length regulatory distance from its users. It places the burden of compliance with local laws on individuals, but the Civil Rights Act of 1964 does not apply to people renting out fewer than five rooms in their own home. So under federal law — local laws may differ — hosts are legally able to reject someone not just for hateful personal beliefs but for all kinds of reasons: they can reject smokers, for example, or a group looking for a place to stay for a bachelor party, or families with young children. During my research, I heard tell of one host who rented only to people from China, because they were a huge potential market of travelers and they "paid well"; and another who rented only to "orientals" because they were "nice, quiet, no problems."

But legal or not, and regardless of whether Airbnb was culpable, discrimination was a crisis of the core for the company. The issue of being friendly and welcoming to one another isn't ancillary, the way, say, Dove soap believes in healthy body image but sells soap, or the way lululemon believes in community but sells clothes. Airbnb sells welcoming and acceptance, and has built its entire brand and mission around the idea of belonging. If there were a polar opposite of belonging, this would be it. "Discrimination to most companies is an adjacency to their mission," Chesky said in an onstage interview at *Fortune*'s Brainstorm Tech conference as the controversy was erupting. "Our mission, most importantly, is to bring people together. This was an obstacle to our mission, and if we merely tried to 'address the issue,' we would probably not accomplish our mission."

And the main culprit was one of the elements that made up the very core of the Airbnb community: its members' online photos and profiles. As the Harvard researchers pointed out, "While the photos are precisely what help create a feeling of humanity on the Airbnb platform, they can just as easily bring out the worst of humanity." Discrimination, the researchers wrote, suggested "an important un-intended consequence of a seemingly-routine mechanism for build-ing trust."

Onstage at the *Fortune* event, Chesky suggested that one reason Airbnb was late to the issue might have been that it was so focused on using photos and identities to keep people safe that it didn't real-ize the unintended consequences of making identities so public. "We took our eye off the ball," he said. Another reason, he added, was that he and his founders simply didn't think about it as they built the plat-form because they were "three white guys." "There's a lot of things we didn't think about when we designed this platform," Chesky said. "And so there's a lot of steps that we need to reevaluate."

Air Rage

Early to bed, early to rise, and work like hell and organize.
— CHRIS LEHANE

SOMETIME IN THE SPRING OF 2010, Chesky got a call from a host in New York City. "He said, 'There's this thing going on in New York, they're trying to push this law through, and you've got to be really concerned about it,'" Chesky remembers. "I'm, like, 'Tell me more about it.'" He says he had no knowledge of the law the host was referring to — and once again, no experience in the subject at hand, in this case municipal government and city politics. Someone suggested Chesky get representation and hire a lobbyist to try to get in front of New York lawmakers. "I didn't even know what a lobbyist was," he says. He says the more he learned, the stranger he thought it sounded. "You can't talk to these people, so you've got to hire people to talk to these people?" he says. "I thought, first of all, that's kind of insane. I'll hire these people to talk to these people because they won't talk to me? OK." The company hired Bolton–St. Johns, a prominent lobbying firm in New York. But there wasn't much time: the law in question was potentially going to be passed in just a few months. "We had to have a crash course," Chesky says.

That crash course would turn into a years-long learning curve regarding the ins and outs of local politics and the powerful forces behind them, not just in New York City but in scores of municipalities around the globe. And it would become the biggest speed bump in Airbnb's young life. As it turns out, the very activity behind Airbnb, renting out one's home on a short-term basis, violates existing laws in many places. The laws are hyperlocal and vary not just state by state or city by city but town by town. And the regulatory patchwork is complex: hosts can run afoul of local laws governing short-term rentals, tax collection, building-code standards, zoning bylaws, and more.

In many markets, Airbnb has worked with regulators to amend these rules to allow it to operate legally. It has forged key agreements over the years with cities like London, Paris, Amsterdam, Chicago, Portland, Denver, Philadelphia, San Jose, Shanghai, and many more to liberalize laws, to create new ones, or to collect taxes. The company is actively engaged in talks with many more municipalities to do the same.

But some places just won't let it go. In a small number of high-profile markets in particular — New York City, San Francisco, Berlin, and Barcelona, among others — regulators and lawmakers have dug in their heels with particular tenaciousness. And as Airbnb has grown bigger over the years, the intensity of the opposition has escalated. (Those same laws govern HomeAway, VRBO, and other short-term-rental platforms, and those companies are involved in some of these same legal fights, too, but none of these companies became as big as fast or were in as many urban places as Airbnb.)

Almost nowhere has the fight been as heated as in New York City, the company's biggest U.S. market, with an estimated $450 million in annual revenue brought in by its hosts. The 2010 law marked the beginning of a protracted saga that took many twists and turns over the years as the company fought for regulatory clearance — and stirred the ire of lawmakers and the entrenched hotel and real estate industries by continuing to operate anyway. In late 2016, the company suffered a major blow when Governor Andrew Cuomo signed a law that made it illegal for individuals to advertise apartments being rented for fewer than thirty days if the resident was not present —

the majority of Airbnb's business in New York. Airbnb immediately filed lawsuits against the city and the state, which it subsequently settled, but the battle has had a major impact on one of the company's highest-profile markets.

The company's experience in New York is also a case study for the kinds of collisions that can happen when new ideas and technologies come out of nowhere to threaten the status quo and incumbent industries — and how the political realities on the ground aren't always as smooth as the ascending line on these companies' unfettered growth charts. It highlights how deeply emotional issues around housing can get. The struggle over Airbnb in New York and elsewhere has also pitted Democrat against Democrat, has brought together strange bedfellows, and has made it hard sometimes to discern just who is the David and who is the Goliath.

New York City suffers one of the most severe shortages of rental housing in the country, with vacancy rates of around 3.4 percent. It is the most lucrative hotel market in the United States. It is one of few places in the country where the labor movement remains robust. And when it comes to rough-and-tumble city and state politics, nothing beats New York City. So, as is the case with many things in the Big Apple, the fight for Airbnb is bigger, tougher, and more colorful than anywhere else.

The law that Chesky received the call about in early 2010 concerned a new amendment to the so-called Multiple Dwelling Law, which would make it illegal to rent out New York City apartments in buildings with three or more units for fewer than thirty days if the permanent resident was not present. The practice already violated most co-op and condo bylaws, but this bill would have made it state law. Sponsored by Democratic state senator Liz Krueger, it was primarily directed at landlords who were operating illegal hotels by converting housing that was intended for long-term rentals into units rented to tourists by the night.

The practice of offering short-term rentals was decades old, but just as it had done with so much else, the Internet had made it vastly easier to get the word out quickly and cheaply. With even the smallest, dingiest studio able to command triple-digit nightly rates and high occupancy levels, landlords, building owners, and some clever entrepreneurs had been turning to websites to more efficiently market their units — whether Craigslist, HomeAway, local operators like IStay New York, or the little-known universe of native-language, country-specific tourism-marketing websites that pipe out New York City lodging deals to the rest of the world. Airbnb was not meant to be the target — in 2010, few lawmakers in the city and state had heard of the quirky start-up from California. So, despite Airbnb's rallying its community of several hundred New York City hosts to write letters to Governor Andrew Cuomo, the bill passed.

As Airbnb gained momentum, though, things started to change. All the conditions that allowed for the company to spread so quickly were particularly ripe in New York: the Great Recession, sky-high rental prices, and large swells of both renters and millennials, the two groups most predisposed to use Airbnb. From 2010 to 2011, as the company sped toward one million bookings, New York, its first market, also became one of its biggest. By 2012, however, the company began to feel the first signs that it might not be so welcome. "We started hearing some rumors that there was going to be a crackdown on our hosts," recalls Belinda Johnson, the company's chief business-affairs and legal officer who at the time had recently joined Airbnb as general counsel.

In September of that year, according to the *New York Times*, a thirty-year-old web designer named Nigel Warren used Airbnb to rent out his room in the East Village apartment he shared with a roommate while he went to Colorado for a few days. With the roommate's OK, Warren listed it for one hundred dollars per night and quickly had a booking from a woman from Russia. When Warren returned from his trip, he learned that the city's Office of Special Enforcement, a multiagency task force that investigates quality-of-life complaints, had paid a visit to the building and slapped his landlord with three violations and fines totaling $40,000. The case took a few turns over technicalities, but several months later a judge ruled that Warren was violating the law and fined his landlord $2,400. Airbnb intervened and appealed on Warren's behalf, arguing that since he was renting a room in his home and not the full apartment, it was within the law, and in September 2013 the city's Environmental Control Board overturned the decision.

Airbnb celebrated the news — the company's then policy head, David Hantman, called it a "huge victory" — and while the ruling clarified that the law allowed apartment-dwellers to rent out a room while the resident was present, it was not necessarily emblematic. More than half of the people who rent out their spaces on Airbnb in New York City use it to rent their entire apartments. The Warren verdict, dealing with a shared-apartment situation, had little to do with those hosts, but a growing coalition of anti-Airbnb forces wanted everything to do with them. The company's fight in New York was just getting started.

Over time, an anti-Airbnb alliance started to form made up of elected officials, affordable-housing activists, and representatives of the hotel union and the hotel industry, whose arguments against Airbnb then were the same that they are today: Airbnb traffic can inhibit quality of life for neighbors, who didn't sign up for having transient tourists parading through their buildings. It creates safety issues both by providing access to residential buildings to strangers and by failing to comply with traditional hotel-safety regulations. Perhaps most critically, they said the proliferation of units dedicated solely to renting out on Airbnb — so-called illegal hotels — removes housing from a market that is already in a serious affordable-housing crisis, driving prices up further for everyone.

A much bigger blow came in the fall of 2013, when New York State attorney general Eric Schneiderman served Airbnb with a subpoena, saying he was going after illegal hotels and seeking records of transactions for some fifteen thousand Airbnb hosts in New York City. Airbnb took the rare move of fighting the subpoena, filing a motion to block the request, alleging it was too broad and too invasive of its customers' privacy. The following May, a judge agreed. But Schneiderman's office came back with a pared-down version asking for information only on Airbnb's biggest players. A week later, Airbnb and the attorney general's office announced they'd reached what they called a "settlement": Airbnb would supply anonymized data on nearly five hundred thousand transactions from 2010 to mid-2014.

When the attorney general's report came out, it said that 72 percent of Airbnb's "private" listings in New York were in violation of state law. And it said that while 94 percent of hosts had just 1 or 2 listings, the other 6 percent were so-called commercial hosts — those who had 3 or more listings regularly through Airbnb — and they accounted for more than a third of bookings and revenue. It said that one hundred hosts had 10 or more listings. The top dozen hosts had anywhere from 9 to 272 listings and made more than $1 million per year each. The biggest user, at 272 listings, had revenue of $6.8 million.

It wasn't so much the illegal activity that was new — after all, given the 2010 law, any Airbnb listing for a full apartment was illegal (unless it was in a house with fewer than three units), and both then and now, thousands of hosts and guests either don't know about the law or willfully ignore it. What was new was that this report — marking the first time a party outside Airbnb had any access to the company's data — revealed the scope of the multiproperty activity on the site. It dovetailed with previous reports that suggested a small percentage of hosts was responsible for a disproportionate share of the company's New York business. Airbnb called the data incomplete and outdated. It said that New York's current rules lacked clarity, and it wanted to work together with the city on creating new regulations to stop bad actors while putting in place "clear, fair rules for home sharing."

The System Gamers

This question of multiunit hosts or "commercial listings" has plagued Airbnb in New York and elsewhere. The company's ideals promote a world where home sharing lets regular people open up their homes to strangers, whether the host is in the residence or out of town, providing a unique and special way to travel. But whether Airbnb likes it or not, it also presents a cold, hard arbitrage to be played — the difference between what a housing unit can pull in each year in nightly rents can be double what it can generate as a longer-term rental. And many people, from property managers to corporate real estate giants to mom-and-pop entrepreneurs, have over the years jumped in to play it. The company has said over and over it doesn't want this behavior and has rooted out professional operators. But it does not share raw data about this, leaving its opponents to fill in the gaps with their own estimates. "The revenue generated by Airbnb rentals is one of those great unsolved mysteries, like the Loch Ness monster or chupacabra," wrote the authors of a 2015 report by Airdna, one of several independent data providers that "scrape" Airbnb's website in order to generate data-and-analytics reports.

No one disputes that the early days of Airbnb in New York City drew a proliferation of bad actors. One of the largest early such players was Robert Chan, a party promoter who went by the name Toshi and operated some two hundred illegal short-term apartment rentals, on Airbnb and other sites, out of fifty residential buildings in Manhattan and Brooklyn; he'd lease multiple units, paying above-market rent to landlords, and rent them out for nightly stays.

The city of New York ultimately sued Chan and won a $1 million settlement in November 2013, but other operators continued to use the platform. In the fall of 2014, Gothamist posted a video of a two-bedroom apartment in the Murray Hill section of Manhattan stuffed with twenty-two mattresses. A pair of renters of a three-bedroom, top-floor apartment in a row house in Elmhurst, Queens, installed Sheetrock to subdivide each bedroom into three smaller bedrooms, which they listed on Airbnb for thirty-five dollars a night. Stories abounded, in New York and elsewhere, of commercial landlords evicting tenants who were seeking the higher yield of a nightly rental.

In 2014, the company began implementing what would become the linchpin of its strategy to push back against its opponents: mobilizing its hosts. Immediately after Schneiderman had issued his subpoena, Douglas Atkin, the company's global head of community, worked with a New York City host to start a petition calling for the New York legislature to change what it called the "slumlord law," which it said failed to distinguish between commercial operators and everyday New Yorkers seeking to rent out their primary home some of the time. The company hired veteran Democratic political strategist Bill Hyers, a partner at Hilltop Public Solutions and the campaign manager behind Bill de Blasio's mayoral victory, who conceived and ran a multimillion-dollar grassroots campaign laser-focused on a single message: that Airbnb helped middle-class New Yorkers. The hallmark of the campaign was a television ad called "Meet Carol," which featured an African American widowed mother who'd lived in her lower-Manhattan apartment for thirty-four years and who had turned to Airbnb after she'd lost her job. In cinematic slow motion, Carol shakes out a fresh sheet over a bed while the sun streams in through the window and flips hotcakes over the griddle for her smiling guests at the breakfast table. "I have on my profile, 'Taking over the world, one pancake at a time,'" she says at the end of the ad.

The middle-class message would become Airbnb's rallying cry in its global regulatory battle for years to come: Airbnb helps everyday people make ends meet. The company argues that it lets longtime residents use what is typically one of their greatest expenses — their home — to make additional income that helps pay the bills. Airbnb says it is a boost to tourism in cities — in particular, spreading tourism dollars to neighborhoods that typically don't see them, since Airbnb properties are typically outside the traditional hotel zones. It says that it helps locals and small businesses in neighborhoods that traditionally wouldn't see any of this spending.

Airbnb has released many reports to support this argument over the years. According to a report issued in 2015, Airbnb hosts had earned more than $3.2 billion in the U.S. over the previous seven years. In a separate report focused on New York City, Airbnb reported that its business brought in $1.15 billion in economic activity in 2014 — $301 million of which went to hosts and $844 million to New York City businesses. Much of the latter funds went to neighborhoods that don't typically see tourism dollars. Of the 767,000 tourists Airbnb says it brought to New York in 2014, 40,000 of them stayed in the Bedford-Stuyvesant section in Brooklyn, where they spent $30 million. In Harlem, they spent $43 million; in Astoria, $10.6 million; in the South Bronx, $900,000. (Airbnb hired HR&A Advisors to do the study.)

Yet none of this appeased Airbnb's opponents, who just accused it of exacerbating gentrification in areas where it had already begun. By the summer of 2014, as the attorney general's investigation was under way and shortly after the company had raised another megaround of funding at a $10 billion valuation, the conversation around Airbnb started getting heated and alarmist. "One person said, 'I don't want al-Qaeda in my building, therefore I don't want Airbnb in my neighborhood,'" Chesky later told me. "Like, it was getting irrational. It wasn't based in reality, and I was, like, 'This is getting dangerous and unhealthy.' And so we went to New York."

While Chesky's reaction when the 2010 bill first appeared was to just fight back — early on, top Silicon Valley minds had advised the company to lie low and stay off the radar or even to be antagonistic — Airbnb's Belinda Johnson brought a decidedly more conciliatory approach when she started, in 2011. She encouraged Chesky to start meeting with his opponents instead. "Belinda taught me that no matter how much somebody hates you, it's almost always better to meet them," he says. He embarked on a "massive charm tour," traveling to New York and meeting with stakeholders: regulators, hoteliers, members of the real estate community, journalists — even Mayor Bill de Blasio ("We had a really great conversation," Chesky says). Meeting face-to-face didn't change their stance in most cases — that would soon become an understatement — but it got them to hear his side.

But the opposition movement continued to gain steam. In late 2014, the city's powerful hotel union, elected officials opposed to Airbnb, and a consortium of affordable-housing advocates and the hotel industry joined forces to form Share Better, a sort of anti-Airbnb political-action committee whose first move was what it said was a $3 million campaign against Airbnb.

The He-Said, She-Said of Home Sharing

Airbnb's response has always been that it doesn't want corporate profiteers, and that over the years it has worked to eliminate them. It stepped up those efforts in the fall of 2015 when it introduced a new "community compact," a pledge to work more closely with city officials and, in particular, to help curb any impact of its business on affordable housing. It released a report filled with data on its operations in New York City, and said it was moving to a "one host, one home" policy there. "We strongly oppose large-scale speculators who turn dozens of apartments into illegal hotel rooms," the report read. "Illegal hotels are not in the interests of our guests, our hosts, our company, or the cities where Airbnb hosts share their space." The most recent report on Airbnb's New York operations showed that 95 percent of its hosts in the city had only one listing, and the median nights booked per listing is forty-one per year.

The issue with critics, however, has been not the percentage of hosts but the volume of the business that comes from commercial interests, whether individual hosts controlling multiple units or even one unit that is dedicated solely to rental on Airbnb. Different studies over the years have shown commercial listings to represent as much as 30 percent of inventory and, depending on the definition, up to 40 percent of revenue or more in some markets. In the summer of 2016, Share Better put out a study of Airbnb's New York activity that identified 8,058 listings it called "impact listings," offered by hosts who had more than one unit rented out for at least three months per year, or a single unit rented for at least six months per year. It said those units reduced the availability of rental housing by 10 percent.

Airbnb has always maintained that the data offered by outside parties is inaccurate. Its most recent data in New York at this writing showed that multiple-listing activity represented 15 percent of its active entire-home inventory in the city and 13 percent of overall host revenue, down from 20 percent of revenue a few months earlier. Its critics say that data doesn't tell the full story; they want the company to release anonymized data showing the location and rental behavior of its individual hosts, which the company refuses to do, to protect its customers' privacy.

Chesky says that a lot of nuances about Airbnb's workings are lost in the headlines. "We really do care deeply about this issue, and we are trying to solve it," he says. He insists that large real estate groups are not what the company wants. "We don't have much differentiation if it's a corporate rental," he says. "It feels like a hotel. There's less belonging."

Purging commercial operators, the company says, is not so simple. Some of the multilisting activity is activity that is legal: units that are rented for more than thirty days, or listings of homes with fewer than three units — say, brownstones in Brooklyn or row houses in Queens — that are exempt from the Multiple Dwelling Law. The company also has a growing number — three hundred thousand spaces globally at last count — of boutique hotels and bed-and-breakfasts that list on its platform. Some hosts, Chesky says, list the same apartment in multiple ways, which can make a single listing look like two. And he points out that even if the company bans a particular host, that host could create another account under a separate name. "We don't know everyone," Chesky says. "We don't interview every single person and ask them why they're doing what they're doing."

This is the biggest issue with members of the hospitality industry: the so-called illegal hotels that they feel are proliferating on the platform. Hotel executives believe that despite what it says, Airbnb has many more such listings than it is letting on, and they believe the company has the power to identify them and police them. "They say, 'We can't get rid of them.' That's absurd," says Vijay Dandapani, president of Apple Core Hotels, a chain of five hotels in midtown Manhattan, and chairman of the Hotel Association of New York City. "Around the world there is a sense they don't play by the rules and they're less than transparent."

Many who make it their business to scrutinize the makeup of Airbnb's listings agree that most of the large-scale professional operators in New York and in other cities have left the site. A lot of them have moved on to Airbnb's competitors. If anything, in New York City and other markets, they appear to have given way to more amateur microentrepreneurs — small-scale, everyday Joes who either amass enough profit to buy or rent a few places for themselves, which they list on the site, or pool together with friends or coinvestors to do so. These are people like Pol McCann in Sydney, who has two listings, is renovating a third, and hopes to retire in a few years to become an Airbnb host full-time; or people like Jonathan Morgan, the previously mentioned host who runs six listings out of three homes in Savannah. Scott Shatford, the founder of Airdna, started his company after developing a business running seven listings in Santa Monica, California. He says he was making $400,000 a year at his peak — money he used to bootstrap his Airdna business.

But these entrepreneurs often go to great lengths to cloak themselves, creating multiple single accounts under different names and curating their listings to generate the individual look and feel that Airbnb wants and that its customers have come to expect. "Everybody wants to play by this very personal experience," says Shatford. (He and others say that, despite what Airbnb's critics say, it's very hard to prevent people from gaming the system. "Anybody who's intelligent at all can get around anything they could put up around managing multiple properties," he says.) But regulators are still waiting to pounce: in 2016, after Santa Monica passed some of the toughest laws regulating Airbnb in the country and Shatford gave an interview about his business, he was charged with five misdemeanor counts. He struck a plea deal with the city, paid $4,500 in fines, and has since relocated to Denver, where he now focuses exclusively on Airdna.

"I think this entire controversy around corporate rentals is only trying to get at a single question," Chesky says when I ask him about it over breakfast ordered in at an Airbnb listing, a modest row house he's staying in in Washington, D.C.'s Georgetown. "Which is, are there units dedicated to Airbnb activity in a city where they have a shortage of housing? I think any other thing about how commercial it is, how many homes they have, is totally beside the point." From a policy perspective, he says, in markets where there is not a housing issue, Airbnb is not against multiple listings. In some places — he uses Lake Tahoe as an example — a municipality may actually want property-management companies to manage listings on Airbnb (and in 2015 the company piloted property-manager partnerships in some vacation-rental markets). It's another way to reach potential vacationers and bring them to the destination. "As a *policy*," Chesky clarifies, "you can't possibly be against that." In cities where there is a real housing issue, however, like New York, he says the policy should very clearly be one listing per host.

From a brand perspective, though, he says it's a different story. "Our core community are ordinary hosts, people renting and sharing the homes they live in. We think that's very special." He points out our surroundings during this interview, with books and trinkets lining the shelves. If this were a dedicated rental, he says, we wouldn't be seeing the human touches around us. "You have a proximity," he says. "There's care. There's a sense of belonging. Not 'service,' but *belonging*. That's the core of the company."

Got that? Airbnb isn't opposed to multiple-unit hosts in cities that are not housing-constrained — but only if the hosts are delivering what Airbnb considers to be a good experience, which it defines as a real human offering the right kind of "hostiness." "We don't want property managers who are going into this for the money," Chesky says. The goal, he says, is what Airbnb's hospitality chief Chip Conley calls "capital 'H' hospitality, and lowercase 'business.'" So, Airbnb argues that in a non-housing-constrained city, microentrepreneurs like McCann in Sydney or Morgan in Savannah should be allowed. (Regulators in Savannah disagree and have slapped Morgan with more than fifteen citations totaling fines of $50,000, which he says he has not paid; in Sydney, McCann had been feeling pressure from a potential tightening of rules there, too; if the government were to place any cap on the number of days a unit can be rented per year, his business would not be viable. But by the time of this writing, a government report had recommended allowing short-term rentals for an unlimited number of days per year in New South Wales; the issue was headed to parliament.)

New Yorkers with Issues

Many of the points the anti-Airbnb camp makes are understandable. Granting transient guests access to residential buildings means that people who haven't been vetted have keys to the buildings' public spaces and could not lock the doors properly or could create other hazards. Residential apartments don't have the same safety precautions as hotels, like sprinkler systems and clear evacuation plans (though New York City building code requires residential buildings, too, to adhere to fire-safety standards). Perhaps most valid for everyday New Yorkers is the quality-of-life issue. People in New York live in small spaces stacked on top of one another, already sharing walls, floors, ceilings, and public spaces.

There are few things New Yorkers treasure more than their personal space and their routines, and having tourists knocking on the door trying to get in or throwing the garbage in the wrong place or tossing cigarette butts on the roof deck infringes upon both. Plenty of New Yorkers I know seem to have some kind of Airbnb-adjacent story involving transient tourists. One longtime resident of a West Village building says she knew her next-door neighbor started listing his studio on Airbnb when she started hearing noises through the walls and noticed different people coming in and out of the place each week. One such party, a family of four, kept the building's luggage cart in the hallway for the duration of their stay; she realized why when she spotted the kids outside the building, gleefully riding the gleaming gold cart up and down Eighth Avenue. Not too far from where I live, there's a listing that's popular with Scandinavian tourists, and neighbors have grown accustomed to seeing clusters of very tall, very blond young men gathered outside the building, smoking and talking late into the night.

Yet even with these nuisances, the argument isn't as straightforward as Airbnb's opposition makes it sound (for one thing, nine out of ten women in New York might tell you they'd welcome any influx of tall men, transient or not). Plenty of New Yorkers know what it's like to deal with a permanent neighbor who's a nuisance year-round.

Over the years, the opposition has focused its argument on the issue of affordable housing: that Airbnb removes units from the market, driving up prices for everyone else. Airbnb indeed has a tremendous number of listings in New York City—more than forty-four thousand at last count. But with more than three million housing units in total, they represent less than 1.5 percent of the total. A much larger number, two hundred thousand units, are vacant for other reasons. There are many forces—zoning laws, the high cost of construction, strict land-use regulations, an influx of wealthy foreign buyers, and a population at an all-time high thanks to a resurgence in big cities—all of which contribute far more directly to the city's lack of housing and sky-high prices than Airbnb does. "We recognize it [Airbnb] might not be causing the issue, but that doesn't mean you shouldn't care and should take thousands of apartments off the market," says Murray Cox, an affordable-housing activist and founder of data provider Inside Airbnb, another outside provider of Airbnb data.

The bigger Airbnb got, the more the conflict in New York escalated. Aside from the law, short-term rentals are forbidden by most landlords, and some began adding riders in their leases prohibiting tenants from using Airbnb, implementing stricter protocols for having guests, and adding cameras and hiring private investigators to catch tenants in the act. Related Companies, the largest owner of luxury residential rentals in New York, with more than seven thousand units, was said to have developed a PowerPoint presentation to teach its property managers how to sniff out tenants who were renting their units out on Airbnb. And in the fall of 2015, Mayor de Blasio pledged $10 million over three years for additional staffing and upgraded technology to better enforce those in violation of the city's short-term-rental law.

There are few things more acrimonious than a political fight in New York City, especially one that combines labor, big business, and the hypersensitive, deeply emotional issue of affordable housing, and as the stakes got higher, so did the level of vitriol. When actor and Airbnb investor Ashton Kutcher wrote a letter defending the company, New York State assemblywoman and longtime Airbnb critic Linda Rosenthal told the *Wall Street Journal* that the letter "won't make a scintilla of difference" and added that "he's trying to punk me." Helen Rosenthal, a city council member representing the Upper West Side (like Linda Rosenthal a Democrat; the two are not related), told *The Real Deal,* "The most important message for me to get out there is that we are going to make life as difficult as possible for Airbnb, who continues to just ignore state law."

In early 2016, Share Better released an ad that mocked the company's "Belong anywhere" motto, titled "Airbnb: Problems Everywhere." ("Thanks anyway, Airbnb, but you're not helping anyone but Airbnb," went the snarky voice-over.) Around the same time, two city council members sent a letter to Airbnb's top thirty investors, notifying them of the illegal nature of Airbnb's operations in New York and warning them it could affect the value of their investment. "For our part, if we were invested in a company that knowingly engaged in so much illegal activity, we would think twice about keeping our money in that company," the authors wrote.

Airbnb dismissed the letter as "theatrics." It amassed more political firepower: It hired a who's who of top New York City lobbying, political-strategy, and communications firms. It hired as its head of policy in New York Josh Meltzer, who'd previously worked for Attorney General Schneiderman. For help approaching the labor unions, it brought on board Andy Stern, former head of the powerful Service Employees International Union. It spent more on advertising. It sponsored marathons. (Perhaps predictably, on the eve of the newly named Airbnb Brooklyn Half Marathon, protesters showed up wearing T-shirts that said "#RunFromAirbnb.")

But it had powerful, well-funded forces lining up against it (REBNY, the real estate lobby, soon joined the fight), and in mid-

2016, at the very end of the state's legislative session, a bill that Assemblywoman Linda Rosenthal had introduced earlier in the year calling for a statewide ban on advertising for short-term rentals started gaining steam. Deliberately written as an "advertising" regulation to get around the legal defense that a website couldn't be held liable for the content its users posted, the bill prohibited apartment-dwellers from simply listing the rental of their unoccupied units for fewer than thirty days and shifted the punishment from the landlord or building owner to the tenant or apartment dweller, who under the bill could be fined $1,000 for a first offense and $7,500 for a third. Despite a PR push from tech-industry heavyweights, including Airbnb investors Paul Graham, Reid Hoffman, and Kutcher, who slammed the bill for preventing innovation and hurting middle-class New Yorkers ("People are going to lose their homes because of this ignorant bill!" the actor tweeted), the bill passed on the last day of the legislative session, dealing a sudden and unexpected blow to Airbnb.

Airbnb maintained that the bill was introduced unfairly, the result of what it said was an eleventh-hour backroom deal brokered by special interests that ignored the voices of thousands of New Yorkers. It launched a million-dollar advertising campaign, removed more than two thousand listings on its platform in New York that it said appeared to be hosts with multiple units, and introduced a proposal to create both a technical tool on its site and a registration process to ban hosts from listing more than one home. But four months after the bill was passed, on a Friday in late October 2016, Governor Cuomo signed it into law. "This is an issue that was given careful, deliberate consideration, but ultimately these activities are already expressly prohibited by law," his spokesperson said in a statement. Linda Rosenthal, the bill's sponsor, weighed in: "I'm gratified that [Governor Cuomo] stood up for the cause of affordable housing and protecting tenants," she told the *New York Times* after the bill was signed.

Airbnb promptly responded: within a few hours of the signature, the company filed a lawsuit against the city of New York and the state attorney general, claiming the law violated the company's rights to free speech, due process, and protection granted to it under the Communications Decency Act. Airbnb circulated a memo titled "Hotels Celebrate Chance to Price Gouge" after a hotel-industry chief executive said in an earnings call that the legislation would positively impact the company's pricing power. (The Hotel Association of New York City's Vijay Dandapani takes issue with this line of attack, saying compression pricing is simple supply-and-demand economics at work, similar to the way airlines price their product.)

A few days later, Airbnb staged a rally outside Cuomo's New York City offices. Some two dozen hosts showed up with signs that said "Each cent pays my rent" and "Freelancers for Airbnb." (One plucky Cher fan held up a sign that read "Cher your home.") They chanted cries of "Airbnb, you and me!" and "Airbnb for NYC!" But they were drowned out by a counterprotest by a group of affordable-housing activists, tenants, union members, and Assemblywoman Rosenthal, who led the charge as the group marched up to the Airbnb protesters and yelled louder and much more forcefully, "Airbnb, BAD for NYC!" and "Homes are not hotels!" A few days later, at another rally, City Council member Jumaane Williams told the *New York Daily News*, "I've never been so happy to see an organization lose."

For the company's community in New York, the news created confusion. Guests who had already booked trips to New York began asking their hosts if they should cancel. Evelyn Badia, the host in Brooklyn with her own consulting business, adjusted her listing so it read, "Legal Comfortable, Spacious 2bdrm apt in House." At the rally, a bystander asked me if Airbnb buys buildings and converts them into rentals.

I spoke with Chris Lehane, the company's global head of public policy, shortly after the rally. "The deck was completely stacked against our hosts," he said. "Bad politics drive bad policy. When the special interests get to write a law and pass it without any public process where hosts have no voice in that, you're going to end up in one of these situations." He says the company will continue to push for a legislative solution for regulations that restrict commercial activity on its platform and allow regular people to rent out their spaces occasionally, a policy proposal that, he says, "by any objective analysis is good for the state." (As this book was going to press, the company settled its suits with both New York State and New York City—in the latter case, with both sides agreeing—in theory—to work together on targeted enforcement of bad actors.)

Neal Kwatra, CEO of the political consulting firm Metropolitan Public Strategies and the chief strategist of Share Better, says, "There's a law on the books since 2010 that has prohibited a huge part of Airbnb's business model, yet they had a very strategic approach here." He says the company "had a very clear understanding that, actual regulation notwithstanding, enforcement of the law wouldn't happen at the kind of scale that would disrupt their business. And I think what we have is a coalition of different constituents principally focused on the impact on affordable housing where Airbnb has driven up rents by removing thousands of units of long-term housing supply."

Assemblywoman Linda Rosenthal says she is "thrilled [the bill] was signed into law, but I think that Airbnb is being dragged kicking and screaming to run its business in accordance with the law and I think they're going to try to get out of it any way they can." She takes issue with what she calls the company's "different business model, which is to go into an area, overwhelm it and then you dictate the policy rather than the government telling you what to do." She says if the company cared about its users, it would have made the law clear on the home page of its website. (On its "Responsible Hosting in the U.S." page, the company encourages its customers to abide by all local laws.)

Airbnb and those familiar with its strategy say it attempted many times over the years to offer to compromise but that lawmakers were not interested in a conversation. "They [Airbnb] were willing to do pretty much any deal," says Hilltop's Bill Hyers, who is not currently working with the company, but he says that various parties were "aggressively not willing to even talk. There was nobody to deal with at the end of the day because of that."

Lehane said the New York situation would likely play itself out over time in a series of battles in a "longer-term war" and that for the next few years the twists and turns of the conflict would be the "mood music in the background." He says the company will continue to push for a compromise that involves getting the underlying 2010 law changed.

Organize, Mobilize, Legitimize

Lehane is friendly and affable when I meet him for the first time at Airbnb's headquarters, months before the law would pass in New York. He seems nothing like the pugnacious war wager he's said to be. Lehane is a political heavyweight: a Harvard-trained lawyer, he's been in Democratic politics since the 1980s. After working on Bill Clinton's 1992 campaign, he was recruited into the special counsel's office of the White House, an elite team that ran damage control for investigations into the Clinton administration (he produced the 332-page report that coined the phrase "vast right-wing conspiracy"). He then served as press secretary for Al Gore's 2000 campaign before decamping for the private sector. Known for his bare-knuckled tactics, pithy one-liners, and skilled opposition-research work, Lehane was famously nicknamed a "master of disaster." In between working for clients like Microsoft, Goldman Sachs, Lance Armstrong, and labor unions, as well as nonprofits like the billionaire Tom Steyer's climate-change-advocacy efforts, he wrote and produced a satirical film about a political strategist called *Knife Fight*. In 2014, Airbnb brought in Lehane as a consultant to help with the company's battle with San Francisco, and he soon joined full-time.

Lehane is slender but cuts a big presence around Airbnb headquarters, where he is almost universally known as "Lehane." Ground zero for his operations is a three-story stand-alone building in an alley behind Airbnb's headquarters, formerly called the Annex, which Lehane rechristened the ADU, shorthand for Accessory Dwelling Unit, a wonky housing term for what's often known as a granny flat or an in-law unit. Such units lend themselves particularly well to home sharing (and they are fittingly, somewhat thorny to regulate). At Airbnb, the ADU houses the entire mobilization team, policy communications and operations, and other departments, including social impact and strategic research — some two hundred staffers all told, many of whom come out of Democratic politics. Lehane modeled the setup after Mayor Bloomberg's design of City Hall in New York, with a bull pen in the middle and different teams clustered around it but near one another so they can interact. "If you ever walked into a global political campaign, it would feel exactly the same," he says.

It falls on Lehane to oversee Airbnb's strategy to push back and get the laws to turn in the company's favor. "It's a wild thing," he says, sitting down for one of our chats in Airbnb's offices. "It's like you're building a car, building the road, building rules, people are throwing rocks at you — it's great!" But he freely admits he is also a consumer of what many by now have referred to as the Airbnb Kool-Aid. He believes the company has the potential to be a driving force for the middle class and says the reason home sharing has caught on with the consumer the way it has is that a series of larger socioeconomic trends have converged. It reinforces social contracts that have become frayed. It enables everyday people to be economically empowered. It brings people together. "At the end of the day, the reason why Airbnb is succeeding at the level that it is is not because of some magic potion or fairy dust that's been put on some algorithm," he told the U.S. Conference of Mayors in 2016. "It is because we've built a platform that allows people to interact with people and have a transformative experience."

Lehane maintains that most cities in the world are opening to partnering, and he is quick to point out the many places Airbnb has worked with local lawmakers to update or amend existing laws to make its activities legal — most recently on the day we speak, in Chicago, which passed a measure legalizing short-term rentals with no caps on the number of days, and allowing for the collection of a 4 percent tax on every rental, which will fund services for the homeless. ("Alternate housing fans touring the Windy City, rejoice," read an article about the rules.) As the New York battle raged, lawmakers passed friendly legislation right across the Hudson River in Newark and Jersey City, New Jersey, and in the same week Cuomo signed the New York bill, regulators forged agreements in New Orleans and Shanghai. (Lehane says that people like to "overindex" New York, but he and others point out that the platform is now so large that no one place is material to the overall company. This appears to be true: Airdna data estimates that total revenue from Airbnb hosts in New York City represents 10 percent of the U.S. total and 3 percent of the company's global host revenue.) Of the top one hundred markets the company has identified as important, Lehane tells me, seventy-five to eighty are "either done or moving in a good direction," ten are "sort of static," and the remaining ten "are always in some type of a conflict," with four at the core: New York, San Francisco, Berlin, and Barcelona.

But in those high-conflict places it's been hard, and the common denominator, Lehane says, is the unique politics that exist. In Barcelona, the government is sensitive to the influx of tourism in its Gothic Quarter. In San Francisco, the issue is a shortage of housing layered on top of a power struggle between the city's progressive roots and its more moderate — and moneyed — technology industry. In Berlin, which banned all entire-home short-term rentals without a permit and instituted fines of up to $115,000 for violators, there are long-standing issues around housing that go back to the reunification of Germany, now exacerbated by a refugee crisis. And New York, of course, is the epicenter of what Lehane calls the "hotel-industrial complex."

Mastering unique politics is Lehane's specialty, and he knew that the key to winning Airbnb's regulatory battles would lie in mobilizing its hosts. He says that Airbnb has something that no other private-sector entity he knows of has: hundreds of thousands of engaged hosts and guests who can be an "army of change." His solution: implement a grassroots mobilizing effort, much like the company did in New York when the attorney general first struck, but one that would be the equivalent in size and scale to a presidential campaign — and would be launched all over the world.

To his way of thinking, Airbnb has two unique elements that make this possible. One is scale: in the United States alone, the company's user base is larger than some of the country's largest special-interest groups, such as the Sierra Club, the American Federation of Teachers, and the Human Rights Campaign. Many in the Airbnb community are casual users; Lehane divides them into "base voters," the hosts, who are the more engaged but much smaller group, numbering just a few million; and "occasional voters," the guests. But the company's polling has shown that even the casual guest can be easily mobilized, and in certain markets as much as 5 to 15 percent of the general electorate uses Airbnb in some fashion. "If there's one thing politicians can do, it's math," he says. "And that's pretty compelling math."

The second unique thing about Airbnb is its economic model. Its "base voters" don't just believe in the cause; they make money from it. Airbnb hosts keep all the revenue that comes in the door but the 3 percent the company charges for its host fee. "These people are making ninety-seven cents on the dollar," Lehane says. "You put all these things together, and that's why I think we can be really politically disruptive."

Some of this groundwork had already been laid when Lehane began his work. Douglas Atkin's effort to build a petition movement during the New York attorney general's investigation was part of a broader effort in 2013 and 2014 to engage the Airbnb community in three cities where it faced opposition: New York, San Francisco, and Barcelona. Called Firestarter, it was a sophisticated mobilization approach that drew on tactics from the Obama presidential campaigns — specifically, the "snowflake" model of community-driven campaigning, a sort of crowd-sourced, bottom-up campaign model that empowers volunteers to organize and train each other. By ratcheting the asks of community members up a "commitment curve," starting with showing up at a meeting or sending a tweet all the way up to writing op-eds, the tactic is designed to extract as much passion as possible out of everyday people. "You can run a bunch of TV ads, and that will have some type of impact," Lehane says. "But getting a couple of hundred calls when you're a city councilperson is an awful lot. And that happens."

Lehane was basically charged with bringing his political advocacy muscle to the Firestarter model, expanding it, and rolling it out to one hundred key cities worldwide. The backbone of his efforts are home-sharing clubs, groups of hosts ranging from ten to fifteen people to a few hundred whom Lehane sees almost as modern-day guilds. Airbnb seeds them and provides infrastructure and support, but the clubs create their own bylaws, set their own goals, and, the hope goes, will become their own political citizenship entity. "These clubs have to be led by you, built by you, made up of you," he told an audience of five thousand hosts as he introduced the idea at the 2015 Airbnb Open in Paris. "We will help provide the advocacy tools, but it's going to be your voice that carries the day."

Lehane's "beta test" for this approach was the mobilization effort in San Francisco in 2015 to defeat Proposition F, a ballot initiative that would have put constraints on short-term rentals and, along with New York, the company's highest-profile regulatory battle. The city and Airbnb had already come to agreement to legalize short-term rentals, passing what became known as the "Airbnb law" in the fall of 2014, with Airbnb agreeing to cap the number of days per year hosts could rent their entire homes and requiring hosts to register with the city. But opposition mounted in the wake of the bill, and Proposition F proposed to reduce the cap, required the reporting of quarterly data, and gave neighbors and housing groups the ability to file legal complaints. With an $8 million budget for the campaign, Lehane deployed a team of veteran field organizers and hundreds of volunteers to mobilize the community's user base. In the end, 138,000 community members knocked on 285,000 doors and contacted 67,000 voters to defeat the proposition. (Its $8 million budget also went toward advertising, including television, with a series of snarky billboards that were perceived as snide and insulting: "Dear Public Library System, we hope you use some of the $12 million in hotel taxes to keep the library open later. Love, Airbnb." After the ads sparked a backlash, the company took them down and apologized.)

The victory was significant — but it would be short-lived. In June of 2016, the Board of Supervisors passed new legislation requiring that short-term-rental platforms vet their own listings to make sure their hosts are registered — or pay fines of $1,000 per unregistered listing per day. A few weeks later, Airbnb filed a lawsuit against the city of San Francisco that, at the time of this writing, was, just as in New York, still moving through the courts.

Scaling "Hostiness"

Airbnb faces a conundrum: it wants to grow its business, in New York City and everywhere. But it wants to do it in an appropriately home-spun way. "The more human interaction, the closer to our mission," Chesky says. But therein lies a challenge: How do you grow the kind of human, hand-held hostiness Airbnb wants? How do you take a one-home, one-host model of cozy hospitality and still scale it? Like most things, the company's founders consider this a design challenge.

One workaround for this is setting up partnerships with landlords. Airbnb is an urban phenomenon, and in many places, regardless of local laws, apartment-dwellers are prevented from hosting on Airbnb because their landlords don't allow it. Many don't want short-term rentals in their buildings because it violates their policy or because it goes against local regulations, and it's often the landlords, not tenants, who get fined. Sometimes these are small-time operators in one-off walk-up buildings. But many people who rent apartments in cities do so from one of a small handful of megalandlords: massive real estate companies like Avalon Bay Communities, Camden Property Trust, and Equity Residential Properties. These companies and others control hundreds of thousands of apartment units all over the country, and they rent to a disproportionate number of young millennials. They typically enlist large-scale property-management groups for the day-to-day management of their buildings, but it's the landlords who make the rules and bake them into their standard leases. Cracking open this group and getting them to change their rules to allow home sharing would let Airbnb notch significant gains — and, ideally, the kind of gains it wants, letting Joe and Jane apartment-dwellers rent out their homes either when they're away or while they're there.

For the past few years, Airbnb has been working on forging alliances with these rental conglomerates. In 2016, *Fortune*'s Kia Kokalitcheva reported on the launch of a new initiative called the Airbnb Friendly Building Program, in which owners and developers of big multifamily buildings can sign up for a partnership with Airbnb. Under the arrangement, the buildings grant their tenants permission to rent space in their units on Airbnb; in return, the developer retains the ability to set certain rules around the practice, like setting hours for check-in and length of stay — and gets a share of the revenue. The booking still takes place on Airbnb, but the company says it will share data with the landlords on the kinds of transactions the tenants are engaging in and in which units. The idea plays to the landlords' interests: their primary goal is to fill their buildings and to secure long-term leases that generate the kind of stable, predictable revenue streams their investors like to see. The case that Chesky and Airbnb are making to them is that their core customers, millennial renters, want to live only in homes that are shareable. They have known Airbnb all their adult lives, and, just as they do about many things, they feel a little entitled to that revenue stream. If you embrace Airbnb and make it legal for tenants to share their homes — or so the pitch to landlords goes — you will have an easier time filling up your buildings, you will have a higher occupancy rate, and, since your tenants may have an additional revenue stream coming in, you will be more likely to collect your rent on time, which will boost the appeal to investors. As of this writing, landlords controlling some 2,000 units had signed on, a fraction of the potential market, but the company hopes to land some of real estate's biggest fish.

In the future, the company hopes to take such partnerships further. Real estate companies also develop new apartment complexes with hundreds of thousands of units, and Airbnb is also in talks with them about designing new apartment layouts expressly for home sharing: apartments with, say, an extra bathroom, or with a layout that's more conducive to having guests, where the second bedroom is in close proximity to its own bathroom and on the opposite side of the living area from the master bedroom.

After he tells me these plans, I point out to Chesky that of course this can't happen yet in New York City, where the most popular form of using Airbnb—renting one's apartment when you're out of town —is illegal. Chesky says landlords are all over the country and not just in New York. "But this idea assumes . . . ," I begin, and he nods and completes my sentence: "a clear-sky horizon."

Early to Bed, Early to Rise . . .

Chesky is optimistic he will get that clear sky. He believes that Airbnb has taken lessons from its battles in New York City, where its opponents have criticized it for having a tin ear for local politics. "What we learned is not to wait for a problem," Chesky told the audience at *Fortune*'s Brainstorm Tech conference in the summer of 2016. "If you want to work with a city, you should get to know a city. If you get there first [and] you come with the best of intentions, you could end up with a partnership. If a city comes to you, you could have many, many years of potential conflict."

Some markets have continued to crack down. In the spring of 2015, despite a protest by one hundred members of the Airbnb community, the city of Santa Monica instituted what was at the time the harshest short-term-rental laws in the United States, with rentals of an entire home for fewer than thirty days banned outright. Only hosts who remain on the premises would be allowed to rent out space in their homes, and only then if they obtained a business license from the city, adhered to city fire and building codes, and remitted a 14 percent hotel tax. (These were the new regulations that got Airbnb host and Airdna founder Scott Shatford in trouble.)

Airbnb has become a big issue in Reykjavik, Iceland, a much smaller market, but one where tourism has surged and hotel capacity has not kept up. Airbnb listings have filled the gap, and the small city now has double the number of Airbnb units per capita than cities like San Francisco and Rome. Researchers have estimated that at least 5 percent of the city's housing stock was being rented out on Airbnb, worsening an already tight housing supply. The city put in place strict regulations — hosts need to register and pay a fee, and they are limited to ninety days of renting per year before being required to pay a business tax. As of this writing, the issue of short-term rentals was heating up in Toronto and Vancouver, and London's new mayor, Sadiq Khan, expressed interest in revisiting the city's short-term-rental laws over concerns about affordable housing and quality-of-life issues for neighbors.

In the meantime, those who use Airbnb have become accustomed to tolerating the lack of clarity in certain markets. Many travelers who book on Airbnb are told by their hosts to tell neighbors they encounter in the hallway that they're a friend or relative visiting. One friend was told on a trip to Los Angeles to look for a key that would be hidden in a stack of bicycles and to say she was a friend visiting to anyone who asked. Even before the short-term-rental bill was passed in New York, landlords might have noticed a growing number of tenants with luggage-toting friends who came in and out frequently to "take care of the cats."

Even those who are renting out rooms in their homes legally are being doubly good about following all rules. "Until this is cleared up, I want to be as close to the line as possible," says Chris Gatto, a New York City host. He rents out a spare room, so his hosting operation is allowable in New York, but he makes sure to give each guest a ten-minute walkthrough of his apartment, pointing out the fire extinguisher and exits, and has installed clear signs throughout the place. Sheila Riordan, the enthusiastic Airbnb traveler from chapter 3, won't stay in any listing where the legality is up in the air. "I don't want to be anywhere where someone might question why I'm there," she says. Companies that have built their business on the back of the home-sharing boom have resigned themselves to the fact that it may be a few more years before things are settled. "It's an externality we just have to kind of live with," says Clayton Brown, CEO of the key-exchange start-up Keycafe. (Meanwhile, a new subset of the Airbnb cottage industry has emerged: companies that help governments and landlords unearth rule-breaking short-term renters.)

At the Open in Paris in 2015, the mobilization efforts were center stage. "You know, being a host, I think a lot of times we're misunderstood," Chesky told the crowd. "Not only are we sometimes misunderstood but I think sometimes we are even attacked." That will soon change, he promised them. "Because they are going to see not just our house but who we are in our hearts." Lehane urged them to take action. "We're going to have more fights and more battles in the days and months and years to come," he told them. "But when this community is empowered to be a movement, it cannot be beat." As they moved forward together, he told them, "Our mantra will be 'Early to bed, early to rise, and work like hell and organize.'"

A Numbers Game

In the long term, though, most experts and observers think that the odds are on Airbnb's side and that it will ultimately be given leeway to operate, even if it means under tighter regulations in some markets, for one reason alone: consumers want it. You don't get the kind of growth Airbnb has seen without striking some kind of deep chord in the consuming public. In that sense, it's not so much the hosts as the one hundred forty million–plus guests, those who book and stay, who may have the ultimate sway on the regulators. "I think in terms of . . . are more people going to be doing this tomorrow than today? Yes. And more the day after that," says Lehane. "The public is already there, and the politicians follow where the public is pretty quickly." Carl Shepherd, the cofounder of HomeAway, thinks regulators who choose not to get on board have their heads in the sand. "It's like they're saying, 'I'm not going to participate in the world in 2015,'" he told the *Los Angeles Times*. "You can either deny this exists, or figure out how to make it safe."

You can measure consumer zeal for Airbnb in a number of ways, but they all show the same thing: it is a freight train. A Quinnipiac poll found that New Yorkers who supported Airbnb outnumbered those who wanted it banned by 56 percent to 36 percent. (Over the course of my reporting, I observed a particularly telling phenomenon of New Yorkers who complained about transient neighbors in their own building but made use of Airbnb when they themselves traveled.)

In New York, outside the hotel industry, the broader business community supports Airbnb, albeit measuredly. "We certainly don't countenance the abuses, and we're not endorsing Airbnb on all terms," Kathy Wylde, president of the Partnership for New York City, the nonprofit made up of the CEOs of the city's largest businesses and private-sector employers, told *The Real Deal*. "But we think there is room to be able to work out an arrangement where everybody wins."

So yes, by planting a flag in markets even when laws specifically prohibited it, the company showed a certain amount of naiveté, moxie, or total disregard for authority, depending on which side of the argument you fall. But there is a reason so many millions of consumers have embraced Airbnb. It wasn't just three guys out to break all the rules. It was a culmination of forces that were more powerful than that: an epic recession that left people with a much greater incentive to travel cheaply or to seize upon the opportunity to turn their homes into something monetizable; a general sense of fatigue with a hospitality industry that had become overpriced and overcommodified; a wave of new millennial values and attitudes that made the idea of a form of travel that was quirkier, more eclectic, more original, and more authentic not just acceptable but a way of life; and declining trust in government, especially among the middle class, and the search for individual, self-sufficient means of economic empowerment. Understanding those forces might help regulators understand why Airbnb caught on the way it did — and why its users are so ready to pick up a sword and fight for the cause. "Tell city leaders we're going to win," says Jonathan Morgan, the host in Savannah who faces $50,000 in fines. "Tell them, 'I'm going to fight this till I die, and I'm younger than you.'"

Plenty of other industries have gone through regulatory issues on their way to becoming accepted: when eBay was gaining ground, it faced fierce resistance from traditional retailers; one of its opponents tried to pass a law requiring that users have an auctioneer's license to sell on the platform. Payment start-ups from PayPal to Square to Stripe had to prove their legitimacy to regulators who were horrified at the idea of exchanging money online. "Success almost always results in legitimacy," says Airbnb board member Jeff Jordan. (Of course, not all popular technologies win out — the peer-to-peer music-sharing service Napster was shut down over copyright-infringement issues, though streaming music would later become standard and the industry figured out a way to charge for it.) None of Airbnb's investors seem too concerned. "I think ultimately we will get to a place where the world is as it should be, and at worst there will be some lower growth in, paradoxically, two American cities [New York and San Francisco] that should be the home of bold tech plays but which are two of the most problematic cities in the world," says Reid Hoffman.

Chesky loves peppering his discourses with quotes from history's great thinkers, often paraphrasing one from George Bernard Shaw: "The reasonable man adapts himself to the environment. The unreasonable man adapts the environment to him. Therefore, all progress depends on the unreasonable man." It's a much-cited reference in Silicon Valley, where legions of start-up founders pride themselves on being unreasonable enough to get gobs of funding and then get the laws changed in their favor.

For this reason, Chesky is not surprised that Airbnb has generated so much pushback. "When we started this business, I knew that if it would become successful, it would be somewhat controversial," he tells me in a moment of reflection in the President's Room at Airbnb's headquarters, a wood-paneled replica of a 1917 executive quarters in the company's offices in 2015. He said that even back in the days of that holiday break in 2007, when, unemployed and discouraged, he started casually talking up the idea of AirBed & Breakfast to people when he was home in Niskayuna, they had a visceral reaction to his new idea: they either loved it or they hated it. "Either it was 'Great, I can't wait to do it' or 'I would never want that in my neighborhood.'" And when he first heard about the 2010 law in New York City, and when the regulators at the time assured him that the law wasn't about Airbnb and wouldn't affect his company's users, he had a sneaking suspicion that it might not always be fine. "It doesn't seem 'fine,' because it's the law," he remembers thinking.

Even George Bernard Shaw might have said that was a reasonable assumption to make.

Chesky is confident that there will be a solution and that "my hair will still be brown when that happens." He thinks eventually a law will pass that will allow people to rent their primary homes and prohibit dedicated rentals and second homes from being rented in New York. He also believes Airbnb will collect and remit taxes to New York. "I think this is going to happen, but I do think there's going to be quite a bit of jockeying over the next couple of years to land there."

If nothing else, this whole saga has caused Chesky to plan a little differently for the future. Back in 2007, it seemed impossible that Airbnb would ever be in ten thousand homes, let alone three million. Now that he has seen the enemy with his own eyes, as he plans out the next phase of the company, its ambitious push into on-the-ground experiences, he has taken care to do so assuming that same kind of growth and all its attendant pushback. "I've been designing this assuming all of that," he says, after giving me a preview of the company's new expansion plans. "What will it do to neighborhoods? Are we going to enrich the communities or take away the communities? This is not going to be without its critics. That's the first thing I've learned."

Others have a different approach: they shrug it off. They say that all of this, while a giant headache, was entirely predictable. "It's one *hundred* percent inevitable," says Michael Seibel, the Airbnb cofounders' very first adviser and the person who, more than anyone else beyond the founders, may be responsible for Airbnb's becoming what it is today. "Whenever you disrupt a massive industry and you try to make room for yourself inside of that industry, the various interests are going to push back," he says. "They didn't build a billion-dollar hotel industry by not knowing how to push back. The more incumbent you are, the more you can use politics to do that." At the end of the day, Seibel says, echoing so many others, it's the consumer who votes and the consumer who usually wins.

Another one of Chesky's favorite quotes is from Victor Hugo. "You cannot kill an idea whose time has come," he paraphrased for the audience at the 2014 Airbnb Open. But Seibel boils it down even more succinctly. "At the end of the day, do people like using Airbnb? Do millions and millions and millions of people want Airbnb? Yes," he says. "Everything else is a solvable problem. It's solvable with the application of smart people, time, and money."

"What you can't solve for," he says, "is if you built something nobody wants."

6

Hospitality, Disrupted

This is where the world is leading us . . .
You need to embrace it.

— Sébastien Bazin, CEO, AccorHotels, to *Skift*

IN 1951, KEMMONS WILSON, a businessman and father of five living in Memphis, was pried away from his work by his wife, who insisted they go on a vacation. He piled the family into the car and set off on a road trip to Washington, D.C., to visit the national landmarks.

Disappointed with the subpar roadside motels they stayed at along the way, which had small rooms, uncomfortable beds, and added surcharges for each child, Wilson saw the opportunity for something better. By the time they arrived in D.C., he'd come up with an idea: to build a chain of four hundred motels across the country, all positioned along highway exits and each within a day's drive of the next, that would be clean, affordable, and, most important, predictable: they would be standardized down to the last square inch, so that guests could expect exactly the same features no matter where they were. After taking meticulous measurements of every room the family stayed in during their trip, he came up with the ideal dimensions, and back in Memphis he had a draftsman draw up the plans. He happened to be watching a Bing Crosby movie at the time called *Holiday Inn,* and on a lark jotted the name down at the top of the plans.

The first Holiday Inn opened a year later, in 1952, outside Memphis on one of the main highways to Nashville, and the following year he built three more.

They were indeed most predictable, clean, family-friendly (there were no surcharges for children), and readily accessible to roadside travelers. And they were revolutionary for their time. The idea took root, spread, and became a global brand, its hallmark being the fifty-foot roadside signs with the company's logo. By 1972, Holiday Inn had 1,400 locations worldwide and had landed on the cover of *Time* magazine as "The World's Innkeeper."

Wilson wasn't the only one with the idea. In Texas, a young man named Conrad Hilton had started buying up hotels in the 1920s during the oil boom. In 1957, J. W. Marriott opened the Twin Bridges Motor Hotel in Arlington, Virginia. Collectively, and along with a few others, they would usher in the era of mass-market, predictable, ubiquitous roadside motel chains, which was as disruptive an idea as the hospitality industry had ever seen. Previously, lodging had for the most part been limited to boardinghouses; small, independent motels; or expensive city hotels and grand vacation estates that were destinations unto themselves. But conditions were ripe for innovation: millions of GIs had returned from the war and started families, the postwar economic boom brought prosperity to a new and rapidly growing middle class, millions of households were still in wondrous awe of their new private automobiles and the mobility and freedom they afforded, and, thanks to President Eisenhower and the Federal Highway Act, the great era of interstate construction was well under way. Once a privilege of the wealthy, travel had been cracked open and democratized.

Wilson, Marriott, Hilton, and a handful of others were the hospitality industry's first disrupters. They shook things up with their novel vision of what travel should look like, built great fortunes, and paved the way for today's modern chain conglomerates.

Now, some sixty-three years later, in October 2015, a representative from the hotel industry's newest disrupter stood on a stage before a group of hotel and real estate executives. "I am one of you," Chip

Conley assured the audience at the Urban Land Institute's (ULI) Fall Meeting 2015, in San Francisco. "I'm evidence for the fact that you can teach an old dog a new trick." The hotel entrepreneur–turned–Airbnb executive was addressing the audience with a talk on the history of innovation in the hospitality business, drawing from his experience as a two-time industry innovator himself: first as a boutique hotel entrepreneur, starting his Joie de Vivre hotel chain in 1987; and now as a top executive at Airbnb. He walked the audience through a modern-day history of hospitality disruptions, from roadside motels to so-called boutique hotels to the rise of short-term vacation rentals, or "home sharing." His message for them: the hospitality industry has been disrupted many times before; the disruptions usually address some underlying need not being met; and, in the end, the big chains get on board and everybody wins. "Over time — and for those of you running big companies right now, this will make you feel better," he says, "over time, the establishment embraces innovations that represent a long-term trend."

The relationship between Airbnb and the hotel industry is complicated and has evolved over time. Airbnb has gone out of its way to say that it is *not* a hotel-industry disrupter and to paint a picture of benign coexistence. "For us to win, hotels don't have to lose," Chesky is fond of saying, and he and his team frequently dispense talking points to demonstrate this. Airbnb stays are longer than traditional hotel stays. Roughly three-quarters of its listings are outside the areas where the big hotels are located. It tends to draw larger groups. It is a different "use case," in technology-industry terms. A large number of travelers stay with friends and family, "so if we disrupt anything, we might disrupt you staying with your parents," Chesky had told the ULI crowd earlier in the conference's program. And the company points out that the hotel industry had record occupancy rates in 2015. If Airbnb were truly disrupting the hotel business, how could that possibly be the case? "No hotels have gone out of business because of Airbnb," Nathan Blecharczyk told the *Globe and Mail*. Chesky says he does not like the word "disrupter." "I never was in love with the term, because I was fairly disruptive growing up in class, and that was never a good thing," he said at the ULI event.

But, of course, Airbnb is having an impact on hotels' business. It sells rooms, by the night, to millions of people. It has grown like a weed. It has captured the imagination of the most important lodging-industry demographic: millennials. So the bigger Airbnb has become, the more hotel companies have seen it as exactly that — a disruptive threat, and one that gets to play by different rules. At the same time, they acknowledge that the company has tapped into something — some fundamental need that wasn't being met — and they admire that about it. ("I take my hat off to them," Steve Joyce, CEO of Choice Hotels, told an audience at the Americas Lodging Investment Summit in early 2016. "They saw an opportunity the rest of us missed.") It all makes for a fascinatingly dynamic situation in which hotel companies are simultaneously funding the fight against Airbnb, cautiously engaging with it, and experimenting how to tap into the short-term-rental trend themselves, whether through trying out their own concepts, buying or investing in other companies, or establishing partnerships with one of the dozens of new start-ups that have emerged in the nascent "alterative accommodations" industry.

For the most part, the hospitality industry was late to see or acknowledge Airbnb as something it should pay attention to. Jason Clampet, cofounder of the travel-news site *Skift*, recalls meeting with the CFO of one of the largest hotel chains in 2013, who said, "What's Airbnb?" when Clampet asked him about it. "They have not been at the forefront of this really until the last eighteen months, tops," Clampet said in the fall of 2016. Most hotel executives maintain that Airbnb serves a different customer. "We've thought about it a lot. We've done a lot of research," said Hilton Worldwide president and CEO Christopher Nassetta on an earnings call in late 2015. "I suspect over time investors . . . will see it for what it is, which is a really good business, but a business that is maybe not 100 percent but largely distinct from what we do, and that there is every opportunity for both of us to have really successful business models." He said it would be hard for Airbnb to replicate the services Hilton provides. "I don't think our core customers suddenly woke up . . . and said, 'We really don't care about consistently high quality products, and we don't need service and we don't need amenities.' I just don't buy it."

Barry Diller, the founder of consumer Internet conglomerate IAC and chairman of online travel giant Expedia.com, told *Bloomberg BusinessWeek* in 2013 that he didn't think Airbnb was stealing much business from urban hotels. "I think it's serving people who didn't travel because they were scared, or couldn't afford it, or use it because it's an antidote to loneliness," he says. "A room in someone's house is not as valuable as a room at the Helmsley." The New York real estate developer Richard LeFrak also chimed in, telling the *Commercial Observer*, "It's not like I'm going to stay at the St. Regis or somebody's house."

David Kong, the CEO of Best Western Hotels and Resorts, remembers speaking on a panel sometime in 2011 and being asked about the sharing economy. "I said at the time it was a niche play — that we can probably coexist and it probably won't have too big an impact," Kong recalls. "Since then it's grown tremendously — it's doubled in size every year."

In 2015, Bill Marriott, the eighty-four-year-old executive chairman and chairman of the board of Marriott International, acknowledged that Airbnb had become a contender. "It's a real disrupter for us," he said, noting that Airbnb had more rooms available in Orlando than Marriott. "Anybody that owns a condo down there — and there are a lot of condos — they're all renting it out on Airbnb," he said. He acknowledged it was a good idea. "It's a great concept," he said, before adding, "You do get concerned about what kind of quality you're going to get . . . The consistency is not there. You may want to bring your own towel," he said with a chuckle.

The leaders of the hotel industry have engaged in a delicate dance with Airbnb. In early 2014, the CEOs or executive teams of four of the top six hotel companies separately visited the company's headquarters for a day or day-and-a-half "immersion." But the bigger Airbnb got, the more the relationship became cooler and more competitive. And while it's true that hotels have had some banner years recently — the industry has been in a surging up cycle for the past several years that saw it hit record numbers for both occupancy and revenue per available room, or "revpar," the industry's key metric, in 2015 — there are signs that the cycle may have reached its peak. Industrywide, supply began to exceed demand in 2016, and as of this writing, occupancy was projected to be flat or down for the year, with demand, occupancy, average daily rate, and revpar all continuing to slow in 2017. Things are particularly weak in New York, where performance has been soft for the past few years.

Much of this weakness is due to other factors, including a strong dollar and an oversupply in certain markets — particularly in New York, where the industry is in the middle of an unprecedented building boom (New Yorkers might have noticed shiny new hotels from affordable brands popping up on side streets in Manhattan and in Brooklyn in recent years). But increasingly the softness is also being attributed to competition from Airbnb. In a September 2016 report, Moody's cited Airbnb's "extracting demand from the market" as a factor in slower industry-demand growth. "Airbnb has and will continue to encroach on the business of the traditional lodging industry," concluded a 2016 report by CBRE called *The Sharing Economy Checks In*. The report, which created an Airbnb Competition Index, found the impact to be highest in New York and San Francisco. "In New York in particular, we've seen very weak hotel performance since 2009, where occupancy came back in the city but lost their pricing power, and we think that can be at least partially attributed to Airbnb," says Jamie Lane, senior economist for the firm.

An oft-cited study in Texas led by researchers from Boston University found that Airbnb had caused a statistically significant decrease in hotel-room revenue, showing that in Austin, Airbnb's presence had led to revenue declines of 8–10 percent for the most vulnerable hotels. The report found that hotels were affected disproportionately during high season by limited pricing power and that the impact fell mostly on lower-end hotels and on those that lacked conference facilities. "Our results suggest the risk to incumbent hotels from Airbnb as a market entrant is both measurable and increasing," the researchers found.

An important way hotels make money is in so-called compression pricing: the ability to send rates way up in times of peak demand. Such nights make up just 10–15 percent of nights but are a critical source of revenue. One of the things about Airbnb that makes hotel executives cringe is that when a big event comes to town, its supply of inventory can expand instantly to meet the demand. Previously, travelers would have paid higher rates or gone as far out as they needed into the suburbs to find a reasonably priced room. Now, they can just turn to Airbnb. "The next time you go to a conference, you can ask a question: 'How many of you are staying at an Airbnb?'" says Best Western's Kong. "And you'd see more and more people raise their hands. So how can the hotel industry say it's got no impact?"

Even for the hotel companies that are still seeing minimal impact on their bottom line, the thing about Airbnb is that however small its impact today, its growth rates, fed by its near-zero marginal cost and ability to expand into new markets almost overnight, mean that that influence will only grow. "Whatever our conclusions on the risks posed by Airbnb today," reads a Barclays investor note, "we should be aware that the threat may be twice as significant within the next year alone, should this pace of growth continue."

Over the past few years, hotel-industry executives, some behind the scenes and others more publicly, have joined the effort to push back against Airbnb. The hotel industry's lobbying arm, the American Hotel and Lodging Association, has been an active participant in the opposition movement against Airbnb in New York and San Francisco. Hotel-industry executives and surrogates say they have nothing against home sharing, but they draw the line at so-called illegal hotels — those units that are dedicated to rental through Airbnb — and say that Airbnb should have to operate on a level playing field with hotels: its hosts should have to abide by industry standards for fire safety, for disease prevention, for compliance with the Americans with Disabilities Act, and in paying their fair share of taxes. Their disrupter, once a cute afterthought and now a heavyweight, has gotten this big, they say, largely on being able to expand totally unchecked, and it's not fair. So while many in the industry have clung to the belief that the two don't compete, that argument is becoming harder and harder to make.

Airbnb can't completely say it's not going after the hotel business, because of an area of expansion that aims at the hotel industry's core: business travel, a lucrative segment of the market in which corporate clients are sticklers for things like the safety of their employees, because if something goes wrong, the employer is responsible. In 2014, Airbnb announced a partnership with the travel-expense-management service Concur to officially recognize Airbnb as a corporate-travel provider, and it has steadily built its program from there. In 2015, Airbnb launched a "Business Travel Ready" program, a credential program for entire-home listings that met certain reviews and responsiveness rates and that adhered to certain standards, like providing twenty-four-hour check-in, Wi-Fi, a laptop-friendly workspace, hangers, iron, a hair dryer, and shampoo. The pitch to hosts: they get a special logo that makes their listing stand out to a new large stream of higher-paying, professional, well-behaved guests; and they're able to fill up empty dates or traditionally slow times on their calendar, since business travelers often book midweek and during slow seasons. "Ideal for any type of business trip," the company's business-travel site claims, touting extended stays, off-sites, retreats, and group trips.

By the spring of 2016, the company said it had some fifty thousand companies signed up. The vast majority of those were small to midsize businesses whose employees travel infrequently, but the company had also signed a few heavy hitters, like Morgan Stanley and Google. A few months later, Airbnb announced partnerships with American Express Global Business Travel, BCD Travel, and Carlson Wagonlit Travel — the heavyweights of the corporate-travel business, who handle the back end of so many companies' travel-purchasing needs. These deals show a growing willingness in the business-travel world to recognize Airbnb based largely on the organic demand that corporate-travel departments were seeing bubble up from their employees. Carlson Wagonlit said its data showed that one in ten business travelers was already using Airbnb, and the figure rose to 21 percent for millennials. "It's time for hotels to really, truly worry about Airbnb," read a headline on the website *Quartz* when the deals were announced.

Conley says business travel will still represent a smaller percentage of sales for Airbnb than it does for traditional hotel companies, estimating it may grow to 20 percent of the Airbnb business. He points out that Airbnb's business travelers are younger and their behavior on the road is different — they tend to stay longer, with an average stay of six days — which Conley attributes to the trend toward "bleisure," or travelers blending leisure with their business trips. But Airbnb is also starting to make a push into meetings and events: Conley gave a talk at an events conference — a conference about the conference business — in which he pitched Airbnb as a way to personalize corporate travel, and suggested it could perhaps be a "peripheral player" in the meetings industry. And while the company hasn't said much about getting into the wedding business, there's a wish list of "ultimate wedding destinations" on the site, including, in the summer of 2016, a sixteenth-century stone house in the United Kingdom, a villa in Italy, and a "Ralph Lauren style ranch house" in Morongo Valley, California. None of them had a "wedding-ready" logo, but that may be only a matter of time.

It's hard for Airbnb to say it doesn't pose a challenge to the hotel industry business at large, given all this. But one of the things that the industry should fear the most is how much Airbnb's users seem to like it. Goldman Sachs commissioned a survey of two thousand consumers to measure attitudes toward peer-to-peer lodging, and while overall familiarity with the concept was relatively low, those familiar with it rose from 24 percent of respondents to 40 percent of respondents from early 2015 to early 2016. About half of those who were familiar with the sites — not just Airbnb but also HomeAway, FlipKey, and others — had used them, and, if they had stayed in such accommodations in the last five years, the likelihood they preferred traditional hotels was cut in half. Even if they'd used these sites to book fewer than five nights, the researchers found, the consumers polled experienced this "dramatic shift in preferences," and the researchers said they found it notable that people tended to "do a 180."

This, of course, isn't the first time the hotel industry has been disrupted. As Conley's talk to the ULI pointed out, in the 1950s the very idea of a mass-market chain was disruptive. But even since then, he went on to say, the industry has weathered plenty of upstarts. In the 1960s, a few entrepreneurs in Europe came up with a novel idea that merged leisure travel with the burgeoning interest in owning real estate: the notion that you could buy a piece of property as a "right to use" instead of outright and that, in this way, your vacation would be something you "owned" instead of rented. This new model caught on and soon spread to the United States; the modern-day time-share industry was born; and, after some time, the big hotel brands entered the market.

In 1984, Ian Schrager and his business partner in Studio 54, Steve Rubell, introduced a new hotel concept when they converted an old building on Madison Avenue and opened the Morgans Hotel in New York. Focusing on design and social spaces above all else, the hotel drew a chic crowd and quickly became a "scene." On the West Coast, Bill Kimpton had pioneered a similar concept with Kimpton Hotels, converting unique properties into small hotels with a focus on design and the atmosphere of the public spaces.

Kimpton added locations across the country, Morgans launched spin-offs — the Delano in Miami and the Royalton in New York — and Conley soon made his own early entry with Joie de Vivre, starting with the Phoenix, a run-down hotel in San Francisco's Tenderloin neighborhood that he relaunched with a sort of rebellious, rock-star attitude, targeting touring musicians.

Conventional hotel chains balked at boutique hotels, but the sector outperformed them, the new breed of individualized, high-design hotels speaking to a new generation of travelers for whom the social and aesthetic appeal of a property was a huge draw. "I think that what we started is the future of the industry," Schrager told the *New York Times* at the time. "If you have something unique and distinctive, people will beat the doors down to come to it." Soon the hotel chains followed; in 1998, Starwood created the pioneering W brand, and many others quickly entered the scene. Most recently, Marriott partnered with Schrager himself to develop a new brand called Edition, a collection of four properties so far (with more in the works) that are hip and high-design and look nothing like your standard Marriott.

In recent years, another big threat to the hotel industry has come from the rise of online travel agencies, or OTAs — websites like Travelocity, Expedia, Priceline, and Orbitz, that allow travelers to access discounted rates across multiple brands on one site. For years, these upstarts represented only a small piece of hotel chains' business, since they charged hefty commissions for access to their large distribution platforms. And since they handled the booking process, they got to "own" the direct relationship with the customer, which the hotel companies were loath to let go. But in the wake of 9/11, when people stopped traveling, the third-party booking sites and their massive platforms became an easy way to fill rooms, so hotels fed them more of their inventory. It's been hard to get that business back — hotels are now waging big ad campaigns to convince travelers to book directly — and over the years the OTAs gained leverage to demand better terms. Today, Priceline is now bigger in market value than Marriott, Hilton, and Hyatt combined.

But, as disruptive as they were, the OTAs were not providing a competing place to lay one's head at night. So, while plenty of other consumer-service sectors have gone through the threat of replacement by Internet entrants, as Goldman Sachs pointed out in the report about its survey results — think Amazon and Walmart, or Netflix and Blockbuster — so-called peer-to-peer lodging, as best exemplified by Airbnb, marked the first time the hotel industry was faced with an actual alternative accommodation to hotels. "Airbnb has had a more radical impact on the travel industry than any other brand in a generation," says *Skift*'s Jason Clampet.

The Disruptive Online Home-Sharing Entrepreneurs of . . . 1995

Of course, Airbnb was neither the first nor is it the only service of its kind. As Chip Conley pointed out in his talk to the ULI, in the 1950s the Dutch and Swiss teachers' unions established a home-swapping practice so that teachers could enjoy affordable travel to one another's countries during the summer. But the modern-day, online short-term-rental industry traces its roots to the mid-1990s, when, for one thing, Craigslist started to gain traction as a place to list a home or apartment, whether for travelers or subletters, just as it became a place for listing almost everything else under the sun.

Around that same time, Dave and Lynn Clouse, a married couple living in Colorado, needed to rent out their ski condo in Breckenridge, which they'd bought as an investment property, and they started a website they called Vacation Rental by Owner, or VRBO .com, to list it. At the time, vacation rentals were handled in a fragmented manner, either by local real estate brokers, in special-interest travel magazines, or by expensive classified ads or 1-800 numbers. The Clouses' idea was that people should be able to transact rental deals between one another directly. Dave Clouse put together a rudimentary database in their basement, got some of their friends to come over and help out, and soon they had a website (the Internet was still in such early days that they called themselves "webmasters").

At the time, it was a disruptive idea; most people still used hotels for vacations, and the nascent industry drew people passionate about the anti-establishment "by-owner" idea and even "rent-by-owner advocates" who espoused the benefits of this new way to travel. (Sound familiar?)

By the mid-2000s, VRBO.com had grown to sixty-five thousand

properties and twenty-five million travelers per year. Vacation rentals by owner had grown from a subset within the travel industry to being much more mainstream, international interest was booming, and there was more demand for vacation rentals than the Clouses could handle without first making big investments in technology and marketing. So in 2006, they sold their company to HomeAway, an upstart founded a year earlier by Brian Sharples and Carl Shepherd in Austin, Texas, with the goal of consolidating these fledgling worldwide vacation-rental sites under one roof.

HomeAway went on to build a hugely successful business, its roll-up strategy allowing it to scale from sixty thousand listings to the more than 1.2 million that the company has today. Like VRBO, HomeAway traditionally focused primarily on second-home rentals. Having bought up every significant player in the industry, HomeAway drew significant funding, raising more than $400 million before going public in 2011.

These sites served a healthy and growing market for years, functioning largely as online bulletin boards, where an owner advertised a space and managed his or her relationship with would-be customers. Payments were handled between buyer and seller directly.

When Airbnb came along, it was different in a few significant ways. It had a more user-friendly interface than anything that had come before it. It brought the owner and customer together in a new, more intimate way, showcasing home renters' personalities and displaying their homes with magazine-worthy photography. It was a self-contained system that handled everything: payments, messaging, and customer service. It had a sophisticated technological back end that benefited from all the novel breakthroughs coming from Silicon Valley's new golden age — cheap and powerful cloud computing, fast horsepower, sophisticated searching and matching. And, perhaps most significantly, instead of focusing on vacation destinations in resort areas, it focused on cities. Despite the attention paid to the treehouses and tepees, Airbnb's actual invention was that it was an almost entirely urban phenomenon from the very beginning, taking root with millennial travelers who were city-focused and millennial hosts who wanted to monetize their small urban apartments.

While it's expanded well beyond that, in 2015, 70 percent of Airbnb's full-home listings were studios, one-bedroom, and two-bedroom units, according to Airdna. So for the first time, short-term rentals were no longer just the big homes in lake, beach, or mountain destinations. They were in the apartment right next door in the heart of every city around the world. That's what made the platform grow so fast, and it's what makes the company so threatening to hotels. But it's also why so many people who were initially drawn to Airbnb, both on the host side and on the guest side, weren't customers of another vacation-rental site who switched; they were an entirely different kind of customer.

After dismissing it for so long, the hotel industry slowly started to confront its Airbnb Problem. Executives started talking openly about it at industry events. At the 2016 NYU International Hospitality Industry Investment Conference, a series of CEOs took the stage and, referring to the "second phase" of Airbnb, pointed out why it wouldn't compete and cited the hotel industry's strengths — that hotels were people- and service-focused, that there would always be a customer for hotels, and that the hotel industry just needed to double down on its strengths. (*Skift* described the CEOs' reactions as "surprisingly tepid and generic, especially compared to the rabid consumer excitement surrounding Airbnb.")

Some, though, said the industry needed to take note. Javier Rosenberg, COO and EVP of Carlson Rezidor Hotel Group, the parent of Radisson Hotels in the United States, told the audience that while Airbnb's customers may be different and more leisure-focused, there was something to study in its success: "What's working is the 'home concept' of Airbnb and this thing about being somebody's host," he said. "The true host and the service he or she provides welcomes you with a smile, really takes care of you for five, six, seven days — how do we, from a leadership perspective, how do we bottle that?"

Airbnb or no Airbnb, the hotel companies were already well under way in reshaping their businesses to win over millennials, their new massive customer base whose habits and tastes are so markedly different from those before them. For the past several years, almost every major hotel chain has been hard at work cooking up new brands targeted at the younger set. Along with the Edition partnership with Schrager, Marriott has also launched Moxy, a global chain of stylish, affordable hotels for young, budget-conscious travelers (Marriott calls them "Fun Hunters"), and AC Hotels by Marriott, a more sophisticated, city-based chain. Hilton has launched two brands, Tru and Canopy, and is said to be considering launching a new chain of "hostel-like" hotels for the younger demographic. Best Western has two new chic boutique hotel brands, GLō for its suburban markets and Vīb, a "stylish urban boutique hotel." Almost every hotel company is adding details and touches it thinks will win the millennial over, whether it's keyless entry, streaming content, charging stations, partnerships with brands like Uber and Drybar, or, in one unique attempt, emoji-only room service.

Hotels are seizing on the same consumer shifts that propelled Airbnb and are now marketing themselves as anything *but* standardized and routine. Royal Caribbean's latest ad campaign touts, "This is not page three of the guidebook," while Shangri-La Hotels and Resorts encourages its customers to "leave boring behind." In the spring of 2016, Hyatt announced the Unbound Collection by Hyatt, a selection of independent, high-end hotels that would retain their own names, the idea being that each would bring its own unique story and "rich social currency" to the collection. It noted that future Unbound properties could include nonhotel products, like river cruising and other experiences, as well as "alternative accommodations." "It's a collection of stays, not just hotels," Hyatt CEO Mark Hoplamazian said in announcing the new brand.

Hoplamazian has also overseen an effort to bring more "empathy" back into the experience for guests, stripping back procedures, policies, and scripts. It's revamped its check-in process, for example, to be less computer-focused and to include more face-to-face interactions. Hoplamazian also put in place a mandate to "unleash [employees] and let them be who they are," doing away with grooming standards, encouraging employees to dress and look how they want (within reason), and instructing them to go "off script" and to feel more free to be themselves. The goal, he says, is to "bring humanity back to hospitality."

In mid-2016, when the boutique-hotel industry gathered at the annual Boutique and Lifestyle Lodging Association's annual investment conference in New York, its original disrupter, Ian Schrager, took the stage and told a crowd of hoteliers that they should be worried. "Airbnb is coming from your kids," he said, adding that it was a major threat to the industry, whether or not the industry wanted to address it. His comments inspired the association to form an official Disruption Committee to figure out how the hotel industry can innovate and adjust to compete.

The most dramatic thing hotel companies have done so far is to test the waters of short-term rentals themselves. Hyatt was the first mover, when in the spring of 2015, it took a stake in onefinestay, a UK-based, fast-growing upstart focused on short-term rentals with added services at the very high end of the market. While Hyatt's investment was small, it marked the first time a hotel company acknowledged that peer-to-peer accommodations were legitimate; headlines called it the "clearest sign yet that a major hotel operator sees home rentals as a viable business." Around the same time, Wyndham Hotels, parent of Ramada and Travelodge, took a stake in another London-based start-up, Love Home Swap, a subscription-based home-swapping platform; and InterContinental Hotels Group forged a partnership with Stay.com, a site based in Norway that offers recommendations for travelers from locals.

In early 2016, Choice Hotels said it would partner with vacation-rental-management companies at a handful of destinations around the United States to launch Vacation Rentals by Choice Hotels, a new service that would provide an alternative to traditional hotel rooms. "It's a huge business," said CEO Steve Joyce at the time. "We don't have to get much of a share to do really well." Marriott has not made a move into short-term rentals, but in mid-2016 it announced the creation of a new collection of urban time-shares called Marriott Vacation Club Pulse.

The most forward-thinking hotel company so far has been AccorHotels, the French multinational hospitality chain and parent to hotel brands Sofitel, Raffles, Fairmont, and others. It is most notable for its aggressive push into the sharing economy. In February 2016 it announced it had taken a 30 percent stake in Oasis Collections, a Miami-based high-end start-up that bills itself as a "boutique hotel" twist on short-term rentals. On the same day, Accor also announced an investment in Squarebreak, a French short-term-rental start-up. A few months later it made its biggest move yet, acquiring onefinestay outright, for around $170 million. The deal was small for Accor, but it was significant in that it was the first validation that so-called alternative accommodations had a place in a traditional hospitality-brand portfolio. Accor CEO Sébastien Bazin was candid about the changes such companies were bringing to their industry: "It would be absolutely foolish and irresponsible to fight against any new concept, offer, or services like this, let alone fighting against the sharing economy," Bazin told *Skift*. "This is where the world is leading us. All of those new services are very powerful and very well implemented and executed. You need to embrace it."

There is in fact now a cottage industry of short-term-rental start-ups. Whether started before or after Airbnb, the category now includes dozens of other companies: Roomorama, Love Home Swap, Stay Alfred, and many more. Some were scooped up by the travel industry's giants — TripAdvisor's FlipKey and HouseTrip, Priceline's Booking .com — and in the fall of 2015, Expedia paid $3.9 billion for industry veteran HomeAway and its 1.2 million–plus properties listed.

Some new entrants are starting to offer their own twist on the concept, evidence of the kind of segmentation that starts to happen when a bold new idea becomes more established. Onefinestay was the first to get significant traction. Founded in 2009 by three friends with backgrounds in tech and business, the company created its own niche in high-end, high-touch short-term rentals (it's often described as "the posh Airbnb"). Would-be hosts have to apply to have their residences accepted (and need to meet certain standards, like a certain number of wineglasses on hand and a certain thickness of the mattress). Each of the properties in its collection is visited by the company's staff in advance of any booking and given a luxury makeover: it's cleaned and de-cluttered, the bed linens are replaced and appropriately anonymized and staged with fluffy duvets and high-end bed linens, and shampoo and soap are provided.

The company, which bills itself as the "unhotel," deploys employees to greet customers at check-in and offers white-glove treatment on the ground, including a personal iPhone to use during their stay, a twenty-four-hour remote concierge, and room service delivered by a network of providers. This high-service model isn't as scalable, since every property needs to be approved and then given its luxury patina, so for now its 2,500 listings are available in only five cities; but, like Airbnb, it has grown largely by word of mouth.

In 2006, Parker Stanberry was living in New York City and had just been laid off from Miramax Films in the wake of its split from Disney. He decided to move to Buenos Aries for three months and needed to find a place to stay. After going through a clunky process involving real estate brokers and Craigslist, he found a place, but once on the ground there, he found himself missing a level of service, in particular the personalized touches and lively bar and social scene that a boutique hotel provided. He came up with the idea for Oasis, a business that would bring the elements of a boutique hotel to the world of short-term apartment rentals. Airbnb didn't exist at the time, but Stanberry's approach was different; it was smaller, did not involve peer-to-peer hosting, and was more service-oriented, with a staffer on-site to check guests in and out, member "clubs" accessible nearby, and free passes to SoulCycle and the like. He calls the model a "deconstructed boutique hotel" (or, as he describes it in comparison to Airbnb, "removing some of the uncertainty with great stuff layered on top"). Oasis now has two thousand listings in twenty-five cities — its prices start at around $120, so it offers more of a broad range than onefinestay — with a goal of reaching one hundred cities. (It lists many of its properties on other sites as well, including Airbnb and HomeAway.)

Oasis has had some successes: during the Summer Olympics in Rio in 2016, the company housed groups from Nike, Visa, and the BBC. "They can come to us and say to one central point of contact, 'We need thirty midlevel units for staff, fifty high-end for VIP retailers, and a few villas for athletes and CEOs,'" Stanberry says. "And we can do that." He acknowledges that there is a "gold rush" for short-term-rental sites in the wake of Airbnb's success. "It's pretty easy to raise $1 to $3 million in a Series A and give it a whirl in San Francisco or London," he says. "But to actually build something that's differentiated enough and scale it is harder."

Another just-launched hybrid: Sonder, the relaunch of a previous company, Flatbook, which bills itself as a "hometel," a short-term rental with the touches of a hotel. Like the others, it takes aim at what it sees as a flaw of inconsistency with larger short-term-rental sites (i.e., Airbnb). It recently raised $10 million in funding. New twists on hotels, too, are emerging, companies like Common, a model of flexible, shared housing with outposts primarily in Brooklyn; and Arlo, a new hotel brand that calls itself "homebase for urban explorers."

It's all part of the rapid mainstreaming of the fast-growing category of "alternative accommodations," and plenty of players in the hospitality industry want in on it. There are many ways to slice it, and in a curious number of these cases, the websites' designs, friendly voices, and review systems all bear an uncanny resemblance to Airbnb. But the idea of something that's not your father's hotel room has taken hold. "It's a really relevant and growing space in the accommodations pie," says Stanberry of Oasis. "And there's no question it continues to grow."

Of course, there will always be a market for hotels, even a robust one. Many people would never be caught dead staying in someone else's home or apartment, no matter how high-end the service. Marriott's

Arne Sorenson observes that one reason Uber has taken off is that the level of quality it offers is dramatically higher than that of a taxi, which can be "awful" and, in many cities, hard to find. "In the hotel business," he told *Surface* magazine, "I still think we can deliver better service, so we don't have quite the same risk." David Kong, CEO of Best Western, points out the many things hotels provide that Airbnb can't: the lobby, a social gathering space; a staff member to greet you; the ability to call the front desk and request an extra blanket or have something fixed if it's not working. "You can only find that in a hotel," he says.

A former colleague of mine for whom travel has been a lifelong passion swears off anything related to staying in someone's home. "I want a place that's bigger than my own apartment, with crisp white sheets, a big TV, and really good air conditioning," she says. And she adores room service: "I love how they roll in the cart, the vase with flowers, everything." If she has a noisy neighbor or something doesn't work, she likes knowing she can call the front desk and they will send someone to fix it or give her a new room. I can see her point: when I can afford the splurge or when my company is paying the bill, I love staying in upscale hotels; there's a reason the Airbnb host I stayed with in Georgetown referred to me as the "Four Seasons lady." And while Nike used Oasis for some of its travel needs during the Olympics, Stanberry points out that the company also booked plenty of hotel rooms, essentially commandeering one of the city's hotels for its workers.

But there's no question the hospitality landscape is changing before our eyes. One former hotel-industry top executive who says he, too, was initially dismissive of the threat posed by Airbnb and its ilk, says in hindsight he now understands why. "I superimposed my own forty-something personal preferences," he says. "What about the sheets, the mattress? How would I get the key? I had all the fears of an older person." The younger generation, he says, has grown up without the fears and biases that he had — and has known only a world with Airbnb in it. Young people are "Airbnb native" in the same way they are "digital native"; for many in this group, staying in a chain hotel room is as foreign as talking on a landline, walking into a bank branch, or watching a television show at the actual time it airs. "Airbnb educated an entire generation," the executive says. And the company's hand becomes even stronger, he says, the more it's able to use its data to accurately predict and deliver exactly what its consumers want. "I would not bet a cent against Uber or Airbnb," he says.

A Future of Partnerships

What may end up happening is that the big hotels will set up more partnerships with short-term-rental sites for collaborations that offer the best of both worlds. Some of this experimentation has already happened. Before Accor bought onefinestay and back when Hyatt was still an investor in the start-up, the two companies tested a pilot program in London where onefinestay guests were able to store luggage at the Hyatt Regency London — the Churchill — if they arrived before check-in, and to use the hotel to shower, work out, or have a meal. Room Mate, a novel chain of low-cost hotels in Europe and the United States, also offers a collection of "handpicked apartments," but guests who choose that option can use the hotel as a sort of concierge center: they can pick up their keys at one of the hotels, then head to the apartment, and even order room service and elect how frequently they want the place cleaned during their stay. Many in the industry see this as a legitimate model for more widespread adoption going forward.

One area in which lodging-industry analysts are already pushing hotels to get closer with Airbnb is distribution. Airbnb has become a robust marketing platform that reaches millions of eyeballs; some hotels already see it as a way to attract guests. Globally, there are more than three hundred thousand homes or spaces classified as professional hospitality providers or actual bed-and-breakfasts on its platform, and Chesky says he is open to this kind of traffic on Airbnb, as long as it provides the right kind of experience. "We want B and Bs," he says. "We're open to some boutiques. I do want small businesses and professionals to realize there's a place for professional hospitality on Airbnb."

But for some hotel-industry leaders, this would be like sleeping with the enemy. Best Western CEO David Kong, who takes a cerebral but firm approach to the issue of Airbnb, says this would be a serious mistake, akin to repeating the one the industry made by becoming too reliant on OTAs. In a blog post about it, Kong wrote, "Celebrated author and playwright George Bernard Shaw said, 'Success does not consist in never making mistakes, but in never making the same one a second time.'" (Kong and Chesky might be surprised to discover they share an affinity for quoting George Bernard Shaw.)

The relationship between the two parties is likely to become more tense. Airbnb still says it wants to befriend hotels and that it doesn't really compete with them. But that friendly-sounding language is at odds with its business model, which as early as the DNC in Denver in 2008 had crystallized as a platform where travelers could book a room in someone's home as easily as they could book a hotel. And the more it evolves, the more its business has gotten closer to hotels, whether it's business travel or a feature like Instant Book, which lets travelers book a room instantly — just as rooms are booked on hotel websites — instead of waiting for approval from the host.

From the beginning, the Airbnb founders talked about encouraging their hosts to deliver "seven-star service," going well above the hotel industry's five stars. During his fireside chat with Sarah Lacy back in 2013, Chesky laid out three reasons people stay in hotels: a frictionless booking experience, knowing what they're going to get, and services. He addressed them one by one: Airbnb, he said, was going to become more and more frictionless; it would be able to deliver a more consistent product over time; and "every one of those services is something that somebody in a city could do."

One of the company's very early mottos was "Forget hotels." And at one point in 2014, while testing out a concierge program, Chesky had flowers delivered to his girlfriend, Elissa Patel, with a note that said, "Dear Elissa, Fuck Hotels. Love, Brian." It had become an inside joke between them after a friend had suggested changing the original motto and was not meant for public view, but a photo appeared on the Internet and got some attention. (Some industry watchers were simply relieved to finally see some proof of actual conflict. "It's *about time* the Airbnb vs. hotel industry beef got real," commented the real estate website Curbed. "This is the rivalry of our time.")

There is one other saying that you hear inside Airbnb's halls. It's a quote often attributed to Gandhi that Chip Conley recited on his first day, back in 2013, when he addressed four hundred employees, and it must still be oft repeated, because at least three executives recounted it to me when I brought up the question of competition with hotels. "There's this great quote from Gandhi," they begin. "'First they ignore you, then they ridicule you, then they fight you — and then you win.'"

Learning to Lead

Design is part of what makes him tick, but he basically
was trained to run a military campaign.

— MARC ANDREESSEN, cofounder,
Andreessen Horowitz

"I JUST WANT TO BRAG on Brian just for one second," says Barack
Obama.

Obama is on a stage in Havana, Cuba, in March 2016, at an event
that is celebrating the opening of U.S.-Cuban business relations. He
has brought with him a delegation of U.S. entrepreneurs who have
been doing business in Cuba since the president restored diplomatic
relations there, including Brian Chesky, as well as the CEOs of Silicon
Valley start-ups Stripe and Kiva.

But Chesky is the only one the president "brags on." He continues:
"First of all, for those Cubans who are not familiar with Brian, you
can see just how young he is. The company that he started, Airbnb,
basically started as an idea with his cofounder, who is also here —
how long ago did you guys start, Brian?" Eight years, Chesky says
from his place on an adjacent dais. "And what's the valuation now?"
Chesky starts to demur. "Don't be shy," the president warns. Chesky
tells him $25 billion. "Twenty-five billion dollars," Obama repeats.
"With a *b*?" Yes, Chesky confirms. Obama goes on to explain to the
crowd how Chesky is one of America's "outstanding young entrepreneurs" and praises the company's platform. He notes how someone

in Germany can now go on Airbnb and look up a house in Cuba and see the hosts and see the reviews. There are even ratings, the president explains, so "when you get there, the room actually looks like the room on the Internet," and so if the guest has used the platform before, the person offering the space can see that "they haven't completely torn up the house."

Besides displaying a level of detailed awareness with Airbnb review systems, the president's overall point was that Chesky was a good example of the entrepreneurial potential that can be unleashed with the right investment in Internet infrastructure. But for Chesky, his team on the ground in Cuba, and those watching back at home in San Francisco, it was a new first: getting "bragged on" by the leader of the free world.

One of the unique aspects of the Airbnb story has nothing to do with its weird, unthinkable idea for a business or its high-profile battles with lawmakers or even the rapid growth of its user base. Rather, it is the lack of traditional management experience of the company's founding team — especially its CEO — and the speed with which they have had to learn how to become leaders of a very large company.

Airbnb is now in its ninth year of so-called hypergrowth, that vertical phase in the middle of the stick part of the hockey-stick growth chart when revenues essentially double, or come close to it, every year. Such a burst typically lasts a year, two, maybe three. Airbnb basically entered this phase in 2009 and hasn't gotten out yet.

But that vertical ascendance can be dizzying for all involved, especially for its top leaders — and especially when they've never done it before. The verb for keeping up with or ahead of this growth in tech-industry parlance is "to scale," and the annals of Silicon Valley history are filled with examples of founding CEOs who left or broke up after the companies grew to a certain size, over power struggles, money disputes, sexual-harassment incidents, or any number of reasons. Chesky, Blecharczyk, and Gebbia are unusual in that they are still in it together, all still steering their rocket ship nine years in. No one I spoke with could name an example of a cofounding trio in the current tech boom or of any tech company that could say the same. Their roles have evolved and changed significantly, especially in the past few years, in ways that suit their individual strengths. It hasn't always been a smooth road, but the way they managed to keep up and learned to lead a company that had come to be Airbnb's size with such little prior experience may offer a new playbook for leadership development.

The path has been especially extraordinary for Chesky, the leader of the company — and the only one of the three who previously had no business experience whatsoever. "It's kind of like, what *did* I know?" Chesky says. "Almost everything was brand new."

Yet there was no time for any of the conventional ways to learn how to become a CEO. Being groomed by a predecessor, running a key division of the business, spending a few years at the company's overseas subsidiaries, acquiring an executive MBA — none of those strategies applied. Even the idea of getting any kind of formalized training would have been laughable; there was no time. The company was growing so fast, it was essentially shedding its skin every few months, crises were hitting left and right, and there was an entire culture to build, with everyone looking directly to Chesky for vision and direction. The company needed him to be a CEO immediately; it couldn't wait for him to get there. "There is basically no time for a learning curve," Chesky says, teeing up another historic-figure paraphrase. "It's kind of like the old Robert McNamara saying — there's no learning curve for people who are in war or in start-ups."

And this start-up was more complex than your average on-demand app, say, or even social network. Airbnb's business is built around a fairly simple idea, but the business and operational challenge behind that friendly website is much more complicated than it looks. At some point in the process, Sequoia managing partner Doug Leone pulled Chesky aside and told him that he had the hardest job of any CEO in the Sequoia portfolio. Beyond all the routine challenges of running a technology company, Leone said, Airbnb was more global than any other: it was in almost 200 countries, so it had to have offices and people in those countries and had to figure out how to operate internationally. It is essentially a payments company, handling billions in transactions around the globe every day, so Chesky had to be concerned with all the fraud and risk potential inherent in that. It had hundreds of thousands of people staying in other people's beds each night, providing so much opportunity for horrible things to happen, let alone everyday misunderstandings and cultural differences. Then there are the regulatory problems and the major amounts of time, attention, and public-policy resources that go into pushing back against those problems on a city-by-city basis.

"A Learning Animal"

Chesky already possessed a couple of key skills that would become essential to his growth as a leader: a knack for ringleading dating back to his days at RISD and a near-pathological curiosity. His solution to acquire the rest of the tools he'd need was to basically hack leadership by seeking out help from a series of expert mentors. But while any new CEO will seek out advice, Chesky's process could best be described as obsessive, methodical, and interminable. He calls his practice "going to the source": instead of talking to ten people about a particular topic and then synthesizing all their advice, he reasons, spend half of your time learning who the definitive source is, identifying the one person who can tell you more about that one thing than anyone else — and then go only to that person. "If you pick the right source, you can fast-forward," he says.

He'd already begun this process with Airbnb's earliest advisers: first, the weekly office-hours sessions with Michael Seibel and Y Combinator's Paul Graham; then, breakfasts at Rocco's with Sequoia's Greg McAdoo. Airbnb's next investment rounds unlocked access to Silicon Valley icons like Reid Hoffman, Marc Andreessen, and Ben Horowitz, all seen as gurus when it came to the art of building tech companies in Silicon Valley. The more successful Airbnb became, the more top people the founders had access to, and as it began to get bigger, Chesky started seeking out sources for specific areas of study: Apple's Jony Ive on design, LinkedIn's Jeff Weiner and Disney's Bob Iger on management, Facebook's Mark Zuckerberg on product, and Sheryl Sandberg on international expansion and on the importance of empowering women leaders. John Donahoe of eBay was a particularly important mentor, schooling Chesky on scaling operations, managing a board, and other aspects of being the CEO of a large marketplace business. In what became a valuable reverse mentorship, Donahoe also quizzed Chesky for his advice on design and innovation and on how eBay could maintain characteristics of being young and nimble. From Jeff Weiner, Chesky learned the importance of removing those managers who weren't performing. From Salesforce.com CEO Marc Benioff he learned how to push his executive team. He also had access to an informal support group among his current-generation start-up peers, including Travis Kalanick of Uber, Drew Houston of Dropbox, Jack Dorsey of Square, and John Zimmer of Lyft, all sharing their individual lessons about everything from running start-ups to balancing friends, relationships, and other elements of young founder life.

A key principle of Chesky's sourcing strategy was to become creative with identifying just who the experts were, and seeking out sources in unexpected disciplines. So, for instance, Chesky approached former CIA director George Tenet, not for trust and safety but to talk about culture ("How do you get people to feel committed in a place where everyone's a spy?" he reasons). For hospitality expertise, he went not to Marriott or Hilton but to the French Laundry, to study how the legendary restaurant treats its customers and plates its cuisine. For recruiting, he posited that an obvious source would be a recruiter, but an even better source would be people in those industries that live and die on talent, like sports agents, or maybe even the leaders of Cirque du Soleil. Halfway through our conversation about this, Chesky stopped, looked at me, and told me I could be a source. "By the way, I'm learning from this," he said, pointing to my notes. "If

I wanted to learn how to interview a candidate, the obvious place to go would be another executive. But the better place to go would be a reporter."

Of course, Chesky is operating at a level of highly privileged access; not everyone can call up Jony Ive or Mark Zuckerberg or Jeff Bezos. But Chesky insists there are always good mentors, regardless of someone's level. "When I was unemployed and a designer, I also met with people, and I was [just as] shameless," he says. In fact, if he had been meeting with some of these heavy hitters when he was an unemployed designer, he points out, it wouldn't have been useful. "There wouldn't have been anything to give back in the conversation. It's a matter of picking people that are, at least, a couple of years in front of you." Sequoia's Alfred Lin says that plenty of CEOs have similar connections to Chesky's but aren't as successful. "I think the network is very helpful, but the potential has to be there," he says.

"Sources" need not be living: Chesky took some of his most valuable lessons from biographies of two of his biggest heroes, Walt Disney and Steve Jobs, as well as historical figures like General George S. Patton, former secretary of defense Robert McNamara, and scores of others; management tomes by the dozens (his favorite is Andy Grove's *High Output Management*); and niche-industry sources like the *Cornell Hospitality Quarterly*. To say Chesky is a voracious reader doesn't quite capture it. He takes his family on vacation once a year, usually around the holidays, when his way of recharging is to ingest as many books as possible. While he's away, "he doesn't stop reading," says his mother, Deb Chesky. "We're at dinner, and he's reading." He also spends the holidays drafting his annual letter to employees, "for hours and days, like, nonstop," Deb says. "And he reads it to us, and we think it's perfect, and then he's gone and changed it fifty times."

Another key source: Warren Buffett. Chesky had some limited communication with the revered investor about helping to expand the number of rooms available in Omaha during the Berkshire Hathaway Annual Meeting, the Woodstock of investing that draws some forty thousand visitors and maxes out the city's hotel supply. But Chesky wanted to make Buffett a source, so he reached out to him and asked him if he could travel to Omaha to have lunch with him. Buffett agreed, and the lunch lasted four and a half hours. ("I thought it was a one-hour lunch," Chesky says. "We were in his office for an hour, and then he said 'Let's go to lunch!' and I'm, like, OK — I thought that was the lunch.") The biggest lesson Chesky took away: the value of not getting caught up in the noise. "He's literally in the center of Omaha," Chesky says. "There's no ticker, no TVs anywhere. He spends all day reading. He takes maybe one meeting a day, and he thinks so deeply." On the way home, Chesky wrote a four-thousand-word recap of his experience to send to his team. (There is some symmetry to this event: when Buffett was around Chesky's age, he traveled to Disney headquarters and lucked into a similar extended meeting with Walt Disney himself. The young investor also recorded everything that happened. "I've still got my notes from that meeting," Buffett says.)

Buffett says he is impressed with Chesky and with Airbnb. "It's a very, very big hosting machine," he says. "It doesn't appeal to everybody. The truth is, at my age and with my habits I'm not going to be doing an Airbnb thing. But it clearly has very strong appeal on both sides, to the customer and the provider." He thinks the social element is a significant part of the appeal too, recalling how he and his family often welcomed visitors in their home. "For many years, we had a lot of people stay at our house just as guests," he says: George McGovern stayed at the Buffett home, as did other political leaders and students from Sudan and all over the world. "It can make for a very interesting experience." Buffett says Airbnb "will be a significant factor. But so will Hilton and Marriott and the rest of the hotel chains." But he is impressed by Airbnb's growth and in particular by how fast it can grow its supply. "It's got a lot of advantages," he says. "I wish I'd thought of it myself."

The most consistent observation from those who know Chesky is that he possesses this extreme level of curiosity, and what could be described as an obsession with constantly absorbing new information. "Brian's biggest strength is that he is a learning machine," says Reid Hoffman. "It's a skill set for all successful entrepreneurs — the phrase I use is 'infinite learner'—and Brian is the canonical example of that." Hoffman recalls doing an onstage interview with Chesky in San Francisco in Airbnb's early years. When they were barely down the steps from the stage, Chesky turned to Hoffman and asked him for feedback on what Hoffman thought Chesky could have done better. "Like, it was literally the first thing he said to me," Hoffman remembers.

Chesky is constantly taking notes. "He may not say anything after a meeting the first time he hears a new idea, but he's always pulling up his Evernote, and if you say something interesting, he writes it down," says Sequoia's Alfred Lin. "By the next time you see him, he went back, looked at the notes, thought about it, talked to a bunch more people about the topic, and then formed his own opinion." That relentless focus on learning, Lin and others say, is the main reason Chesky has been able to scale with the company. "Yes, he's product-minded, yes, he's very, very focused on providing a great customer-value proposition," Lin says. "But we know a lot of people who are also that who don't scale as CEO."

Marc Andreessen says one of the things that makes Chesky distinctive is that he's up for the challenge. "I've never had a conversation with Brian where he's like, 'Oh my God, it's so much.' He's always trying to figure out the next new thing."

"He is a learning animal," says eBay's Donahoe.

Chesky is just as obsessive about sharing the lessons he picks up, and e-mails like his four-thousand-word missive to his staff after the Buffett meeting are common. Since 2015, most Sunday nights he has sent out an all-staff e-mail about something new he's learned, or something on his mind, or a principle he wants to convey. "In a large company, you have to be fairly strong at public speaking or writing, because that becomes your management tool," he has said. "In the early stage, you're around a kitchen table, and it's four people, so your interactions are different." One of his early missives was a three-part series on—fittingly—how to learn.

It's a safe bet that Chesky came out of the womb with this kind of intense focus. "You could see at a very young age, anything he tackled, he just did it full force," says Deb Chesky. Chesky's childhood was as normal as they come: he grew up in Niskayuna, New York, a suburb of Schenectady, the son of Deb and Bob, both social workers (his younger sister, Allison, was the editorial director of teen-content publisher Tiger Beat Media and recently left to start her own company). Chesky's first passion was ice hockey; he started skating at age three and soon decided he would be the next Wayne Gretzky. When he got hockey equipment for Christmas one year, he insisted on going to sleep in it, pads, skates, stick, helmet, and all ("We said he looked like a crustacean," says his mother).

When it became clear he wasn't destined to be the next Gretzky (as Chesky puts it, "Sports is the only thing where you learn your limitations quickly"), hockey gave way to art. An early hobby drawing and redesigning Nike sneakers revealed a serious talent as an illustrator, and after he was in high school, his art teacher told his parents he had the potential to become famous as an artist. Chesky poured himself into his work, often disappearing to the local museum for hours, where he would draw replicas of the paintings. On a family trip to Florence one year, he stood in front of the statue of David for eight hours, meticulously drawing it. "We were, like, 'Well, we want to go and see other things,'" his mother says. "But it didn't matter what we were doing; he had his own path and he was just going to do it."

It was at RISD that he began to show early potential as a leader, first through the hockey team, where he'd gotten up to his antics with Gebbia promoting RISD's sports leagues, and then when he gave his memorable commencement speech to his class. Predictably, Chesky threw himself into the task, devouring every commencement speech he could find. To calm his nerves the night before, he stood at the podium for hours and watched as the event staff set up the few thousand chairs, one by one. "Who does that?" says Deb Chesky.

But while the learning came easy, mastering the nuts and bolts of dealing with people took some time. He learned the hard way, if two people had a disagreement, not to automatically take one person's side of the story. Hard-earned experience taught him that his words and actions can carry major influence throughout the company. (Picking up a green marker on the table in front of us, he says, "It's kind of like if I use this green marker. And then someone says, 'Brian only likes green markers. Get rid of all the non-green markers in every room!' And I might have just randomly picked up a green marker for maybe no reason.")

He was slow to hire a senior leadership team and delegate to them — the company had reached a few hundred employees, and he was still involved in thousands of minute details — and he initially had a hard time interviewing candidates who had decades more experience than him. ("You're sitting across from them, and they've had to do this on the other side of the table fifty times, and you're doing it for the first time with somebody who's much more seasoned than you, and you're kind of, like, 'This is very strange.'") When executives didn't work out, he was slow to let them go. Once he had his full executive team — the company calls the group the "e-staff" — in place, he then had to figure out how to get them to take things up a notch. "How do you get people to play at the next level when they're all tired, they haven't seen their families that much, and they just need to have a rest — and you're like, 'Yes, *but I need you to do ten times more*'?" The answer, which came from a consultation with "source" Marc Benioff, was that he couldn't ask them to work harder, but he could ask them to "massively up-level their thinking." ("Up-level" is a common Cheskyism that means taking it up a notch. Other Chesky terms include "skip-leveling," talking to different people at different levels of the company; and making a "step change," not just an iterative step but a new way of thinking about something. And he is always talking about having a "North Star," a phrase you can hear repeated throughout the halls of Brannan Street and even among hardcore Airbnb hosts and travelers.)

The sourcing came in handy when Airbnb faced some of its biggest crises. During the EJ ransacking incident of 2011, probably still the company's largest and most existential crisis to date, Marc Andreessen helped Chesky broaden his thinking by adding another zero to the $5,000 guarantee the company created. When the Samwer brothers were going after Airbnb in Europe, Paul Graham advised

Chesky that they were mercenaries and Airbnb were missionaries, and "missionaries often win." It helped Chesky make the decision to build Airbnb's own European business in order to compete with the Samwers. In the more recent crisis around the widespread discriminatory behavior on the Airbnb platform — even bigger in some ways than the EJ crisis — he pulled in outside sources like former attorney general Eric Holder and ACLU veteran Laura Murphy, but he also went to Andreessen Horowitz cofounder Ben Horowitz and his wife, Felicia, as well as to TaskRabbit CEO Stacy Brown-Philpot.

Those closest to him praise Chesky for his vision. "You take a picture of Brian's mind, [and] he's in 2030 or 2040 already," says Lisa Dubost, one of the company's first employees, who worked on culture and then moved to the business-travel team before leaving the company in 2016 to move to Europe to be with her family.

"Brian is this amazing visionary that looks not one, not two, not three, but ten steps ahead," says Belinda Johnson, his number-two executive and the person who, besides or perhaps more than the founders, spends more time with him than anyone else. "He's very inspirational — probably more than any manager I've ever had," Johnson says. "I say this, but I think he'll be known as one of the great CEOs of our time."

This kind of praise starts to feel a bit saccharine after a point. But it is also repeated over and over. And while much of Airbnb's language and messaging can be eye-rolling to those not "championing the mission," as one of its original core values implores, Chesky's fanatical belief in and devotion to what he sees as Airbnb's higher purpose seem to be the things that drive him more than anything else. He believes in home sharing "down to his toes," says Chip Conley, and he talks about the company's mission, "belonging anywhere," relentlessly, not as a CEO talking up the tagline that sells the product his company makes but as the reason he was truly put on this earth.

Paul Graham says what drives Chesky is not the things that often drive founders: wealth, influence, success. "He is not working for Brian Chesky," says Graham. "Really, honestly. I have seen so many different founders — literally, thousands. And I can tell the opportunists from the believers. It's way beyond money or even fame for him." For that reason, Graham says, Chesky may not be cut out for just any CEO role. "He's the kind of leader who leads people to do things that he himself believes in," he says. "You could not hire him as the CEO of some random company."

Warren Buffett sensed this, too. "He feels it all the way through," he says. "I think he would be doing what he's doing if he didn't get paid a dime for it."

Indeed, while every Silicon Valley CEO talks his or her own book, for Chesky, Airbnb seems more a calling than a job. "We have a mission to create a world where you can belong anywhere," he explained to me over lunch at one point. He believes that if more people in the world were hosts, "the world would be an inherently more hospitable and understanding place." Later, I ask him about his tangible business goals. "As far as a goal for 2020," he begins, "I think we're oriented on how many people can experience belonging in a deep, meaningful, transformational way." He has said that nothing takes precedence over making the mission of anyone belonging anywhere real: it comes before shareholders, it comes before the valuation. It comes before profits, it comes before product, it comes before everything. He wants Airbnb's value to peak sometime after he dies.

It isn't just Chesky; Gebbia and Blecharczyk espouse these beliefs, too, and they permeate the air at the company's headquarters. The company likes to say that it is "the UN at the kitchen table," bringing people together from different worlds and uniting strangers. "Maybe the people that my childhood taught me to label as strangers were actually friends waiting to be discovered," Gebbia said in a TED talk he delivered on how the company built its platform for trust. When asked about his goals for the company, Chip Conley told one of my colleagues that he would like to see it win the Nobel Peace Prize within ten years.

While no one doubts that any of this is sincere, the high-minded, "save the world for humanity" ethos has drawn its share of ribbing: "None of this is done with much of a sense of humor," wrote Max Chafkin in *Fast Company*, referring to a sign on the wall at the time that read "Airbnb is the next stage of human evolution." "Even Coca-Cola's famous 'Hilltop' ad — 'I'd like to buy the world a Coke / and keep it company' — had a certain sense of proportion."

During one of our conversations, I ask Chesky if anyone has ever told him he's overly idealistic. "I think it was Tom Friedman who had a great quote," he says, paraphrasing the *New York Times* columnist. "He said, 'Pessimists are usually right, but it's the optimists who change the world.'"

Even world changers have weaknesses. Chesky's vision and ambition can lead him to set goals that sometimes seem impossible to reach. Paul Graham says Chesky needs to take things less personally. "When anybody says anything bad about Airbnb — and when you get big enough, people are always saying bad things about you, it's an automatic consequence of being big — it hurts him," he says. "It really hurts him, as if someone had hit him. But it would save him from a lot of pain if he didn't take things so personally. But maybe it's impossible. Maybe it's a necessary consequence of leading by believing."

Marc Andreessen, who has seen his share of young founders try to scale with their companies, says that Chesky "is one of the best new CEOs since Mark Zuckerberg." He attributes this to a little-known fact: before transferring to Niskayuna High School, Chesky spent two years at a private school that taught military procedure and leadership. It's an easy mistake, Andreessen says, to assume Chesky is just a designer. "The twist with Brian is, he has the soul of the designer, but the precision and discipline of a military-school student," Andreessen says. "There's nothing abstract or fuzzy. Design is part of what makes him tick, but he basically was trained to run a military campaign."

One year in start-up years is like seven anywhere else, and as Chesky has evolved, so have his "sources." These days his mentors have given way to paid consultants. Stanley McChrystal, the former army general, was brought on to help him increase transparency and engagement between the company's top and mid-level leaders. Airbnb has hired Simon Sinek, the author and expert on finding and articulating an organization's "why," or purpose. And while not in the paid category, there's also that new bigwig Chesky shared the stage with in

Cuba: President Obama. The two have spent an increasing amount of time together: they first met in the Oval Office, when Chesky was tapped for the Presidential Ambassador for Global Entrepreneurship (PAGE) program, an elite group of entrepreneurs including fashion designer Tory Burch, AOL founder Steve Case, and Chobani founder Hamdi Ulukaya. In addition to the Cuba initiative, Chesky was part of the president's official delegations to global entrepreneurism summits in San Francisco and Nairobi, Kenya — where Chesky joined the State Dinner at President Kenyatta's house and met Obama's Kenyan family. It's a long way from the company's more peripheral relationship with Obama in its early days: relaunching Airbnb at his over-capacity 2008 DNC acceptance speech, fashioning the Obama O's around him, and "crashing" his inauguration in 2009.

Back home in upstate New York, Deb and Bob Chesky still can't fully grasp their son's journey. "All we can say is, it's been surreal," Deb says. "I don't even know how else to say it."

"The Bad News You Need to Hear"

As the Airbnb CEO, Chesky gets the spotlight and most of the media attention, but Joe Gebbia and Nate Blecharczyk also cast a large day-to-day presence throughout the company. If Chesky has found his calling as a leader of the troops and the captain of the ship, his cofounders have had leadership journeys of their own, both very different from Chesky's and from each other's. Like Chesky, Gebbia has sought out help from mentors: Chip Conley, he says, is one who has been very helpful to him; David Kelley, the founder of the design firm IDEO, is another, advising him on how to maintain a creative culture as the company has grown so much bigger. "How do you keep an environment creative, where people feel safe proposing new and maybe sometimes scary or risky ideas without them getting shot down?" Gebbia asks.

But if scaling as a leader came easy to Chesky, it was harder for Gebbia, who was more in his element conceiving bold, out-of-the-box ideas in a small team than managing a large chunk of the organization — which is what he soon found himself doing. As the company started to get bigger and bigger in 2013 and 2014, the growth and the pace started to become overwhelming. "There were so many moving parts," he says. "At one point you could keep your eye on everything, and at a certain point you couldn't." He felt a growing level of anxiety. "The teams are getting bigger. The numbers are getting bigger," he recalls. "Everything's kind of growing around you. So how do you grow with that?" He says he couldn't. "I have to admit," he says, "I hit a wall."

To help find the answer, the company had an outside consultant come in to administer a 360-degree review. Candid, anonymized interviews with the dozen or so people who worked most closely with Gebbia delivered some painful results. People saw him as an optimistic, upbeat leader, but he had a reputation as a perfectionist, and people were afraid to be candid with him when projects weren't working out. "That was a big one," he says. Anytime anyone gave him bad news, his body language would shut down, they said, and he became defensive; so after a while, they just didn't give it to him. "Problems would fester and become worse, and then I would hear about them, and then they would be harder to deal with," he says.

That perfectionism also meant that simple decisions often took a very long time to make, and he would sometimes become a bottleneck in his own company. He also didn't quite realize that just because he had a strong work ethic — the same drive that led him to create two companies before starting Airbnb — it didn't mean everyone else did. The 360-degree review revealed to him that people on his team hadn't had dinner with their significant others in weeks and weren't doing things like going to the gym, and in truth some of them were thinking about leaving. "My drive for perfection was burning people out," he says.

Thus began a huge education process for Gebbia. With the help of a coach (who was "brutally honest," he says), he had to learn that it was OK to have products go out the door if they were less than perfect, and that a fast decision is sometimes better than a fully informed one. His team was behind him, and they even came up with a new mantra for him: "80 percent equals done." "That was a very uncomfortable thing for me up until that point," Gebbia says. Gradually he started asking people, in meetings and individually, "What's the bad news I need to hear?"

He came to realize that some of this behavior had spread through the rest of the company. "People look to the leaders for how to behave," he says. "So if I wasn't creating a space where people could have candor and be open about what was going on, that was showing up elsewhere in the company." So in mid-2014, Gebbia turned what he had learned into a candid talk delivered in front of a few hundred employees and beamed out to the company's offices worldwide. "We have a problem with candor at our company," he began, before revealing in great detail the feedback he'd received about himself and how he worked to change his approach. He then introduced a theory he'd learned. Called "elephants, dead fish, and vomit," it was a set of tools designed to encourage difficult conversations: An "elephant," he explained, is a big truth everyone knows but doesn't talk about; a "dead fish" is a personal grievance that needs to be aired out, usually with an apology, or it risks getting worse ("I had quite a few dead fish to deal with," he told the audience); and "vomit" sessions were time put aside for people to get things off their chest without interruption and without risk of judgment. He revealed the specifics of his actions that he'd learned in the feedback that related to each one.

After he delivered the last line, he breathed a deep sigh. "It was a very scary talk," he said later. "You could hear a pin drop." But it had a significant impact throughout the company. Division managers started creating time dedicated solely to talking about "elephants" and "dead fish"; the terms are still used across divisions. Today, Gebbia gets e-mails from people around Airbnb with all-caps subject lines: JOE: THE BAD NEWS YOU NEED TO HEAR. Taped to the top of his computer monitor, he has a sign that says "80 percent equals done."

Around this same time, Gebbia had already started to chart a different course for himself, one that hewed much closer to his design roots and his passion for conceiving and incubating new ideas. "My superpowers weren't being utilized," he says. "I was managing managers." An opportunity came in late 2013, when the company held an executive off-site meeting in New York. The previous year, the founders had laid out a vision for the future of the company in an important internal project they called Snow White.

With the help of professional animators, they "storyboarded" the Airbnb experience, detailing "frame by frame" what happened for both traveler and host from the moment a customer first logged on to the site to the moment he or she returned home from a trip. The big revelation from the project was that Airbnb itself was part of only a few of the frames, those that involved the accommodations, and they needed to work to fill in the rest of them. Months later, at the off-site, the founders realized they hadn't been making enough progress toward that expanded vision for the future of the company: to own not just the accommodations but the full trip.

It was time to start moving into those other "frames," and soon it was decided that Gebbia would run an immersive prototyping exercise to start exploring how. He pulled together six people in design, product, and engineering and moved them all to New York City for three months, a timeline and setup modeled after Y Combinator. (They even drafted their own core values.) Living and working around the clock out of an Airbnb loft in Brooklyn, they hacked together several different in-app tools, outfitted a small group of international Airbnb tourists with phones that contained the jerry-rigged software, and sent them out to test their ideas. At the end of the three months, they would have a Demo Day back at Airbnb headquarters. The concepts they tested were all over the map: an "arrival tracker," a sort of Uberlike geolocator that made it easier for the host to know when to expect the guest to check in; a "smart house manual"; and something called Local Companion, a virtual-assistant tool that let travelers request anything they needed, whether a local restaurant recommendation, food delivery, or answers to questions about the city. It also had a "magic button" users could tap to get an unknown, ultracustomized experience that would be tailored to their interests.

One traveler who was a licensed pilot hit the button and got a helicopter ride above Manhattan; another got a custom nail manicurist who came to her door. A third asked for help planning his engagement, a challenge the Local Companion team took up with glee, organizing a post-proposal carriage ride in Central Park complete with a harpist; dinner and a night out; and brunch the next day where, instead of a bill, the waiter presented them with a photo album documenting their experience.

Back in San Francisco, the prototype operation morphed into a team called Home to Home, led by Gebbia, to explore and test more ideas. One in particular showed promise: the Experience Marketplace, a platform where hosts with a particular skill or knowledge set could offer city experiences to guests in their city for a fee. Some hosts were already doing this; a guy in Park City touted in his listing that he would take guests skiing on local-only trails; a Boston host would take guests on a personal tour of Kendall Square. The team ran a pilot in San Francisco and Paris to recruit and build out more of these experiences. One host in Paris, Ludovic, told the team he made $3,000 from hosting people in his home but had earned $15,000 from giving walking tours around Le Marais.

The project ran for most of 2014 and saw some traction, but this was right around the time that Gebbia had hit his wall, and he soon realized he was having trouble scaling and "operationalizing" the ideas. Out of the experience came a realization for Gebbia that he was more drawn to the creation of new ideas than the implementation of existing ones. He gradually started conceiving an idea for a new division of Airbnb that would be dedicated solely to advanced research and design. In 2016 the company launched Samara, an in-house design studio, overseen by Gebbia, that explores large-scale concepts, including the future of shared housing and new models for architecture and tourism that could help create social change. Its first project was the Yoshino Cedar House, a new model for a community center–meets–hostel located in rural Japan: Airbnb travelers can stay there, locals can set up stations to craft there, and the two can interact in ways that might also bring economic benefit to a declining rural area. Other explorations include iterations on the "magic button" that would better divine exactly what would most "delight" each individual user.

Alongside Samara is something called The Lab, a small team focused on the short-burst iteration of products and ideas that are more experimental but can be quickly tested.

Both teams were launched out of Gebbia's home, an industrial loft a block away from Airbnb headquarters, and moved to a new space behind the Airbnb building in mid-November 2016. This kind of independent Skunk Works operation is common at other large companies, and it is Gebbia's sweet spot. It brings him back to the Rausch Street days, when he and Chesky would come up with new ideas over fierce and sweaty games of Ping-Pong. "I want to be a creator of safe space for the invention of ideas," Gebbia says.

"The Inspector"

While Brian Chesky and Joe Gebbia have received the lion's share of the media attention over the years — and there has been a lot of media attention — Nate Blecharczyk's path is in many ways the most interesting. By all accounts, he is a technical and coding genius. Chesky has said of the early days that having Blecharczyk on board was like having three engineers. He was the one who created all kinds of free ways to grow: Airbnb's early hack into Craigslist, the dynamic ad campaigns that could target specific cities, and the special technology to interface with Google AdWords. The payment system he built is legendary in the engineering community. With a less talented person in AirBed & Breakfast's chief technical role, it may not have gotten off the ground.

But Blecharczyk has always had more of a business-oriented mind than the average engineer. He took the GMAT after college and thought seriously about applying to business school. He also went pretty far down the road trying to start his own social-advertising network before committing to Chesky and Gebbia and AirBed &

Breakfast. A methodical and disciplined thinker, he is especially good at thinking through complex issues and then simplifying the ideas. "I'm a very analytical person," he says. "If there's one skill that I have, it's taking complex things and boiling them down." When the entire executive team took the Myers-Briggs Type Indicator personality test at an off-site one year, Blecharczyk registered as an ISTJ personality type, which correlated with the "inspector" role in the related Keirsey Temperament Sorter personality questionnaire. The characterization made the executive team laugh in recognition. ("That's how they know me," he says, "as someone who probes the details.")

Over time, Blecharczyk developed an interest in strategy, especially when, as CTO, he began to see more of the insights that were coming out of the data-science department, which reported directly to him. In the summer of 2014, after the executive team was beginning to realize the company wasn't fully aligned on its many initiatives and goals, Blecharczyk started an "activity map" to document every project being worked on throughout the company. He identified 110 of them, but they were extremely fragmented, with different executives overseeing multiple projects in the same area. He then did a deep analytical study of the company's growth, which made him more acutely aware of the imbalance between Airbnb's limited supply (hosts) and its fast-growing demand (guests). "In the short term that's not a huge problem, but in the long term it becomes a problem," he says.

He became drawn to the idea of coming up with ways to increase the rate of supply growth. Much of those 110 disparate projects involved hosts, so beginning in 2015, Blecharczyk took on a much broader role, becoming responsible for homes and hosting strategy and operations. "What I'm leveraging is my understanding of our technical systems, having the context of the last eight years and the moral authority of cofounder," he says, to bring disparate hosting-project teams together throughout the company and to think through its overall strategy more broadly. Blecharczyk's CTO title hasn't changed as of this writing, but he says it's "a little bit dated and at this point may be misleading."

The Myers-Briggs test also revealed something else: that Blecharczyk was the most different from anyone else on the team and from the general composition of the team. "The general competence of the team is inverse to whatever I am," he says. The coaches administering the session said that was important and advised the group that Blecharczyk's perspective was so different that he should be a part of any important conversation the company was having. He was already privy to much of that as a cofounder, but it became more evident that he represented a different and important point of view. "That was very important to lay the groundwork for my strategy role today," he says.

Over the years Blecharczyk has also leaned on books, like Jim Collins's *Good to Great; The Five Dysfunctions of a Team*, by Patrick Lencioni; and Geoffrey Moore's *Crossing the Chasm*. He's learned how to be more visible. "My temperament is to be an introvert," he says, but some of the feedback he's received over the years is that employees value hearing from all three founders individually — not just Chesky. "I've had to learn an important leadership lesson in being visible," Blecharczyk says.

People around him say Blecharczyk is also a calm, steadying force. "He, more than anyone else on the leadership team, keeps us grounded," says Mike Curtis, a top engineering executive at Facebook whom Blecharczyk hired as Airbnb's VP of engineering in 2013. "We have so much ambition as a group," Curtis says, "and Nate is the methodical, disciplined thinker who takes all the inputs from all different people and he can pull all those things together and read it back out to the group so that we can make decisions."

The differences among the three founders do not go unnoticed. "Ask anybody in the company and they'll tell you we all have such different personalities," Gebbia says. Mike Curtis agrees. "The three of them have such different points on the spectrum," he says. "The way they balance each other out is pretty wild." (Do they bicker? "Oh, totally!" Curtis says.) A few years ago, the founders took another personality test that placed them into one of three sections of a circle. When the administrators plotted their results, each of the three founders landed in a different section, perfectly equidistant from each other. "They came back and said, 'We've never seen this before,' Gebbia says. "It was like a perfect isosceles triangle."

They say these differences are what has led them to succeed. "No one of us alone could have done this," Gebbia says. "Two of us alone couldn't have done this. But the combination of what Nate brings, what Brian brings, what I bring, put that together, and I think that's how we've persevered through all the challenges that have come our way the last couple of years." Investors in Airbnb usually list the founding team, and specifically the combination of the three of them together, as one of the top few factors that drew them to back the company. Chip Conley makes a popular analogy for this. "It's like the Beatles," he says. "The four Beatles could do their own individual albums, but they'll never be as good as all together."

"Don't Fuck Up the Culture"

The company's culture could almost be its own character in any story about Airbnb. A common fixation among Silicon Valley start-ups, culture has been an obsessive focus of all three founders ever since they exited the Y Combinator program. But it didn't truly hit home for Chesky until 2012, after the company closed its Series-C round of funding, a $200 million round that was led by Peter Thiel's Founders Fund. The Airbnb founders invited Thiel to the office, and Chesky asked him for advice. Thiel said simply, "Don't fuck up the culture." He said that Airbnb's culture was one of the reasons he had invested, but he said it was basically inevitable that after a company got to a certain size, it would "fuck it up." Chesky took this as a challenge, and he has had a somewhat maniacal focus on Airbnb's culture ever since. "If you break the culture, you break the machine that makes your products," he wrote in a blog post on the topic. The stronger the culture, he argued, the more trust there would be for employees to do the right thing and the less need there would be for formal rules and processes. And the fewer the processes and the lighter the oversight, the better the conditions for innovation.

According to Chesky, the way to not fuck up the company culture is both by making it a top priority and — naturally — by designing it. This has been an enormous area of focus for Airbnb. It's why Chesky stood onstage at the company's all-hands meeting in 2015 and told workers that what will kill the company is not regulators or competition or anything like that but rather losing their ability to be "crazy"; why he obsessively writes Sunday-night e-mails; and why he personally interviewed every job candidate until the company got to be more than three hundred people.

Airbnb's workspace is one important pillar of that culture. In 2013 the company moved into its current headquarters, a 250,000-square-foot space that takes up five floors of a former battery factory in San Francisco's SoMa neighborhood. Depending on whom you talk to, the headquarters are either a work of art or almost shrine-like, as one person familiar with the company described it. Most of the conference rooms, of which there are more than two dozen, are exact replicas, down to every last wall hanging and tchotchke, of Airbnb listings throughout the world. There's the living room of the Rausch Street apartment, a replica of the famous Mushroom Dome in Aptos, California, and a recent addition, a Viennese parlor with a player piano that starts playing only when you lift up a secret book on one of the shelves. ("Only the necessities — that's what we invest in," Chesky deadpans when we sit down in this room for a meeting and he learns about the secret book for the first time.)

There are pantries and minikitchens on every floor that stock coffee, other beverages, and nut-free seaweed snacks. There is the Eatrium, a no-waste oasis serving up all the kinds of meals you'd expect from a Silicon Valley company with a multibillion-dollar valuation, plus innovations like a row of forty-eight silver taps dispensing sparkling water, wine, beer, kombucha, and Redbnb, a house-made, artisanal Red Bull made from hibiscus, green tea, and yerba mate.

The collective group of Airbnb employees is referred to as the "Air-family," or "Airfam" for short, and employees can avail themselves of many special perks and events. These include "Air Shares," sessions where employees can share skills like photography or tie-dying. There's a Toastmasters program and a mindfulness group. There is a lot of dressing up at Airbnb, whether it's Mad Men days, a Halloween-costume contest, or an annual Oktoberfest party where Blecharczyk traditionally shows up in lederhosen. Much of this is replicated at Airbnb offices around the globe.

And there's that idealism again. Employees across disciplines, from financial planning to project management, bring up the company's "belonging" mission unprompted. Recently, community chief Douglas Atkin has been developing a version of the "belong anywhere transformation journey," the metamorphosis Airbnb intends for its guests to experience, that applies to its internal culture, calling it the "belong *here* transformation journey." The goal is the same: you arrive as a stranger and you edit yourself; then you become welcomed, you feel in a safe space, you can be your full self. As one employee in Portland told Atkin, "I can be the full-fat version of myself here, not the skim-milk version."

It seems way over the top — the full-fat version of over the top — yet most people seem to buy in. "Airbnb has brought out the best of me and a part of me I didn't know existed," says VP of product Joe Zadeh. Says engineering head Curtis, "All my previous jobs were leading up to this." Jonathan Golden, the first product manager at the company and a veteran of Dropbox and HubSpot who worked in finance before that, calls Airbnb "the most expansive and iterative culture I've been in. There's always a question of 'Why not?'" He says it's also the "most collaborative culture I've ever worked in, by far." The negative that comes with that, Golden says, is not as much efficiency — more people tend to be involved in e-mails and meetings, because many people get brought into conversations — but he thinks the openness leads people to aspire to do more.

"They pump something into the air," says Andreessen Horowitz's

Jeff Jordan. "How do you build a culture — from the top to the bottom — where everyone believes they're changing the world?" In 2016, the company ranked number 1 on Glassdoor's Employee's Choice Awards, beating out Google, Facebook, Twitter, Salesforce, and others.

This kind of environment can help smooth things over when there are internal near-disasters, like the one Mike Curtis experienced one afternoon in early 2015. One of the company's engineers accidentally typed a bad command into a console, and in a single keyboard stroke he deleted almost the entire data warehouse of the company, "like, in one fell swoop," Curtis says. Almost all of Airbnb's capabilities and much of its future potential were rooted in the vast repository of data it had accumulated about how people travel around the world. And in an instant, it was gone.

"It was a massive, massive data-loss event," Curtis says. It was like the tequila bottle resting on the delete key in the famous episode of HBO's *Silicon Valley*, only it was bigger, and real, and worse, and it was an actual command typed in by an engineer (and one of the department's stars, at that). "Blood was draining from my face," Curtis recalls. After working twenty-four hours a day for the next few days, a small team identified a fix, and they were ultimately able to recover all of it — a process that took two weeks — but there were a few days before they found the solution when it was unclear whether there would actually be one. "That was a terrifying day," Curtis says. Curtis says Chesky's reaction was to give him the space he needed to figure it out. "Whereas he could have completely flipped out, he did not," he says. The rest of the team rallied behind the culpable engineer (who is still there, by the way), making him a T-shirt with the proper command on it that still hangs in the department.

There are issues, of course. The same elements of Airbnb's culture that make it so touchy-feely can also breed a tendency toward nonconfrontation, which led to Gebbia's elephant/dead fish/vomit talk. It is a work-hard environment, and Chesky can be demanding. When the team working on entry to Cuba worked tirelessly to recruit hosts and to identify five hundred listings in a matter of weeks, the team members brought the results to their CEO — who told them that was great, but he wanted it doubled to one thousand listings in three weeks. A few years ago, when the company was growing faster than expected, Zadeh said he "worked himself into the ground" and ended up getting pneumonia.

As the company has gotten bigger, it has brought in new employees and top executives who don't always exhibit the same values as its early employees, many of whom still identify with the company's scrappy roots. In those days, employees often had to describe to their friends what Airbnb was; people hadn't heard of it, and that played a role in the pioneer types who joined. Over the years, though, as the company became larger, it started to attract more people with MBAs and others who joined precisely because it had gotten so big, seeing great opportunities to jump on a rocket ship and to build their careers. The Glassdoor surveys have "pro" and "con" sections, and a common complaint on the "con" side was that there were new Airbnb managers who were inexperienced and that the company culture did not extend to every team. "Toxic people do exist," one employee wrote. (Other cons were the lack of a 401[k] match for employees and that dinner was not available to go.)

Chesky thinks one thing that can help scale its culture is to make sure the company remains transparent as it adjusts to its new size. Implementing an idea he gleaned from Stanley McChrystal, in order to foster better communication from the top to the bottom of the organization, the company instituted a new weekly call for executive staff members plus every one of their direct reports (about one hundred people).

As of this writing, the founders were working very closely together on a major new effort, quarterbacked by Douglas Atkin, to revamp the sacred charter of the company, the six core values instituted in 2013 (among them, "Be a host," "Champion the mission," "Embrace the adventure," and "Be a 'cereal' entrepreneur"). These principles worked well when the company was smaller, but over time it became clear that there were too many of them, some of them conflicted with others, and they were too "cute and cryptic," says Atkin. Worse, some employees were co-opting them to their own advantage; if someone didn't agree with an employee's suggestion, he or she could then accuse the person of not "embracing the adventure."

Working for months, Atkin and the founders ("the boys," as he calls them) whittled the values down to three, which weren't finalized as of this writing but were coalescing around being "host-y" or empathetic; forging one's own path and being unconventional; and — surprise — putting the mission before everything else. Atkin was masterminding relaunch day, when employees would be "dunked into the core values like a tea bag" and become fully inculcated in them. The company's next One Airbnb, its all-employee gathering, he told me, would be the "climax of the introduction process."

One other aspect of its culture the company is trying to address is that, like many of its Silicon Valley peers, Airbnb is too white. This is an issue at all technology companies, but Airbnb also had a major issue with discriminatory behavior by hosts on its platform. Many (including the company's founders) say a lack of diversity in the company — starting with its founders, three white men — is one reason that it failed to anticipate that its platform might enable such behavior.

In the summer of 2016, when Chesky and Belinda Johnson appeared onstage together at *Fortune*'s Brainstorm Tech conference, the last question from the audience came from Kimberly Bryant, founder of the nonprofit Black Girls Code: "I wonder, do you not recognize that some of the issues in the design of the product as is, [are] being driven by the fact that it's not inclusive design? Perhaps it's because there's only 2% black people that work at Airbnb, there's only 3% of Hispanics that are part of the Airbnb community, and if we go down further into the tech ranks, it's like 1%." The room was silent. "So while I appreciate the redesign efforts, I really would challenge you to look at what are the employee makeups of your companies." According to Airbnb's most recent diversity report, black employees are 2.9 percent of the total, Hispanic or Latino employees 6.5 percent, and men 57 percent. Those numbers put Airbnb ahead of Facebook, which is 2 percent black, 4 percent Hispanic, and 67 percent male; and Google, which is 2 percent black, 3 percent Hispanic, and 69 percent male. But Airbnb's figures for black and Hispanic or Latino employees declined slightly since the preceding year, as did the percentage of women (though the percentage of women in leadership roles increased). The company has acknowledged this is a problem and is working on it: there is a new head of diversity, a goal to boost the percentage of underrepresented minorities among its U.S.-based employees from 10 percent to 11 percent, and a suite of new recruiting partnerships and policies — like the requirement that all candidate pools for senior-level positions have to include women and underrepresented minorities. "We have to do better," Chesky said.

As of this writing, Chesky, Gebbia, and Blecharczyk had a new management challenge before them: taking Airbnb from a one-product company to a multiproduct company. They were readying the launch of the next chapter in their company's history, the entry into the market for the rest of the trip beyond accommodations. It was a project two years in the making and, as we will see, a significant departure. "I know how to start a product — I started one," Chesky told an audience at Reid Hoffman's "Blitzscaling" course at Stanford. "But how do you start a new product inside an existing business that's successful?"

Chesky assumed it would be just like getting the original product going the first time, he said, but, as he discovered, it was much more complicated: you may have more funding and many more resources, but people don't understand why you're pushing them to do something else; they want to stay focused on their original mission. "Shifting from a single-product company to a dual-product company, that's a pretty big shift," Chesky said. To help him, he pulled in a new "source": Geoffrey Moore, a management consultant with a particular specialty in helping executives grow a one-product company into a multiproduct company.

But in Chesky's mind, the expansion was also critical for Airbnb's future. Most tech companies that were really big, he pointed out, had more than one product. Apple had computers first, then the phone and the watch. Amazon had books, then everything else. "I think all enduring companies have to do that," he said. "Because if you're a technology company, you can't presume your original invention is the thing that you're selling many years from now."

For Airbnb, the new thing it was about to start selling was the rest of the trip.

8

What's Next?

AT THE TIME OF THIS WRITING, the company was putting the final touches on its plans for the annual Airbnb Open, the three-day festival for its hosts that Airbnb puts on each year to rally and commune with its troops, drench them in the company's mission, and sprinkle "belonging" fairy dust to thousands of its most passionate disciples. A sort of smaller-scale of mash-up of Woodstock, a TED conference, and the Berkshire Hathaway Annual Meeting for the sharing-economy set, it is a spectacle of "hostiness" and a chance for the company to preach, teach, and pay homage to its most converted. The 2016 event was set to take place in Los Angeles in mid-November. Anyone who is signed up as a host on Airbnb gets an invitation, but the event typically draws around five thousand of the most engaged in the community. Attendees fly in from all over the world on their own dime (which means airfare, lodging—on Airbnb of course—and tickets that range from $25 for a single event to $300 for the whole shebang). In 2016, Airbnb guests would be invited too, and there are always a few investors, board members, and friends and family of the founders in tow, but the Open is really for the hosts. Critics could say it is a masterful execution of a company's celebration of its most important stakeholder group wrapped in the cozy warmth of hospitality, and they wouldn't be wrong: Airbnb uses its megaphone at the Open to rally the audience to mobilize in support of changing laws around the country and to convey its principles of hospitality to the people who are responsible for delivering it.

This year, though, the Open would be much bigger than before. It was to be the setting for the long-planned introduction of Airbnb 2.0, a "new" direction for Airbnb marking the first second act in the disruptive, controversial company's young life. (It would also be the first Open since the 2015 event in Paris, which was cut short by terrorist attacks.) Speakers were set to include Gwyneth Paltrow, Ashton Kutcher, *Eat, Pray, Love* author Elizabeth Gilbert, the movie producer Brian Grazer (*A Beautiful Mind*), the chef and entrepreneur Danny Meyer, and a roster of other top names. Talks and meetings would be spread out among various venues in downtown Los Angeles, and one of the highlights would be the Bélo Awards, the company's annual Oscars of hosting — named for Airbnb's squiggly "Bélo" logo — hosted by the comedian James Corden.

For months, close observers could glean that something new was in the works. At a launch event for the company's "live like a local" campaign several months earlier, Chesky preached that the company's new app would help its community of users escape the soulless emptiness of modern mass tourism and closed his remarks with a tease — "The question becomes, What if Airbnb *did* go beyond the home?" — before exiting with a "See you in November" and a pretty well-executed mic drop. Shortly thereafter, travelers in a few key markets were invited to beta-test a new program tentatively called City Hosts, a collection of multiday excursions with locals available to Airbnb guests in certain cities.

The Open in Los Angeles would mark the announcement of the project, code-named Magical Trips and expected to be launched as just "Trips," that Airbnb had been working on since late 2014. By now, if Airbnb has had its way, plenty of ink will have been spilled about the new venture. But in a preview before the November event, Chesky walked me through a demo. It wasn't yet complete — the company would still make plenty of changes after we spoke — but it would mark the launch into a whole new category of travel products, services, and experiences, all rolled into a new app that would host both the "old" and the "new" Airbnb.

As of this writing, the most significant element of the expansion was to be the City Host venture, renamed as Experiences and intended as off-the-tourism-grid activities travelers wouldn't otherwise be able to do that would be offered by locals, curated and vetted by Airbnb, and designed to play up the unique expertise and character of the people offering them. On the beta launch, the choices included "Viktoria, the Perfumer," a professional "nose" offering a tour of hidden perfume houses of Paris; and "Willy, Elite Runner," who offered a four-day stay at the high-altitude training center where Kenya's elite runners live and train. In Miami, an expert fire spinner would indoctrinate you into the world of "fire bending"; in Italy, you could go truffle hunting with a third-generation truffle hunter; and so on.

The way it was coming together, these experiences would cost around $200, would include three or four different activities spread over a few days, and would be offered to multiple people at a time, so you might show up for your truffle hunt and find a handful of other like-minded, Airbnb-user truffle enthusiasts. The hosts would keep 80 percent of the fee, so, the idea goes, they make money, the guests get a unique experience they can go back home and tell their friends about, and, if all goes as Chesky hopes, it will initiate an Airbnb viral-like spread all over again. There were also plans for a parallel marketplace for smaller, à la carte experiences, like surfing or rock climbing, that users could partake in either when traveling or in their home city.

The overall idea isn't new: over the past several years, a mini cottage industry has emerged of start-ups offering peer-to-peer experiences, but none has broken out. According to Chesky, this is because the quality hasn't been that good and the experiences have been too touristy and not unique. And none of them have a built-in platform of millions of engaged users to market to. Airbnb's offerings are meant to be one-of-a-kind, hyperlocal excursions that give a view of a niche, expertise, or neighborhood. "These are deep, insider immersions into somebody's world," Chesky says. "We think this is a totally unique vertical that doesn't exist today."

These items were just one part of the launch: other areas of focus would include a new push into events, a way for guests to book tickets to both large events coming to town and a collection of Airbnb-exclusive pop-up concerts, salons, and the like in Airbnb hosts' living rooms or at the corner bar; and an upgrade to the company's guidebooks feature that would include local recommendations from influencers as well as location-enabled suggestions from Airbnb hosts. There would be a "smart itinerary," a kind of digital calendar to corral all these new bookings that Airbnb hopes its guests will make. Another section of the app would provide routine services like rental equipment, SIM cards, connectivity, and the like. The company also expected to make a big push into travel content, because, Chesky says, "that's the top of the funnel." All of the new introductions would be browsable on the Internet but bookable on mobile devices only, and the various elements would be displayed with a heavy focus on video over photos. "We think travel in the future will be sold through videos and immersive experiences," Chesky says.

Chesky's hope is that these new offerings will turn conventional tourism on its head in the same way its rental of homes has disrupted hospitality. When Chesky wants to describe something he thinks is truly inventive upgrade, he uses the phrase "the thing *after*." The guidebooks tool is "the thing *after* guidebooks"; the new Verifi the company also has in store will be "the thing *after* Verifi the sharing economy is "the thing *after* mass production believes Airbnb is introducing the thing *after* travel. "My at the end of this launch, everything you knew about different," he says. "You might still call it a trip, you travel, but it's going to make all the travel you kn very, very different."

In many ways, this plan is a logical exter core business. It doubles down on its focu the "anti-Frommer's" approach to touris in on in the past few years. During the iteration process, the company plucked a tourist named Ricardo out of Fisherman's Wharf and followed him with a photographer for a few days, documenting him at Alcatraz Island, trying to gaze through a fogged-out view of the Golden Gate Bridge, and eating at Bubba Gump Shrimp Company. Airbnb tallied up his receipts and found he spent most of his money on chain franchises based in other cities. The Magical Trips team re-engineered what might be a perfect trip for that same tourist, plunging him into a 1920s-themed dinner party, sending him on a walking tour of the city's Bernal Heights neighborhood led by a local, and presenting him with instructions to show up for a spontaneous midnight "mystery" bike ride, where sixty riders outfitted their bikes in neon lights and rode all over the city until 2 or 3 a.m. "Right now, travel is oriented around being an outsider, having limited access to public places," Chesky says. "This is going to be about being an insider and immersing in a community. And that is a profound shift."

Beyond the travel experiences, the events and guidebooks also signal an attempt to get Airbnb users to use Airbnb in their home cities. "This is the beginning of Airbnb becoming integrated into your daily life," Chesky tells me. "This is not just a new way to travel but it is a new way to live, in some ways." The new venture will be called Trips, but he said that he hopes that one day the company will lose that distinction and all the products and services it offers on its platform will become known simply as Airbnb. Renting homes, he says, might ultimately represent less than half of the company's revenue.

The business case for getting into these new enterprises is that Airbnb can offer a range of experiences throughout a trip, it can [make] additional revenue across all activities throughout the trip [and] even in one's home city — and, critically, it can significantly [deepen i]ts relationship with its customer. The new offerings also have [the potent]ial to make the platform significantly bigger — but all while [staying d]own on its brand mission to offer unique experiences and [bring simi]lar people together. "The reason we're doing this is be[cause] Trips is the end game," Chesky says. "It's kind of where [it's all be]en."

That's, of course, assuming the new venture takes off. As magical and inventive as it is, it may be a heavy ask for some people to spend most of their weekend away on an activity that's directed by someone else, with other strangers tagging along, and to pay a few hundred dollars for it. Airbnb is putting its unique spin on travel, but it's entering a crowded market and taking on a variety of existing players across the spectrum: traditional tour operators, Yelp, Foursquare, TripAdvisor, and even Lonely Planet and *Condé Nast Traveler* all at once. When Airbnb blazed its disruptive trail in shared accommodations, it did so by accident, tapping into something unexpectedly wondrous and huge and viral. With this launch, it is attempting the exact opposite of that: it is an idea that was conceived, engineered, tested, and tweaked by Airbnb's team of specialists, and then formally introduced to the market. Success may not be as easy as it was the first time around. It begs an interesting question: Can true disruptions be planned and strategized, or are they more powerful when they're accidental?

This is also a significant new foray for a company whose core business is still growing so fast. But Chesky has been antsy to pivot for a while. He and the founders have been well aware of the ability of once-mighty tech giants to stick too close to their core product and become irrelevant over time. (BlackBerry, Blockbuster, TiVo — the annals of tech history are filled with such examples.) Chesky studied some of the big and lasting tech companies, like Google, Apple, and Amazon, and came to two conclusions: the survival of a tech company depends on a willingness to branch into new categories; and the CEO has to have the discipline to put the new venture ahead of the existing business and to take the new project on personally. For close to two years, Magical Trips has been Chesky's main focus, taking up one-third to one-half of his time.

To figure out how Airbnb would make this leap, Chesky found inspiration in companies that had done something similar and succeeded — in particular, Disney. He modeled the operating processes for Magical Trips on Walt Disney's creation of Walt Elias Disney Enterprises, WED, the separate company that was established in the

1950s to create Disneyland (and that was ultimately acquired by the parent company and renamed Walt Disney Imagineering). "No one saw Disneyland coming," Chesky says. "Disneyland saved the company in the '80s. There would be no Disney without Disneyland." He met with Disney CEO Bob Iger but also brought in Jay Rasulo, the former Disney CFO who later ran all its theme parks; and the company's former chairman for theme parks and resorts, Paul Pressler (who later served as CEO of Gap Inc.). "This product was designed around the principles of Disneyland," Chesky says. He also met with his sources at other companies that had branched out: Jony Ive at Apple, and in probably the best, if aspirational, model for what Chesky is trying to do, Jeff Bezos, who had turned Amazon from an online bookseller into a mega-retailer.

Chesky also says he took some advice from Elon Musk of Tesla. Musk cautioned him against becoming a company that gets so big that it enters what he calls the "administration era": a phase of 10 or 20 percent growth that a company settles into after the "creation era" and then the "building era" and signals a mature business. "Airbnb will never be in an administration era," Chesky vows. "It will always be in a building era. It will always be in a phase 1, phase 2 era. And this is why we're going to be launching a lot of stuff in November — and then many, many things after that."

"This launch is going to mean something profoundly different for Airbnb," he says.

There is something else profoundly different for Airbnb coming sometime soon: an initial public offering. As of this writing, Chesky and the company still deny that an IPO is in the works anytime soon. In the spring of 2016, Chesky told Bloomberg West that it did not have plans to go public over the next two years and that it didn't need capital, and again when I asked him in the fall he said there were no plans for an IPO in the near future. He said the company had plenty of money: as of this writing, it has raised $4 billion, including $555 million in September 2016, and has taken specific steps that remove pressures to go public, taking on $1 billion in debt financing and including in its most recent round of funding a $200 million secondary offering to provide liquidity to early employees. Chesky has reiterated that Airbnb's investors are patient; many of them invested early on and have already seen a significant upside. (Since making its first investment, in 2009, Sequoia has participated in every fund-raising round except the latest, and only then because the company wanted to focus on strategic investors. Its 15 percent of the company is worth roughly $4.5 billion today.) Even if it wanted to go public, Airbnb likely would need to wait until its legislative and regulatory issues in New York and San Francisco are cleared up. But whenever it chooses to do so, an IPO is where the company is ultimately headed. In 2015 it hired Laurence Tosi, former CFO of the private equity firm Blackstone Group, as CFO.

Chesky says there is less pressure on him from his investors to enter the public markets than people would think, because the company is founder-controlled and has carefully chosen investors who share the founders' vision for their company. "You choose, at the end of the day, who you listen to and the kind of courage you're going to have," Chesky says. "And it's up to us to build the kind of company we want. We're very transparent. We say we're going to build a long-term company. There's risk involved." He says that during meetings with investors in the company's biggest funding round in 2015, he spent ninety minutes explaining the company's vision and culture and its commitment to a long-term horizon. "A bunch of people passed," he said. "That wasn't the kind of company they wanted. They wanted to know we were going to go public in a couple of years. I couldn't give them that view." He says he's doing a lot of things that will actually slow the company down, like spending much of 2016 re-architecting its mobile apps instead of optimizing its website, and incubating the Magical Trips project for two years at considerable investment.

Citing a theory he learned from Reid Hoffman, Chesky says he wants Airbnb to become a "Tier 1" tech company — a company with a multi-hundred-billion-dollar market value, like Apple, Google, Facebook, and Amazon — rather than a "Tier 2" company, those companies with a valuarion of $10 billion to $80 billion, which Airbnb is now. "I think it's hard to be a 2" in the public markets, he says. "You want to grow into a Tier 1." So he wants to grow big enough to become that kind of company. "And I would say that almost all of our investors would say that my ambitions are significantly higher for the company than theirs." Investors familiar with the company say that it has a ten-year goal to become the first online travel company with a $100 billion market value.

But venture capitalists and public markets are different animals, and the latter will care a lot more about the company's ability to continue to sustain its high growth levels and might not want to think in ten-year cycles. They will also likely care a lot more about the regulatory risk, which its venture investors seem less concerned about. Other risks include competition: while Airbnb is dominant, Home-Away has more than 1.2 million listings and a new deep-pocketed owner in Expedia. In 2015, HomeAway announced a push into urban markets — Airbnb's core — with a new Cities Initiative, complete with a collection of city guidebooks with local recommendations. "Airbnb has helped create the market for alternative accommodations, but that doesn't mean they win most of the economics of that market," says RBC Capital Markets analyst Mark Mahaney. "There are two very good operators in Priceline and Expedia and they already have a hell of a lot of traffic."

But the general consensus is that there is plenty of runway for Airbnb. For all its growth, the company has yet to register significant awareness among the general public. Surveys from research firms like Cowen and Goldman Sachs found that fewer than half of respondents had heard of Airbnb; Cowen found that fewer than 10 percent had used it, suggesting that Airbnb could grow two to three times bigger from brand awareness alone. The firm also found that of those who knew of Airbnb but had never used it, more than 80 percent said they would be willing to try it, and 66 percent said they planned to do so within the next year. "We expect Airbnb to become many times larger than it is today and to become one of the largest two to three players in the global lodging industry," the Cowen researchers said. There is also significant opportunity in China among both domestic and outbound Chinese travelers, a group that grew 700 percent on Airbnb in 2015. Smaller U.S. cities and vacation markets are also an important area for growth. "Obviously all companies hit some kind of saturation point," says Reid Hoffman. "And to go and rent an apartment from a different person isn't for everybody. But nominally it could get many orders of magnitude larger than it currently is."

That saturation point is still looking far away: as of this writing, the company was said to be adding 1.4 million guests and forty-five thousand listings per week. Its figure of 140 million total guest arrivals from late 2016 was projected to hit 160 million by February 2017 and to climb past that number soon after. Airbnb doesn't release its financials, but investor estimates put revenue at $1.6 billion for 2016, with earnings before interest, taxes, depreciation, and amortization (EBITDA) of $156 million; $2.8 billion in 2017, with EBITDA of $450 million; and as much as $8.5 billion in revenue and $3.5 billion in EBITDA by 2020.

It is the combination of these numbers, along with the company's efficient business model, its lead in a category with high barriers to entry, its strong founding and management team, and the size of the travel industry — $7.2 trillion — that has kept investors coming back. "What makes [Airbnb] interesting right now is they'll probably be the most successful of this whole crop," says Max Wolff, market strategist for 55 Capital Partners. He says the company is "smarter and more grown up [than some of its tech brethren] and has the potential to be an absolutely transformative killer in hospitality."

The "Stock-Sharing" Economy?

Whenever Airbnb does choose to make its entry into the public markets, there's one group of people outside of Wall Street that will be paying close attention: some of Airbnb's hosts. There's no doubt that many of the millions of Airbnb hosts will see the occasion as a victory and an important milestone for the company that has afforded them an income stream. But some are starting to feel that they should get some shares, too. They helped build the business, after all, and they control the product and experience that makes the platform possible.

Hans Penz and his wife rent out two rooms in their house in Staten Island, New York. Penz, thirty-eight, is a baker and originally started hosting as a way to raise money to grow his business; now, the couple do it because they like the extra income and having people from all over the world stay with them. Penz loves hosting and is one of those people who genuinely believes Airbnb "is making the world a better place." He also feels that hosts, or at least the most engaged hosts, should be able to get pre-IPO shares. "The hosts are the company," he says. He says he's talked about this with other hosts and with the company. He says that if he were one of the company's existing investors, "I would definitely ask the company how they're going to make sure hosts stay with Airbnb and don't decide to start their own business."

When I ask Chesky about this issue, he says the company has looked into it and talked about it internally. He says it's hard to give a million people equity in the private market, where every investor must be given access to the company's financials. "It's not without its complications." This same issue came up way back when eBay went public, but that company in the end did not end up granting shares to its sellers. There are many potential problems with the idea, among them that hosts could wind up unhappy if the stock doesn't perform. That said, if Airbnb doesn't find a way to reward hosts, it could turn the spectacle and celebration of an IPO into a potential moment of resentment for some in the company's most important stakeholder group.

Much bigger questions are these: What happens to the company's soul should it become a public company? What happens to the mission of "belonging"? What happens to changing the world? What happens to "the United Nations at the kitchen table"? Can you have a social mission and be a big behemoth on Wall Street? Plenty of tech-industry giants, of course, claim they have missions. Facebook's is "Make the world more open and connected." Google had "Don't be

evil" until its new parent, Alphabet, changed it to "Do th̶̶̶̶̶̶̶̶
But balancing mission and Wall Street expectations is a tric̶̶̶̶̶

"I really like these guys — they are genuine," says Jessi Hemp̶
head of editorial for the online technology publication *Backchannel,*
about the Airbnb founders. "But the bigger question is, is an Internet company that has to scale a flawed endeavor? If you believe in a
mission, start a nonprofit. Be a Wikipedia, or a Craigslist," she says,
referring to Wikipedia's nonprofit model and what Craigslist refers
to as its noncommercial, public-service nature (it is a for-profit company but did not take venture funding). Hempel's point is that the
moment a technology company takes its first dollar of venture capital, it becomes hostage to investors' desire to maximize returns. "The
peculiar parameters of venture-based start-ups are that the demand
for growth is so important that it takes precedence over everything,"
she says.

Chesky recognizes this conflict. (For a fleeting moment in 2008,
back when he knew nothing about business, Chesky himself felt that
a nonprofit was the right direction.) But he says that as a private company that is founder-controlled and -run, "if you control the board,
it's your decision." Being public is another matter entirely. "I do think
there's an issue with being public that I haven't sorted out," he says.
"The mandate of a public company is to act in the best interest of
your shareholders. But the problem is, you don't pick your shareholders." Their interests might just be short-term returns. "It's hard to
reconcile," he says. He points to strong-willed CEOs like Steve Jobs
and Jeff Bezos: "I don't think Steve ever listened to an investor. And
maybe Bezos has been able to, like, just drown them out. But a lot of
CEOs haven't."

Airbnb investor and board member Jeff Jordan takes a stronger
view. "People think it's evil [to go public or to take venture funding],
but to build an enduring long-term company where your invention
will last for long periods of time, almost all of them are public companies," he says. "Google, Facebook, Alibaba — these are the companies
that are changing the world. If you want to build something that will

last and you want to control your own destiny, going public is the way you do it."

Clearly, Airbnb has grown by leaps and bounds. No one would confuse it with a nonprofit these days. But as any company gets to the size of Airbnb, it inevitably reaches a point of backlash, where its early users start to complain that it has grown too large and has lost the essence of what made it so special in the early days. Some of Airbnb's earliest users, who prided themselves at being in the forefront of a new paradigm and part of a counterculture movement of sorts, take issue with the fact that the company's platform has gotten so big and gone so mainstream.

Rochelle Short, a host in Seattle, started using the site in 2013, became a Superhost, and started a popular blog, *Letting People In* — but, as she recounted in an article on the web outlet *The Verge*, she stopped hosting in 2015, because the people using it had, in her view, become too conventional. "I think the demographic started to change." In 2013, she said, it felt like a true social experiment, "pioneering new territory, attracting people who were open-minded, easygoing, don't worry if there's a fleck on the mirror in the bathroom." She said that by 2016, it "became the vanilla tourist who wanted the Super 8 motel experience. I don't like these travelers as much as [in] the early days." Phil Morris, a host in Barcelona who created the host website Ourbnb, expressed similar sentiment in an oral history of Airbnb published by the producers of the *Get Paid for Your Pad* podcast. "We do feel from time to time that the old Airbnb was much more fun and personable," he said.

Chesky hopes the new foray into trips will help bring back some of that early-adopter sense of social experimentation. The company's Trips product, he says, will allow it to get closer to the company's roots. By better segmenting its business, he hopes that different parts of the site can appeal to different kinds of travelers at the same time. Blecharczyk, too, feels that this is an opportunity for innovation: "How do we make sure we have the right experience for an early community member who loves personal hospitality a host might provide, and also provide it for the person who wants to have a luxury experience? That's the challenge and the opportunity." But the company still has to walk a fine line without seeming too corporate or "vanilla." The Airbnb Open in 2016 had a "presenting partner" for the first time, American Express, as well as secondary sponsors, including Delta.

In fact, the move into Trips may come as a surprise to Airbnb's critics. It lends no further evidence to the argument that the company is secretly seeking the biggest-spending corporate customers at all costs as it races toward an IPO. It's not an evil land grab for more homes or more commercial properties. Chesky says that if the company wanted to be big at all costs, it could have easily done so with its existing platform. "We have such low penetration of housing and hospitality that if we just wanted to be big, we could be big," he says. Instead, the expansion into the trips business is a move that doubles down on the "uniqueness" element of Airbnb, at least for now. (While the company may eventually face a similar issue of professional tour operators seeking to offer their experiences on the Trips platform, for now all experiences are approved and vetted by Airbnb.) If this is the future of Airbnb, it is one that seems to lend itself to less pushback from entrenched industries.

Still, opposition to Airbnb has only grown stronger. When I spoke to a number of parties engaged on the opposition effort as this book was heading to the printer, they told me they believe Airbnb continues to mask the true numbers of dedicated rentals and so-called illegal hotels on its site. Airbnb continues to say the data that's been put out there is misleading, it wants nothing to do with that business, and it's doing everything it can to stop it, including releasing more of its own data. Chesky says he believes he will be proved right over time. "I think the truth is going to come out," he says. "History has a way of being more wise and more truthful than the present, because the present is cloudy and foggy." But as the company and its platform base continue to get bigger, the issues around the way Airbnb has impacted some communities will likely intensify, too. "Even for those who love Airbnb, what's going on in Reykjavik feels kind of devastating," says *Backchannel*'s Hempel, speaking of the housing challenges brought on by the rapid rise of short-term rentals in that market that the company and its peers have enabled.

Chesky has taken one big lesson away from the experience: he planned the next chapter of Airbnb's business assuming it would face enemies. When the founders started Airbnb, they had no assumption that it would become so big or so polarizing and so detested. This time around, Chesky says he has been designing the new Trips business with that assumption baked in — and with "eyes wide open" to all possible consequences the business could have on neighborhoods and established players. "Having lived through eight years in homes, and all the protests and the criticisms, this is not going to be without its critics," he says. Now, with access to the top legal and policy minds, he designed against possible backlash. "Social-good" experiences, conceived in concert with local nonprofits, represent 10 percent of the experiences Airbnb will offer. The company has an ambitious partnership with the Make-A-Wish Foundation to host "wish trips" and help build experiences. And Chesky and his team deliberately chose cities to launch Airbnb's experiences business in by picking those they felt would most benefit and most welcome it, like Nairobi, Detroit, Havana, and Cape Town. "We're not launching in New York," he says. (He says they included San Francisco, one of its conflict markets, in the launch only because the company needed to be able to test the product in its own backyard.)

The regulatory uncertainty around Airbnb's core product has not stopped businesses from planning for a future with the home-rental giant in it. In some markets, landlords have already begun pricing the expectation of an Airbnb revenue stream into the rents they charge. Builders are designing apartment complexes with shareable layouts and fewer parking spaces (not to mention landing pads for Amazon drones on the roof). KB Home, one of the nation's biggest home builders, has designed a new prototype with "Airbnb-inspired" bedrooms, with beds and desks that fold up and moveable walls that can convert, say, half of a living room into a spare bedroom. Subscribers to home-design catalogs may have noticed increasing space given to the display of products like sleeper sofas designed to make it easier to host "guests."

Back at the Airbnb mother ship, employees are working on the company's next big iterations. The engineering and product teams are doubling down on improving the company's matching technology, using machine learning and artificial intelligence to better help predict not only hosts' and guests' behavior patterns, based on prior booking behavior on the site, but also their individual personal and aesthetic preferences (whether you prefer ultramodern or classical architecture, whether your music tastes trend toward Rachmaninoff or The Weeknd). There is a new tool that lets hosts enlist a "co-host" to help run their listing and share revenue. Gebbia's innovation teams, meanwhile, are focused on creating more new concepts within the Samara unit, like a current project to try to develop a non-networked method of communication designed for large migrating groups of people such as refugees, who have phones but who lose access to power.

Chesky and Gebbia are also working on creating new metrics for the company's performance. Currently, its "North Star" is how many nights it has booked, but because the quality of those nights is all over the map, they are hoping to get at something that's a better measure for, yes, belonging. When I asked how the Trips product fits in with the company's business goals, Chesky turned to me and said, "The end business goal, our mission, is to create a world where you can belong anywhere."

There hasn't been a company quite like Airbnb. It has grown from zero to $30 billion in value in nine years. It has taken an old idea and popularized it on a scale not really seen since eBay first came up with an online version of the flea market. Few leaders have zoomed to the top of the business world with as little prior management experience as Chesky, Gebbia, and Blecharczyk. And all while growing a business that is far more complex than it seems on the surface: there's a reason Sequoia's Doug Leone told Chesky he has the hardest job of any CEO in the firm's portfolio. While many other disruptive technology companies have blazed polarizing paths, it's hard to think of a modern conflict between business and regulators, or between old industry and new industry, that has gotten as emotional and as heated as the fight over Airbnb. All for a business built around a concept that, at first blush, most people thought was really weird.

The business has had ripple effects beyond its own business. CEOs with a design background are now considered desirable by venture funds looking for the next hot thing, much in the same way that two PhDs from Stanford or a social-networking entrepreneur from Harvard had become the de facto model in the wake of the successes of Google and Facebook. Many of the investors who said no or almost said no have reformatted the way they evaluate pitches.

By every account, Airbnb should never have happened. It was three guys who came up with a business idea quite accidentally, while looking for something else they hoped would be the next big thing. They had little business experience and remain self-taught. They did things that, by conventional business standards, would be counterintuitive: instead of focusing on growing their business as fast as they could in the early days, they showered all of their attention and resources on a tiny number of users three thousand miles away. They invested in the expensive, cumbersome service of providing individual professional photography to every customer who wanted it. They made something that was seen as odd and strange and fraught with all kinds of risks into something not only acceptable but viral. It is a rags-to-riches story on a major scale.

They did all these things with a rare combination of skills that enabled them to overcome huge obstacles and to conquer issues that might have been too complex for another trio: creating a global payments platform, building a search-and-matching methodology, sketching out systems that would, if not eliminate risk, then foster as much safety as they could — all innovations that were later incorporated as standards on other similar platforms. Their quirky idea paired with a smooth, fast, friendly, and easy-to-navigate site quickly found a hungry audience. And then they took all this and scaled. It is often overlooked how Airbnb was and remains an execution machine.

The three founders had hustle, of course, which is why they didn't give up when the business failed to take off after three launches, and why they ambushed early advisers like Michael Seibel and Paul Graham for time, advice, and feedback. And they had plenty of moxie and nerve, whether it was smooth-talking their way into the design conference in 2007 by saying they were bloggers; or entering markets where their business was illegal; or standing up to forces others might have found too threatening by saying no to the Samwer brothers' request to buy them; or resisting the New York State attorney general when he issued them with a subpoena.

They made plenty of mistakes along the way and in eight years have probably learned a lifetime of lessons. More mistakes, and bigger lessons, are no doubt still to come. More bad things will happen on Airbnb. At the same time, the competition is closing in: HomeAway is inching into Airbnb's core market, the traditional hotel industry is slowly moving in on the "alternative accommodations" category that it once mocked, and a new crop of upstarts is coming up with ideas for experimental hybrids and twists on the idea. Lots and lots can happen from here.

Chesky, Gebbia, and Blecharczyk also got a giant assist from entering the market at the right time — and from a consuming public that was ready for an unorthodox idea like Airbnb to take off. The Great Recession had weakened the spending power of consumers on a global level just as cities were becoming increasingly expensive places to live. The surge of millennials and their dramatically different value system represented a fertile consumer base, with their preference for authentic experiences over things, their anticorporate and antiestablishment leanings, their hunger for anything that claimed to have a purpose or mission, and their desire to seek out community wherever they could find it. The chance to connect, the spirit of adventure, the quirky product, and the low prices that Airbnb offered were a no-brainer. And, thanks to social media and this generation's having grown up conditioned to believe that anyone can instantly be a "friend," they also were already accustomed to instant intimacy; it wasn't that odd for them to use those same platforms to reserve a room inside someone's home.

There are specific reasons that Airbnb took off among the rest of us nonmillennials, too — namely, a long, slow, general decline of human connection in today's complicated world. A growing separation of society had already pushed people into solitary boxes, whether in big suburban homes, in cars on grinding daily commutes, or, increasingly, into our own solitary smartphone trances. This goes even deeper: as Sebastian Junger points out in his book *Tribe*, we are the first modern society in human history where people live alone in apartments and where children have their own bedrooms. The gradual decline of trust in societal institutions over the years, meanwhile, from business to government, accelerated in the wake of the Great Recession, making people more receptive to a "fringe" idea than they might otherwise have been (see Bernie Sanders and President Donald Trump). Add on a growing sense of unease over geopolitical risk and the sense that horrible and unpredictable things are happening in the world, and the urge to connect with others becomes an unarticulated desire in all of us. Whatever you think about "belonging," these forces really were a large part of what made people more open to trying this new, quirky, affordable travel experience. Airbnb touched on so many different things at once that it's hard to imagine its taking off in the same way at any other time.

As odd as this whole crazy story is, and for everything they've been through, the founders don't really get very nostalgic. "Who has time?" Gebbia said to me when I asked him the question. Chesky has little time for reflection either, though one moment that he has said stands out for him was when his parents visited the Rausch Street apartment for the first time after they'd started the business and saw that what their son had been talking about for so long was an actual company, with multiple chairs around a table. Chesky's father, who had not been convinced this was a good move, saw the first proof that they had a real business. "It was a pretty moving moment," Chesky said, recounting the moment to a group of new Airbnb hires.

In the present day, there is too much to keep busy with. The founders are settling into their new roles and getting ready for the next leg of the wild ride they've been on, with the company's big pivot. They have started to come to terms with the kind of responsibility that comes with the wealth they have amassed (each of the three is said to be worth $3.3 billion). They have all joined the elite group of billionaires who have signed the Giving Pledge, the campaign created by Warren Buffett and Bill and Melinda Gates to encourage the über-wealthy to commit to giving away the majority of their wealth in their lifetimes. In addition to his new role at the company, Blecharczyk has another responsibility, as a father; he and his wife have a toddler. In addition to starting Samara and the experimental lab, Gebbia has been spending a lot of time on the company's involvement with solutions to the global refugee crisis. That includes providing accommodations to relief workers in Greece and Serbia and launching a "livelihood" program in Jordan that helps refugees living in camps earn income by giving tours and providing other "local experiences" to travelers visiting Jordan. In the fall of 2016, Gebbia joined a group of private-sector leaders — including George and Amal Clooney — in a roundtable discussion with President Obama to discuss solutions to the crisis. (Gebbia still occasionally gets an order for his CritBuns seat cushions, and in those moments he goes into his garage, where he pulls out a roll of packing tape, carefully assembles a box, and ships them off.)

In recent years, Chesky says he has learned to step back and try to find more balance. A lot of that is due to his relationship with Elissa Patel, his girlfriend of four years. The two met on Tinder in 2013 — their first date almost didn't happen because of an iMessage glitch — and he says that she has gotten him to change some of his habits; for example, his compulsion with answering e-mails. (She has told him that his behavior with e-mail resembles the way a dog is with dog food: "She tells me, 'You would eat the whole bag if you could,'" he says.)

Chesky, Gebbia, and Blecharczyk are all fully aware that what happened to them happened against all odds. "We weren't visionaries," as Chesky told me in one of our earliest conversations. "We are ordinary guys. And this isn't that crazy of an idea."

But it's also true that not just any three ordinary guys could have pulled off what they pulled off. "We had instincts and we had courage," Chesky says. But he thinks one of their biggest strengths was precisely how little they knew. "I think if we knew better, we probably would have known better than to do this," he says. "Because in hindsight, everything had to click. Like, it was kind of a weird million-to-one shot. And if we lived another thousand lives, it would be hard to imagine if everything were to click in the same way."

Epilogue

THE ORPHEUM THEATER in downtown Los Angeles is packed by the time Chesky takes the stage. He is standing in front of some two thousand hosts, guests, press, and Airbnb employees. In a highly stylized keynote, he walks the audience through the company's big reveal: a vast menu of five hundred new, bookable experiences, ranging from burlesque dancing to astrophotography to Korean embroidery, all hosted by locals. Chesky unveils a whole suite of bells and whistles: local meetups, restaurant reservations, recommendation tools organized by passion (gluten-free Los Angeles, anyone?), a series of guided audio walks. He teases that car rentals, add-on services, and something involving flights are coming soon. It will all live on the new Trips platform, of which homes will be just one part. "Everything that we do, and everything that we will do, will be powered by people," he says.

The audience members cheered and rose to their feet. They were a concentrated core of the most engaged members of the Airbnb community: The hosts who made the pilgrimage to LA had sheltered a collective 745,000 guests among them, and over the next three days, they were drenched in all things Airbnb. They heard CMO Jonathan Mildenhall talk about building the "world's first community super-brand." They learned about the company's social good efforts, got interior design tips, and communed with the data science team at the Dashboard & Insights Bar. James Corden had a field day ribbing the Airbnb concept during the Bélo awards, accusing the audience of secretly staying in hotels and insisting that he'd caught the founders trying to make some extra cash by renting out their front-row seats. Later that night, there was even a surprise performance by Lady Gaga.

And yet amid all the festivities, there was an undercurrent of the serious challenges still facing the company. After Chris Lehane's talk, during which he reported that Airbnb community members had formed more than 100 home-sharing clubs and sent 350,000 emails to elected officials in 2016, a number of hosts lined up at microphones to ask pressing questions: why did New York institute "draconian rules"; what can the company do to fix it; and, more importantly, *can* the company fix it? A Superhost from Dallas asked: How we can be great neighbors when regulators' biggest concern is party houses?

Outside on the last day, members of the local Unite Here hotel workers union staged a loud and angry protest, marching down South Broadway waving signs, banging a drum, honking horns, and shouting through a bullhorn. Moments later, during a fireside chat between Chesky and Ashton Kutcher, a protester crashed the event and made her way onto the stage, decrying the company's listings in Israeli-occupied settlements in the West Bank. (Kutcher leapt from his chair and defused the protester with a friendly greeting before launching into an impassioned plea for Airbnb: "If we share our homes with one another, we can get to know each other and bring each other together in a peaceful unity that doesn't have borders!" he shouted as the audience members rose again to their feet. "This company is about bringing people together and about loving one another!")

But the disruptions were hardly noticed by most attendees. The final session of the last day was a Q&A with the Airbnb founders. The hard work of the new platform launch was behind them and they were finally able to relax and even reminisce a bit about the company's earliest days. Chesky and Gebbia recalled Blecharczyk's state of almost constant exasperation with their ideas. They told the story of the investor presentation they put together one night that projected their revenue three years in at $200 million. When Blecharczyk told them that number was ridiculous and investors would see right through it, Chesky and Gebbia agreed to change it to $20 million. But the next day, when the slide appeared during the pitch, it read $2.5 billion. ("I wish we had a picture of Nate's face as he was sitting in front of a VC with us saying the market size was $2 billion," Gebbia said. Blecharczyk pointed out the number referred not to market size, but to the company's revenue: "There's a big difference.")

It was a rare moment of nostalgia just at the moment the company was stepping into the future. But the past may always be with this company. As big as Airbnb has become, the odd, strange peculiarity of the original idea — letting strangers sleep in other strangers' homes — is something that still runs through its DNA. This, too, was reflected in the conversations on stage. "Being an early adopter involves being brave," Gebbia had told the audience earlier. "It means being OK with being called 'weird.'" He pointed out that when cars were first invented, regulators forced them to go four miles an hour, and that even the fork was once considered the "tool of the devil." Lehane, for his part, compared resistance to Airbnb with resistance to the introduction of electric street lights in the late 1800s.

It makes for a fascinating study in the trajectory of a disrupter. Airbnb is one of the largest privately held technology companies ever, in the midst of a major step into new businesses, with many of the biggest names in the corporate world behind it. And yet it's a company that is, in many ways, part of a fringe counterculture still in search of recognition.

Time will tell whether the new Airbnb businesses are a success. After the Open, it was right back to business as usual — which included, in New York City, beginning to figure out exactly what working with the city on enforcement would look like.

Navigating all of this is precisely the challenge that comes with bold ideas and big change, and it should be no surprise that the challenge only becomes bigger and the stakes higher the larger the disrupter gets. As Gebbia pointed out in his talk, there are "no blueprints" for what the company is doing. "With global hosting, we're charting new territory," he said. Nine years in, Airbnb is indeed still doing just that — with all the attendant opportunities and consequences. And for that reason, as colorful and complex and successful and fraught as this company's history has been so far, the Airbnb story is likely still just beginning.

Acknowledgments

This book came together quickly and with a village of help, but there are two people without whom it would not exist. The first is Rick Wolff at Houghton Mifflin Harcourt, to whom I am indebted for his passion for the project, his vision and skillful editing, and his patience. The second is *Fortune* editor and Time Inc. chief content officer Alan Murray, who immediately and generously agreed to give me the time needed to pursue this book even though *Fortune* did not have resources to spare. That Alan did not bat an eye shows his commitment to storytelling, and I am indebted to him for it.

I have long thought the Airbnb story was one waiting to be told, and I'm extremely grateful to Brian Chesky for trusting me to tell it and for opening the doors to his company to me. I'm thankful to Joe Gebbia and Nathan Blecharczyk for the same and for sharing their perspectives. My deepest gratitude to Kim Rubey, who was a champion of this project from day one and who worked swiftly to make it happen, and to Maggie Carr for calmly and capably steering me through dozens of interviews and mountains (and mountains) of questions. My thanks also go to the rest of the Airbnb communications team, and to the Airbnb executives and employees who spent time with me. (Thanks, too, to the company and to Jonathan Mann for permission to reprint lyrics from the "Obama O's" jingle.)

Thanks to Melissa Flashman at Trident Media Group for her

enthusiasm and expert guidance, and to Lew Korman for his wise counsel. I'm grateful to the talented and supportive team at Houghton Mifflin Harcourt: Rosemary McGuinness, Debbie Engel, Emily Andrukaitis, Loren Isenberg, Megan Wilson, and to the grace and patience of Rachael DeShano, Kelly Dubeau Smydra, and Tammy Zambo. Special thanks go to Jamie Joseph of Virgin Books for his keen interest in the project.

I am indebted to Nicole Pasulka, who contributed invaluable reporting help and counsel and then fact-checked the book on a super-tight timeframe as if it were her own. Deep thanks go to High Water Press, i.e., Brian Dumaine and Hank Gilman, for fast and skillful reads and edits, and to Jonathan Chew and Tracy Z. Maleef for their research. And special thanks to Mary Schein, who always makes everything easier.

I'm grateful to Clifton Leaf and my colleagues at *Fortune* who made do without me for a stretch — especially Mason Cohn and the talented and unflappable Megan Arnold, who kept *Fortune Live* humming (with critical hosting assists from Andrew Nusca, Aaron Task, and Anne VanderMey). Pattie Sellers, Nina Easton, Jennifer Reingold, Lisa Clucas, Elizabeth Busch, Michal Lev-Ram, Beth Kowitt, Leena Rao, Kristen Bellstrom, and Valentina Zarya held down the MPW fort, and Leena also steered the 40 Under 40. Additional thanks to *Fortune* colleagues including Adam Lashinsky, Brian O'Keefe, Nick Varchaver, Matt Heimer, Erin Griffith, Kia Kokolitcheva, Scott De-Carlo, Michael Joseloff, Kelly Champion, and Kerri Chyka.

Many others contributed help or guidance along the way: Bethany McLean, Doris Burke, John Brodie, Peter Kafka, Dan Primack, Joanne Gordon, Kate Kelly, Sarah Ellison, Rana Foroohar, Charles Duhigg, Alison Brower, Laura Brounstein, Todd Shuster, Rimjhim Dey, Dan Roberts, Deb Roth, Davidson Goldin, Verona Carter, Alice Marshall, Irina Woelfle, and April Roberts. Arun Sundararajan, Jason Clampet, Bill Hyers, Jessi Hempel, Will Silverman, Jana Rich, Scott Shatford, Jamie Lane, Maryam Banikarim, Sheila Riordan, Kathleen O'Neill, Raina Wallens, Kathleen Maher, and Bethany Lampland were all generous with their insight and perspectives. I'm grateful to Marc Andreessen, Reid Hoffman, Alfred Lin, Jeff Jordan, Paul Graham, Michael Seibel, Kevin Hartz, Sam Angus, Greg Mc-Adoo, and others close to Airbnb for sharing their knowledge about the company. Deep thanks to Neil Carlson and Erin Carney and their Brooklyn Creative League for providing an inspiring and welcoming place to work.

And lastly, thanks to my family: to all the Kreiters, especially Gil, Noa, and Ava for putting up with my absences, and Zeb and Anna for always being interested. Thanks to Drew and Adrienne for their support from afar, and Jake and Rocky Gallagher for inspiring videos and general cuteness. Thanks to my parents, Jack and Joan Gallagher, for their support as always, and to the extended Gallagher and Pelizoto clans, especially Carl and Daryl. And to Gil, my deepest thanks go to you for providing perspective, support, and endless amounts of Blue Apron dinners and strong coffee. I owe you a really nice vacation, whether it's in a fancy hotel or an Airbnb treehouse — you pick.

Notes

Unless otherwise noted, all quotes in the text are from my own direct interviews.

Chapter 1: The Hustle

page

2   *cheeky bathroom humor:* The RISD hockey team was called the Nads (preferred cheer: "go-NADS!"); the basketball team was called the Balls (slogan: "When the heat's on, the Balls stick together"). The teams' mascot was Scrotie.

     "sporting event on a Friday night?": Austin Carr, "Watch Airbnb CEO Brian Chesky Salute RISD, Whip Off His Robe, Dance like Michael Jackson," *Fast Company*, February 17, 2012, https://www.fastcompany.com/1816858/watch-airbnb-ceo-brian-chesky-salute-risd-whip-his-robe-dance-michael-jackson.

5   *"'they said it would be at RISD'":* Sarah Lacy, "Fireside Chat with Airbnb CEO Brian Chesky," *PandoDaily*, YouTube video, posted January 14, 2013, https://www.youtube.com/watch?v=6yPfxcqEXhE.

7   *trapped in his job:* Ibid.

10   *in his underwear:* Ibid.

11   *friends would ask:* Reid Hoffman, "Blitzscaling 18: Brian Chesky on Launching Airbnb and the Challenges of Scale," Stanford University, November 30, 2015, https://www.youtube.com/watch?v=W608u6sBFpo.

13   *("until we got customers"):* Ibid.

18   *"travel related businesses":* Brian Chesky, "7 Rejections," *Medium*, July 12, 2015, https://medium.com/@bchesky/7-rejections-7d894cbaa084#.5dgyegvgz.

19   *Urban Land Institute:* Brian Chesky and Connie Moore, "Impact of the

Sharing Economy on Real Estate," Urban Land Institute Fall Meeting, October 6, 2015, https://www.youtube.com/watch?v=03kSzmJr5c0.

20 *losing their patient:* Brian Chesky, "1000 days of AirBnB," Startup School 2010, YouTube, uploaded February 12, 2013, https://www.youtube .com/watch?v=L03vBkOKTrc.

21 "have some please?": "Obama O's," YouTube, uploaded January 12, 2012, https://www.youtube.com/watch?v=OQTWimfGfV8.

22 *to launch Facebook:* Lacy, "Fireside Chat."

24 *"I just ruined it,"' says Chesky:* Ibid.

25 *as* Fortune *called it:* Leena Rao, "Meet Y Combinator's New COO," *Fortune,* August 26, 2015, http://fortune.com/2015/08/26/meet-y-combinators -new-coo/.

28 *(log on to his account):* Brian Chesky, "1000 days of AirBnB," Startup School 2010, YouTube, uploaded February 12, 2013, https://www.youtube .com/watch?v=L03vBkOKTrc.

Chapter 2: Building a Company

35 *"How to Start a Startup":* Sam Altman, "How to Start a Startup," lecture with Alfred Lin and Brian Chesky, video, accessed October 10, 2016, http:// startupclass.samaltman.com/courses/lec10/.

36 *(six new core values in 2013):* The six core values put in place in 2013 were "Host," "Champion the Mission," "Every Frame Matters," "Be a cereal entrepreneur," "Simplify," and "Embrace the Adventure."

41 *in the first half of 2016 alone:* "Uber Loses at Least $1.2 Billion in First Half of 2016," *Bloomberg BusinessWeek,* August 25, 2016, https://www .bloomberg.com/news/articles/2016-08-25/uber-loses-at-least-1-2-billion -in-first-half-of-2016.

45 *a surge in bookings:* Owen Thomas, "How a Caltech Ph.D. Turned Airbnb into a Billion-Dollar Travel Magazine," *Business Insider,* June 28, 2012, http://www.businessinsider.com/airbnb-joe-zadeh-photography -program-2012-6.

46 *according to TechCrunch:* M. G. Siegler, "Airbnb Tucked In Nearly 800% Growth in 2010; Caps Off The Year with a Slick Video," TechCrunch, January 6, 2011, https://techcrunch.com/2011/01/06/airbnb-2010/.

47 *just $7.8 million:* Tricia Duryee, "Airbnb Raises $112 Million for Vacation Rental Business," AllThingsD, July 24, 2011, http://allthingsd .com/20110724/airbnb-raises-112-million-for-vacation-rental-business/.

48 *Lacy, then at TechCrunch:* "Brian Chesky on the Success of Airbnb," interview by Sarah Lacy, TechCrunch, video, December 26, 2011, https:// techcrunch.com/video/brian-chesky-on-the-success-of-airbnb/517158894/.

49   *claimed ten thousand listings:* Alexia Tsotsis, "Airbnb Freaks Out Over Wimdu," TechCrunch, June 9, 2011, https://techcrunch.com/2011/06/09 /airbnb.

("Technology-Enabled Blitzscaling"): Reid Hoffman, "Blitzscaling 18: Brian Chesky on Launching Airbnb and the Challenges of Scale," Stanford University, November 30, 2015, https://www.youtube.com /watch?v=W608u6sBFpo.

55   *"How do I not die?"":* Ibid.

Chapter 3: Airbnb Nation

59   *Punta Mita, Mexico:* Francesca Bacardi, "No Resort Necessary! Gwyneth Paltrow Uses Airbnb for Mexican Vacation with Her Kids and Boyfriend Brad Falchuk," *E! News,* E! Online, January 19, 2016, http://www.eonline .com/news/732247/no-resort-necessary-gwyneth-paltrow-uses-airbnb-for -mexican-vacation-with-her-kids-and-boyfriend-brad-falchuk.

$10,000 per night: Carrie Goldberg, "Inside Gwyneth Paltrow's Latest Airbnb Villa," *Harper's Bazaar,* June 23, 2016, http://www.harpersbazaar .com/culture/travel-dining/news/a16287/gwyneth-paltrow-airbnb-france/.

61   *"on Airbnb?":* Greg Tannen, "Airbnb-Tenant Reviews of the Candidates," *The New Yorker,* July 8, 2016, http://www.newyorker.com/humor/daily -shouts/airbnb-tenant-reviews-of-the-candidates.

"Dreams Come True": Natalya Lobanova, "18 Fairytale Airbnb Castles That'll Make Your Dreams Come True," BuzzFeed, June 15, 2016, https:// www.buzzfeed.com/natalyalobanova/scottish-airbnb-castles-you-can -actually-rent?utm_term=.ss2Kvbx6J#.abpLnz0PW.

64   *"yearning to belong":* Brian Chesky, "Belong Anywhere," Airbnb, July 16, 2014, http://blog.airbnb.com/belong-anywhere/.

65   *"hippy-dippy concept":* Ryan Lawler, "Airbnb Launches Massive Redesign, with Reimagined Listings and a Brand New Logo," TechCrunch, July 16, 2014, https://techcrunch.com/2014/07/16/airbnb-redesign/.

66   *("equal-opportunity genitalia"):* Douglas Atkin, "How to Create a Powerful Community Culture," presentation, October 30, 2014, http:// www.slideshare.net/FeverBee/douglas-atkin-how-to-create-a-powerful -community-culture.

68   *wander the globe:* Prerna Gupta, "Airbnb Lifestyle: The Rise of the Hipster Nomad," TechCrunch, October 3, 2014, https://techcrunch.com /2014/10/03/airbnb-lifestyle-the-rise-of-the-hipster-nomad/.

69   *most e-mailed articles that week:* Steven Kurutz, "A Grand Tour with 46 Oases," *New York Times,* February 25, 2015, http://www.nytimes.com /2015/02/26/garden/retirement-plan-an-airbnb-travel-adventure.html.

Chapter 4: The Bad and the Ugly

81 *floors, walls, and furniture:* Julie Bort, "An Airbnb Guest Held a Huge Party in This New York Penthouse and Trashed It," *Business Insider,* March 18, 2014, http://www.businessinsider.com/how-an-airbnb-guest-trashed-a-penthouse-2014-3.

90 *Airbnb in Madrid:* Ron Lieber, "Airbnb Horror Story Points to Need for Precautions," *New York Times,* August 14, 2015, http://www.nytimes.com/2015/08/15/your-money/airbnb-horror-story-points-to-need-for-precautions.html.

91 *(cleared of charges):* Ibid.

on Cosmopolitan.com: Laura Beck, "If You've Ever Stayed in an Airbnb, You Have to Read This Horrifying Tale," Cosmopolitan.com, August, 15, 2015, http://www.cosmopolitan.com/lifestyle/a44908/if-youve-ever-stayed-in-an-airbnb-you-have-to-read-this/.

93 *the author Tim Ferriss:* "Chris Sacca on Being Different and Making Billions," interview by Tim Ferriss, *The Tim Ferriss Show,* podcast audio, February 19, 2016, http://fourhourworkweek.com/2015/05/30/chris-sacca/.

96 *vacation together:* Zak Stone, "Living and Dying on Airbnb," *Medium,* November 8, 2015, https://medium.com/matter/living-and-dying-on-airbnb-6bff8d600c04#.8vp51qatc.

carbon monoxide: Ibid.

98 *a USA Today investigation:* Gary Stoller, "Hotel Guests Face Carbon Monoxide Risk," *USA Today,* January 8, 2013, http://www.usatoday.com/story/travel/hotels/2012/11/15/hotels-carbon-monoxide/1707789/.

An earlier study: Lindell K. Weaver and Kayla Deru, "Carbon Monoxide Poisoning at Motels, Hotels, and Resorts," *American Journal of Preventative Medicine,* July 2007.

According to the National Fire Protection Association: Richard Campbell, "Structure Fires in Hotels and Motels," National Fire Protection Association, September 2015.

100 *relative to nonblack hosts:* Benjamin Edelman and Michael Luca, "Digital Discrimination: The Case of Airbnb.com," Harvard Business School Working Paper, no. 14-054, January 2014.

compared with white guests: Benjamin Edelman, Michael Luca, and Dan Svirsky, "Racial Discrimination in the Sharing Economy: Evidence from a Field Experiment," *American Economic Journal: Applied Economics,* September 16, 2016, https://ssrn.com/abstract=2701902.

101 *rejections stopped:* Shankar Vedantam, Maggie Penman, and Max Nesterak, "#AirbnbWhileBlack: How Hidden Bias Shapes the Sharing Economy," *Hidden Brain,* NPR, podcast audio, April 26, 2016, http://www

.npr.org/2016/04/26/475623339/-airbnbwhileblack-how-hidden-bias
-shapes-the-sharing-economy.

"your XXX head": Elizabeth Weise, "Airbnb Bans N. Carolina Host as
Accounts of Racism Rise," *USA Today*, June 2, 2016, http://www.usa
today.com/story/tech/2016/06/01/airbnb-bans-north-carolina-host
-racism/85252190/.

102 *the experts' recommendations:* Laura W. Murphy, *Airbnb's Work to Fight
Discrimination and Build Inclusion*, report to Airbnb, September 8, 2016,
http://blog.airbnb.com/wp-content/uploads/2016/09/REPORT_Airbnbs
-Work-To-Fight-Discrimination-and -Build-Inclusion.pdf.

104 *"we would probably not accomplish our mission":* "Airbnb Just Hit 100
Million Guest Arrivals," onstage discussion with Brian Chesky and Belinda
Johnson, moderated by Andrew Nusca, at *Fortune*'s Brainstorm Tech confer-
ence, Aspen, Colorado, uploaded on July 12, 2016, https://www.youtube.com
/watch?v=7DU0kns5MbQ&list=PLS8YLn_6PU1no6n71efLRzqS6lXAZp
AuW&index=25.

Chapter 5: Air Rage

108 *fines totaling $40,000:* Ron Lieber, "A Warning for Hosts of Airbnb
Travelers," *New York Times*, November 30, 2012, http://www.nytimes
.com/2012/12/01/your-money/a-warning-for-airbnb-hosts-who-may
-be-breaking-the-law.html.

110 *revenue of $6.8 million:* New York State attorney general Eric T.
Schneiderman, *Airbnb in the City*, New York State Office of the Attorney
General, October 2014, http://www.ag.ny.gov/pdfs/Airbnb%20report
.pdf.

111 *data-and-analytics reports:* Scott Shatford, "2015 in Review — Airbnb
Data for the USA," Airdna, January 7, 2016, http://blog.airdna.co/2015
-in-review-airbnb-data-for-the-usa/.

in November 2013: Jason Clampet, "Airbnb's Most Notorious Landlord
Settles with New York City," *Skift*, November 19, 2013, https://skift
.com/2013/11/19/airbnbs-most-notorious-landlord-settles-with-new
-york-city/.

twenty-two mattresses: Ben Yakas, "Check Out This 'Luxury' Manhattan
2BR with 22 Beds," Gothamist, August 29, 2014, http://gothamist.com
/2014/08/29/check_out_this_luxury_manhatt.php

thirty-five dollars a night: Christopher Robbins, "3-Bedroom Apartment
Transformed into 10-Bedroom Airbnb Hostel," Gothamist, December 10,
2015, http://gothamist.com/2015/12/10/airbnb_queens_hostel.php.

112 *the end of the ad:* "Meet Carol: AirbnbNYC TV Spot," Airbnb Action,

YouTube, uploaded July 16, 2014, https://www.youtube.com/watch?
v=TniQ4OKeQhY.

113 *(to do the study):* "Airbnb: A New Resource for Middle Class Families,"
Airbnb Action, October 19, 2015, https://www.airbnbaction.com/report
-new-resource-middle-class-families/.

114 *on affordable housing:* "The Airbnb Community Compact," Airbnb
Action, November 11, 2015, https://www.airbnbaction.com/compact
detaileden/.

*forty-one per year: Growing the Economy, Helping Families Pay the
Bills: Analysis of Economic Impacts, 2014,* findings report, Airbnb, May 2015,
https://1zxiw0vqx0oryvpz3ikczauf-wpengine.netdna-ssl.com/wp-content
/uploads/2016/02/New-York-City_Impact-Report_2015.pdf.

rental housing by 10 percent: BJH Advisors LLC, *Short Changing New
York City: The Impact of Airbnb on New York City's Housing Market,* Share
Better, June 2016, https://www.sharebetter.org/wp-content/uploads
/2016/06/NYCHousingReport_Final.pdf

a few months earlier: "One Host, One Home: New York City (October
Update)," Airbnb, October 2016, https://www.airbnbaction.com/wp-content
/uploads/2016/11/Data-Release-October-2016-Writeup-1.pdf.

117 *(in some vacation-rental markets):* Drew Fitzgerald, "Airbnb Moves into
Professional Vacation Rentals," *Wall Street Journal,* May 19, 2015, http://
www.wsj.com/articles/airbnb-signals-expansion-into-professional-vacation
-rentals-1432051843.

119 *renting their units out on Airbnb:* Andrew J. Hawkins, "Landlord Related Cos. Cracks Down on Airbnb," *Crain's New York Business,* October 2, 2014,
http://www.crainsnewyork.com/article/20141002/BLOGS04/141009955
/landlord-related-cos-cracks-down-on-airbnb.

120 *"he's trying to punk me":* Mike Vilensky, "Airbnb Wins Big-Name Allies
in Albany Battle," *Wall Street Journal,* August 9, 2016, http://www.wsj.com
/articles/airbnb-wins-big-name-allies-in-albany-battle-1470788320.

"ignore state law": Rich Bockmann, "Airbnb Is Not Taking It Lying
Down," *The Real Deal,* March 1, 2016, http://therealdeal.com/issues_articles
/as-opponents-line-up-airbnb-fights-to-win-legitimacy-in-nyc/.

(snarky voice-over): "New Ad Highlights Airbnb's Problem with the
Law, from Los Angeles to New York, San Francisco to Chicago and Everywhere in Between," Share Better, accessed October 9, 2016, http://www
.sharebetter.org/story/share-better-releases-new-ad-airbnb-problems-every
where/.

the authors wrote: Rosa Goldensohn, "Council Members Threaten Ashton Kutcher, Jeff Bezos with Airbnb Crackdown," *Crain's New York
Business,* March 11, 2016, http://www.crainsnewyork.com/article/20160311

/BLOGS04/160319990/new-york-city-council-threaten-ashton-kutcher
-jeff-bezos-with-airbnb-crackdown.

as "theatrics": Ibid.

("#RunFromAirbnb"): Lisa Fickenscher, "Activists Call on Brooklyn Half
Organizers to Dump Airbnb as Sponsor," *New York Post,* May 20, 2016, http:
//nypost.com/2016/05/20/activists-call-on-brooklyn-half-organizers-to
-dump-airbnb-as-sponsor/.

122   *"to see an organization lose":* Erin Durkin, "Airbnb Foes Celebrate Win
after Gov. Cuomo Signs Home-Sharing Bill, Orders Company to Drop Lawsuit Blocking Legislation," *New York Daily News,* November 1, 2016, http:
//www.nydailynews.com/news/politics/airbnb-foes-win-cuomo-signs-bill
-orders-biz-drop-suit-article-1.2854479.

125   *(about the rules):* David Lumb, "Chicago Allows Airbnb to Operate
Under Restrictions," *Engadget,* June 23, 2016, https://www.engadget
.com/2016/06/23/chicago-allows-airbnb-to-operate-under-restrictions/.

130   *partnership with Airbnb:* Kia Kokalitcheva, "Inside Airbnb's Plan to
Partner with the Real Estate Industry," *Fortune,* September 13, 2016, http:
//fortune.com/2016/09/13/airbnb-building-owners-program/.

131   *in the summer of 2016:* "Airbnb Just Hit 100 Million Guest Arrivals,"
onstage discussion with Brian Chesky and Belinda Johnson, moderated by
Andrew Nusca, at *Fortune*'s Brainstorm Tech conference, Aspen, Colorado,
uploaded on July 12, 2016, https://www.youtube.com/watch?v=7DU0kns5
MbQ&list=PLS8YLn_6PU1no6n71efLRzqS6lXAZpAuW&index=25.

132   *San Francisco and Rome:* Andrew Sheivachman, "Iceland Tourism and
the Mixed Blessings of Airbnb," *Skift,* August 19, 2016, https://skift
.com/2016/08/19/iceland-tourism-and-the-mixed-blessings-of-Airbnb/.

an already tight housing supply: Kristen V. Brown, "Airbnb Has Made It
Nearly Impossible to Find a Place to Live in This City," *Fusion,* May 24, 2016,
http://fusion.net/story/305584/airbnb-reykjavik/.

133   *"make it safe":* Tim Logan, "Can Santa Monica — or Anyplace Else — Enforce a
Ban on Short-Term Rentals?," *Los Angeles Times,* May 13, 2015, http:
//www.latimes.com/business/la-fi-0514-airbnb-santa-monica-20150514
-story.html.

134   *"everybody wins":* Bockmann, "Airbnb Is Not Taking It."

Chapter 6: Hospitality, Disrupted

138   *national landmarks:* "Holiday Inn Story," Kemmons Wilson Companies,
accessed October 9, 2016, http://kwilson.com/our-story/holiday-inns/.

139   *"The World's Innkeeper":* Victor Luckerson, "How Holiday Inn Changed

the Way We Travel," *Time*, August 1, 2012, http://business.time
.com/2012/08/01/how-holiday-inn-changed-the-way-we-travel/.

during the oil boom: "History and Heritage," Hilton Worldwide, accessed
October 9, 2016, http://hiltonworldwide.com/about/history/.

in Arlington, Virginia: "Meet Our Founders," Marriott, accessed October
9, 2016, http://www.marriott.com/culture-and-values/marriott-family
-history.mi.

140 *"a new trick":* Chip Conley, "Disruptive Hospitality: A Brief History
of Real Estate Innovation in U.S. Lodging," lecture, Urban Land
Institute Fall Meeting, October 6, 2015, https://www.youtube.com
/watch?v=XHlMnKjH50M.

hotel chain in 1987: "About," Joie de Vivre, accessed October 9, 2016,
http://www.jdvhotels.com/about/.

conference's program: Brian Chesky and Connie Moore, "Impact of the
Sharing Economy on Real Estate," Urban Land Institute Fall Meeting,
October 6, 2015, https://www.youtube.com/watch?v=03kSzmJr5c0.

told the Globe and Mail: Shane Dingman, "A Billionaire on Paper, Airbnb
Co-founder Feels 'Great Responsibility' to Do Good," *Globe and Mail*, December 17, 2015, http://www.theglobeandmail.com/report-on-business/careers
/careers-leadership/a-billionaire-on-paper-airbnb-co-founder-feels-great
-responsibility-to-do-good/article27825035/.

141 *("the rest of us missed"):* Nancy Trejos, "Study: Airbnb Poses Threat to
Hotel Industry," *USA Today*, February 2, 2016, http://www.usatoday.com
/story/travel/hotels/2016/02/02/airbnb-hotel-industry-threat-index
/79651502/.

142 *"an antidote to loneliness":* Diane Brady, "IAC/InterActiveCorp Chairman
Barry Diller's Media Industry Outlook for 2014," *Bloomberg BusinessWeek*,
November 14, 2013, http://www.bloomberg.com/news/articles/2013-11-14
/retail-expert-outlook-2014-iac-interactivecorps-barry-diller.

"or somebody's house": Gary M. Stern, "Airbnb Is a Growing Force in New York,
But Just How Many Laws Are Being Broken?", *Commercial Observer*, October
12, 2015, https://commercialobserver.com/2015/10/airbnb-is-a-growing
-force-in-new-york-but-just-how-many-laws-are-being-broken/.

143 *industry-demand growth: Lodging and Cruise — US: Lowering Our Outlook to Stable on Lower Growth Prospects in 2017,* Moody's Investors Service,
September 26, 2016, https://www.moodys.com/.

The Sharing Economy Checks In: Jamie Lane, *The Sharing Economy
Checks In: An Analysis of Airbnb in the United States*, CBRE, January 2016,
https://cbrepkfcprod.blob.core.windows.net/downloads/store/12Samples
/An_Analysis_of_Airbnb_in_the_United_States.pdf.

the most vulnerable hotels: Georgios Zervas, "The Rise of the Sharing Economy: Estimating the Impact of Airbnb on the Hotel Industry," Boston University School of Management Research Paper Series, May 7, 2015, https://pdfs.semanticscholar.org/2bb7/f0eb69a4b026bccb687 b546405247a132b77.pdf.

144 *"pace of growth continue":* Kevin May, "Airbnb Tipped to Double in Size and Begin Gradual Impact on Hotels," *Tnooz,* January 20, 2015, https://www .tnooz.com/article/airbnb-double-size-impact-hotels/.

146 *deals were announced:* Alison Griswold, "It's Time for Hotels to Really, Truly Worry about Airbnb," *Quartz,* July 12, 2016, http://qz.com/729878 /its-time-for-hotels-to-really-truly-worry-about-airbnb/.

the meetings industry: Greg Oates, "Airbnb Explains Its Strategic Move into the Meetings and Events Industry," *Skift,* June 29, 2016, https://skift .com/2016/06/29/airbnb-explains-its-peripheral-move-into-the-meetings -and-events-industry/.

from early 2015 to early 2016: "Airbnb and Peer-to-Peer Lodging: GS Survey Takeaways," Goldman Sachs Global Investment Research, February 15, 2016.

148 *"to come to it":* Susan Stellin, "Boutique Bandwagon," *New York Times,* June 3, 2008, http://www.nytimes.com/2008/06/03/business/03boutique .html.

149 *to list it:* "VRBO/HomeAway Announcement," Timeshare Users Group, June 6, 2005, http://www.tugbbs.com/forums/showthread.php?t =35409.

151 *according to Airdna:* Scott Shatford, "2015 in Review—Airbnb Data for the USA," Airdna, January 7, 2016, http://blog.airdna.com/2015-in-review -airbnb-data-for-the-usa/.

("surrounding Airbnb"): Greg Oates, "CEOs of 5 Leading Hotel Brands on Their Hopes and Fears in 2016," *Skift,* June 7, 2016, https://skift.com /2016/06/07/ceos-of-5-leading-hotel-brands-on-their-hopes-and-fears -in-2016/.

152 *the new brand:* Greg Oates, "Hyatt Hotels Launches Its New Brand: The Unbound Collection," *Skift,* March 2, 2016, https://skift.com/2016/03/02 /hyatt-hotels-launches-a-new-brand-the-unbound-collection/.

153 *"a viable business":* Craig Karmin, "Hyatt Invests in Home-Rentals Firm," *Wall Street Journal,* May 21, 2015, http://www.wsj.com/articles /hyatt-invests-in-home-rentals-firm-1432232861.

154 *"really well":* Nancy Trejos, "Choice Hotels to Compete with Airbnb for Vacation Rentals," *USA Today,* February 23, 2016, http://www.usatoday .com/story/travel/roadwarriorvoices/2016/02/23/choice-hotels-compete -airbnb-vacation-rentals/80790288/.

"to embrace it": Deanna Ting, "AccorHotels CEO: It's Foolish and Irresponsible to Fight Against the Sharing Economy," *Skift*, April 6, 2016, https://skift.com/2016/04/06/accorhotels-ceo-its-foolish-and-irresponsible-to-fight-against-the-sharing-economy/.

155 *shampoo and soap are provided:* Michelle Higgins, "Taking the Work out of Short-Term Rentals," *New York Times*, June 19, 2015, http://www.nytimes.com/2015/06/21/realestate/taking-the-work-out-of-short-term-rentals.html.

157 *"the same risk":* Christina Ohly Evans, "The Many Sides of Marriott's Arne Sorenson," *Surface*, August 5, 2016, http://www.surfacemag.com/articles/power-100-hospitality-arne-sorenson.

159 *"a city could do":* Sarah Lacy, "Fireside Chat with Airbnb CEO Brian Chesky," *PandoDaily*, YouTube video, posted January 14, 2013, https://www.youtube.com/watch?v=6yPfxcqEXhE.

160 *got some attention:* Sam Biddle, "Love Note from an Airbnb Billionaire: 'Fuck Hotels,'" *Valleywag*, April 4, 2014, http://valleywag.gawker.com/love-note-from-an-airbnb-billionaire-fuck-hotels-1558328928.

"'and then you win'": This quote is often attributed to Gandhi, but it is widely believed to have originated in a 1918 speech by labor activist Nicholas Klein, addressing the Amalgamated Clothing Workers of America: "First they ignore you. Then they ridicule you. And then they attack you and want to burn you. And then they build monuments to you. And that is what is going to happen to the Amalgamated Clothing Workers of America." Eoin O'Carroll, "Political Misquotes: The 10 Most Famous Things Never Actually Said," *Christian Science Monitor*, June 3, 2011, http://www.csmonitor.com/USA/Politics/2011/0603/Political-misquotes-The-10-most-famous-things-never-actually-said/First-they-ignore-you.-Then-they-laugh-at-you.-Then-they-attack-you.-Then-you-win.-Mohandas-Gandhi.

Chapter 7: Learning to Lead

162 *"torn up the house":* "Remarks by President Obama at an Entrepreneurship and Opportunity Event — Havana," Press release, White House Office of the Press Secretary, March 21, 2016, https://www.whitehouse.gov/the-press-office/2016/03/21/remarks-president-obama-entrepreneurship-and-opportunity-event-havana.

172 *Nobel Peace Prize within ten years:* J. P. Mangalindan, "Meet Airbnb's Hospitality Guru," *Fortune*, November 20, 2014, http://fortune.com/2014/11/20/meet-airbnb-hospitality-guru/.

173 *"sense of proportion":* Max Chafkin, "Can Airbnb Unite the World?," *Fast Company*, January 12, 2016, https://www.fastcompany.com/3054873/can-airbnb-unite-the-world.

187 *"makeups of your companies"*: Kia Kokalitcheva, "Fixing Airbnb's Discrimination Problem Is Harder than It Seems," *Fortune,* July 12, 2016, http://fortune.com/2016/07/12/airbnb-discrimination-hiring/.

188 *"business that's successful?"*: Reid Hoffman and Brian Chesky, "Blitzscaling 18: Brian Chesky on Launching Airbnb and the Challenges of Scale," Stanford University, November 30, 2015, https://www.youtube.com/watch?v=W608u6sBFpo.

Chapter 8: What's Next?

198 *had heard of Airbnb:* Julie Verhage, "One Wall Street Firm Expects Airbnb to Book a Billion Nights a Year Within a Decade," Bloomberg, April 11, 2016, http://www.bloomberg.com/news/articles/2016-04-11/one-wall-street-firm-expects-airbnb-to-book-a-billion-nights-a-year-within-a-decade; *Airbnb: Survey Says . . . It Is Having a Bigger Impact; Consumers Like It,* Goldman Sachs Global Investment Research, May 2, 2016.

208 *their own bedrooms:* Sebastian Junger, *Tribe: On Homecoming and Belonging* (New York: Twelve, 2016).

209 *(worth $3.3 billion):* "Forbes 400: The Full List of the Richest People in America, 2016," *Forbes,* October 4, 2016.

Index

AccorHotels, 154
affordable housing. *See* housing shortage
AirBed & Breakfast
  cereal gimmick, 20–23
  challenges faced by, 27
  investors, 17–18
  lite version, 12–14
  media and press coverage, 19–20
  original idea, 8–9
  redefining of, 28
  Y Combinator and, 23–29
Airbnb
  advantages, xiii
  company building, 35–38
  competition (*see* competitors)
  consumer support for, 133–37, 146–47
  contact phone number, 95–96
  core values, 36, 186–87
  diversity in, 187–88
  forces behind, 134
  home-sharing history, xvi–xvii
  initial public offering, 196–202
  investors in, 30–32
  love/hate reaction to, 10, 135–36, 203–4
  naming of, 28
  obstacles faced by, xiv–xv
  payment system for, 14
  platform, 43–47, 125
  pop culture and, xv–xvi
  product evolution, 59–60
  safety, 50–55
  scale of, 126–27
  super-users, 67–69
  user experience, 41–47
  valuation of, xii, 31, 47, 161
  workspace, 183–84
Airbnb Friendly Building Program, 130
"Airbnb law," 128
Airbnb Open, x–xi, 69, 74, 76–78, 133, 190–91
Airdna, 111, 116, 126, 131, 151
Airizu, 49–50
AllThingsD (website), 47
Americans with Disabilities Act, 98, 144
Andreessen, Marc, 34, 47, 52, 54, 161, 168,
    170, 173
Arlo, 156
Atkin, Douglas, 64, 66, 78–79, 111–12, 127,
    184, 186–87
authenticity, of travel experience, 62–63, 66,
    79, 116

Badia, Evelyn, 73–74, 122
Barcelona, 126, 127
Bassini, Rachel, 81, 99
Bazin, Sébastien, 138, 154
bed-and-breakfasts, 158
Bélo, 64–65, 191
"belong anywhere" (mission), 64–67, 78–79,
    117, 171, 172, 194, 205
Benioff, Marc, 165, 170
Benner, Katie, 65
Berlin, 126

Best Western, 152, 157, 159
Bezos, Jeff, 166, 196, 201
Blecharczyk, Nathan
  on cereal gimmick, 21
  early skepticism of, 12, 15–16, 25
  family background, 11
  fiancée, 31
  growth hacks, 38–41
  on hotel vs. Airbnb market, 140
  leadership of, xviii, 178–82
  payment system, 42–43
  site crashes, 45–46
  South by Southwest launch, 12–14
  Y Combinator and, 23–29
"bleisure," 146
Boatbound, 56
Bolton–St. Johns, 105
Botton, Alain de, 77
Bowerman, Bill, 1
brand awareness, xii, 38, 40, 58–59, 198
Brannan Street, 170
Brown, Clayton, 75–76, 132
Brown-Philpot, Stacy, 171
Bryant, Kimberly, 187
Buffett, Warren, xvi, 166–67, 172, 209
Burch, Tory, 174
Bush, George W., 60
business travel, 145–47

Campbell, Michael and Debbie, 68–69
Cap'n McCain's, 21–23
Case, Steve, 174
castles, xii, 59–60, 61
Chafkin, Max, 172–73
challenges, 80–104
  deaths and, 96–97
  EJ incident, 50–55, 80, 93
  fines and violations, 108–9
  key exchange, 75–76
  Paris Airbnb Open, 77–78
  parties, 81–90
  sexual assault incident, 90–93
Chan, Robert "Toshi," 111
Chesky, Allison, 169
Chesky, Brian
  on accidents, 97
  at Airbnb Open, 76, 77
  background of, 3–4, 11, 42–43, 169
  on corporate rentals, 115, 116–17

  on culture, 182–83
  on EJ safety crisis, 53–55
  on future directions, 193–94, 197–98
  on future regulations, 136
  on home sharing, 130
  hospitality and, 70–72
  on hosts and brand, 117
  on hotels, 140, 159
  on law enforcement, 91–92
  Los Angeles move, 4–5
  on mission of Airbnb, 172
  on NYC and politics, 105, 113, 133
  praise for, 161–62
  on public companies, 201
  on racism, 101, 102, 103
  on rebranding, 64–65, 78–79
  at Rhode Island School of Design, 1–4, 169
  on safety, 48
  San Francisco move, 6–7
  strengths, 167–69
  on Wimdu competition, 49–50
  Y Combinator and, 23–29
Chesky, Deb and Bob, 3–4, 23, 32, 166,
        168–69, 174, 208–9
Chicago, short-term rentals, 125
Choice Hotels, 153
Cianci, Buddy, 2
City Hosts, 191
Civil Rights Act, 101, 103
Clampet, Jason, 93, 141, 148–49
Clinton, Bill, 124
Clooney, George and Amal, 209
cloud computing, 45
Clouse, Dave and Lynn, 149–50
Collins, Jim, 181
commercial listings, 110–13, 114, 115
Common, 156
"community compact," 114
competitors, xi–xii, xvii
  Couchsurfing.com, 13, 14, 41, 46
  Craigslist (*see* Craigslist)
  HomeAway (*see* HomeAway)
  tourism, 112–13, 191–96
  VRBO.com, xi, xvii, 41, 87, 106, 149–50
  Wimdu (Samwer brothers), 48–50
  See also hotels
compression pricing, 144
Conair internship, 1–3
Concur, 145

conferences
  Airbnb and corporate travel, 145–46
  Berkshire Hathaway Annual Meeting,
      166–67
  Fortune's Brainstorm Tech, 103, 131, 187
  International Council of Societies of In-
      dustrial Design/Industrial Designers
      Society of America, ix, 1, 7–10
  South by Southwest, 12–14, 39
Conley, Chip
  on business travelers, 146
  on Chesky, 171
  on company goals, 117, 172
  on home-sharing history, 149
  on hospitality industry, 73, 76–77, 139–40,
      147
  in joining Airbnb, 70–72
Corden, James, 191
core values, 36, 186–87, 219
Cornell Hospitality Quarterly, 70, 166
Couchsurfing.com, xi, 13, 14, 41, 46
Craigslist, 38–39, 41, 51, 82, 100, 108, 149,
    179
crisis management, 48–50, 51–54, 77–78,
    90–93
CritBuns, 5–6, 11, 209
Crittenden, Quirtina, 100–101
Crossing the Chasm (Moore), 181
Cuba, 161–62, 185–86
Culting of Brands, The (Atkin), 64
culture, of company, 35–38, 165, 174–75,
    182–88
Cuomo, Andrew, 106–7, 108, 121, 126
Curtis, Mike, 77, 181, 184, 185
customer-service platform, 44, 52–54, 56,
    86–90, 94

Dandapani, Vijay, 115, 122
de Blasio, Bill, 113, 119
Democratic National Convention (Denver),
    15, 18–20
Diller, Barry, 142
Dimon, Jamie, x
discrimination controversy, xv, 99–104, 171
Disney, Walt, 166, 167, 197
diversity, 187–88
DogVacay, 56
Donahoe, John, 71, 165, 168
Dorsey, Jack, 165

Drybar, 152
Dubost, Lisa, 171
dukana, 56

Ecolect.net, 11
Edition, 148, 152
Eisenhower, Dwight, 139
EJ incident, 50–55, 80, 93
emergency reaction policy, 91
"entrepreneur," as term, 11
European market, 48–50
Everbooked, 75
Expedia, 142, 148, 154, 198
Experiences, 192

Federal Highway Act, 139
fee structure, 39–40
Ferriss, Tim, 93
fines and violations, 108–9, 117, 129, 134
Firestarter, 127
Five Dysfunctions of a Team, The (Lencioni),
    181
Flatbook, 156
FlipKey, 146
Friedman, Tom, 173
future directions, 130–31, 145–47, 177–79,
    188–210

Gandhi, 160, 227
Gates, Bill and Melinda, 209
Gatto, Chris, 132
Gebbia, Joe
  background of, 42–43
  culture, of company, 185
  hometown, 12
  leadership of, xviii, 174–79
  prototyping/design studio, 177–79
  refugee crisis, 209
  at Rhode Island School of Design, 1–3
  San Francisco, ix, 5
  TED talk, 172
  Y Combinator and, 23–29
Gilbert, Elizabeth, 191
Giving Pledge, 209
Glassdoor survey, 185, 186
GLō, 152
Golden, Jonathan, 184
golf party incident, 82–90
Gonzales, Emily, 89, 90

Good to Great (Collins), 181
Google, 145, 188, 195, 197
Google AdWords, 38, 179
Gore, Al, 60, 124
Gothamist, 111
Graham, Paul
    on Chesky, 171–72
    interview with, 23–24
    mentoring of Airbnb founders, 26–27,
        28–29, 164, 170–71
    on Wimdu competition, 49–50
    Y Combinator and, 15, 25–26, 59
Grandy, Nick, 36
Grazer, Brian, 191
Grove, Andy, 166
growth, xii–xiii, 38–41, 46–47, 56, 144, 162,
        198–99
guest arrivals
    August 2009, 35
    average age of, 66
    fee structure, 39–40
    growth of, xii, 41, 58–59, 180
    number of, 26–27, 199
    as term, ix–x
Guesty, 75
Gupta, Prerna, 67–68

Hantman, David, 109
Hartz, Kevin, 31
Hempel, Jessi, 201, 203–4
Hewlett, Bill, 1
High Output Management (Grove), 166
Hilton, Conrad, 139
Hilton hotels, 141–42, 152, 167
hiring, 25, 35–38, 49–50, 55, 56–57
Hoffman, Reid
    as adviser, 49–50, 164, 197
    "Blitzscaling" course, 188
    on Chesky, 167–68
    on growth, 56, 199
    as investor, 46–47
    NYC politics, 121
    on uniqueness, 62
Holder, Eric, 102, 171
Holiday Inn, origin, 138–39
home sharing, xvi–xvii, 125–26, 149
HomeAway, xvii, 41, 82, 106, 108, 133, 146,
        150, 154, 198
HonorTab, 75

Hoplamazian, Mark, 152
Horowitz, Ben, 47, 52, 164, 171
hospitality, 70–73, 115, 117, 129–31, 139–45,
        151–53, 165, 166
Host Assist platform, 76
Host Guarantee, 82, 86, 87, 88, 89, 94
hosts
    as asset and lobbyists, 111–12, 126–29
    average age of, xii–xiii, 65
    as career choice, 73–75
    from Cuba, 185–86
    data and behavior, 114–15
    defined, x
    discrimination, 99–102
    experiences offered by, 178
    fee structure and earnings, 39–40, 73, 110,
        112–13
    growth challenges, 40–41, 180
    hospitality and, 70–73, 117
    initial public offering, 199–200
    liability and legal issues, 97, 106, 109–10,
        122, 128–29
    matching with guests, 44–45
    Verified ID, 95
    See also Airbnb Open
hotels
    vs. Airbnb, 41, 62–63
    business travel, 145–47
    campaign against Airbnb, 113
    civil rights laws, 103
    compression pricing, 144
    crime and safety, 92–93, 97–98, 109
    legislation, 122
    millennials and, 152
    online travel agencies, 148
    origin of, 138–39
    short-term rentals, 153–54
housing shortage
    corporate rentals, 114, 116–17
    Denver, 18–19
    New York, 107, 123
    Reykjavik, 131–32, 203–4
    San Francisco, 126
Houston, Drew, 165
Hsieh, Tony, 36
Hugo, Victor, 137
humanity. *See* authenticity; challenges
Hyatt, 152, 153, 158
Hyers, Bill, 112, 123

idealism, 64–65, 78–79, 97, 102, 117, 171–73
Iger, Bob, 165, 196
illegal hotels, 107, 109, 114, 115, 144
initial public offering, 196–202
in-law unit, 124
Innclusive, 102
Instant Book, 102, 159
InterContinental Hotels Group, 153
International Council of Societies of Indus-
        trial Design/Industrial Designers
        Society of America (IDSA), ix, 1, 7–10
interview process, 37–38
interviewing, 165–66, 170
investors
    in 2010, 46–48
    cons of, 201
    first investors, 30–33
    initial public offering, 196–202
    meetings with, 15, 17–18
    on political challenges, 135
    safety and, 93
    warning letter to, 120
    Wilson meeting, 29
ISIS-coordinated attacks, 77–78
IStay New York, 108
Ive, Jony, 165, 166, 196

Jefferson-Jones, Jamila, 102
Jobs, Steve, 42, 166, 201
Johnson, Belinda, 55, 77, 108, 113, 171, 187
Jordan, Jeff, 52, 135, 184–85, 201
Joyce, Steve, 141, 153
Junger, Sebastian, 208

Kalanick, Travis, 165
Karim, Jawed, 31
Kat (original guest), 8, 10
Katie C., 86–88
Kay "Plush," 82–90, 95
KB Home, 204
Kelley, David, 174
key exchange, 75–76, 83, 85
Keycafe, 75–76, 132
Khan, Sadiq, 132
Kimpton, Bill, 147
King, Mark and Star, 81–82, 99
Klein, Nicholas, 227
Knife Fight (film), 124
Kokalitcheva, Kia, 130

Kondo, Marie, 77
Kong, David, 142, 144, 157, 159
Krueger, Liz, 107
Kuok, Elaine, 67–68
Kutcher, Ashton, 120, 121, 191
Kwatra, Neal, 123

Lab, The, 179
Lacy, Sarah, 5, 20, 22, 48, 159
landlords, 107–9, 111, 119–20, 129–31, 204
Lane, Jamie, 143
launches, 7–10, 12–14, 19–20
law enforcement, 86–87, 90–93, 94
Le, Tiendung, 13, 39
leadership, 161–89
    advisers and mentors, 164–65
    anomalies of, 162–63
    Blecharczyk and, 179–82
    books on, 166, 181
    Chesky's growth as CEO, 164–74
    culture, company, 182–88
    Gebbia and, 174–79
    new directions, 188–89
    overview of, 206–8
    praise for, 161–62
leases and short-term rentals, 119
LeFrak, Richard, 142
legal issues, xiv, 105–10, 116–17, 126–29,
        133–37
Lehane, Chris, 77, 122–29, 133
Lencioni, Patrick, 181
Leone, Doug, 163–64, 205
liability coverage, 89, 97
Lin, Alfred, 35, 49, 166, 168
lobbying, 105, 120
logo (Bélo), 64, 65, 191
London, 132
Lopez, Jacob, 90–92
Loughlin, Barbara, 82–90, 95
Love Home Swap, 153, 154
Luca, Michael, 99–100, 103
Lynch, Kevin, 68

Madrid incident, 90–93
Magical Trips, 191–96, 202–5
Mahaney, Mark, 198
management. *See* leadership
Maples, Mike, 19
market penetration, xii, 38, 41, 58–59, 198

marketing
  Blecharczyk and, 11, 38–39
  for Democratic National Convention,
    18–20
  hotels and, 152–53, 158
  rebranding (2013), 64–67
  at RISD, 2–3
  uniqueness of experience, 63
Marriott, 148, 154, 167
Marriott, Bill, 142
Marriott, J. W., 139
Maslow, Abraham, 70–71, 92
Mason, Andrew, 49
matching (guest and host), 44–45
McAdoo, Greg, 30–31, 35–36, 164
McCann, Pol, 74, 116, 117
McChrystal, Stanley, 173, 186
McGovern, George, xvi, 167
McNamara, Robert, 166
media and press
  Airbnb in pop culture, xv–xvi, 60–61
  at conventions (2009), 38
  Democratic National Convention coverage,
    19–20
  "Meet Carol" television ad, 112
  negative exposure, 50–55, 80–82, 86, 91
  presidential inauguration, 28
"Meet Carol" television ad, 112
Meyer, Danny, 191
Michael (original guest), 8, 10
Mildenhall, Jonathan, 64
millennials
  as Airbnb early adopters, xii, xiii, 59, 66,
    150–51, 157–58
  apartments and, 129–30
  hotel industry and, 141, 152
  as mobilizing force, 134
  New York and, 108
mission statement, xiv, xix, 36, 64–67, 78–79,
    117, 171, 172, 194, 205
Moore, Geoffrey, 181, 188
Morey, Elizabeth, 31
Morgan, Jonathan, 74–75, 116, 117, 134
Morgan Stanley, 145
Morris, Phil, 202
Moxy, 152
multifamily buildings, 129–31
Multiple Dwelling Law, 107, 115

multiunit listings, 110–13, 116–17
Murphy, Laura, 102, 171
Mushroom Dome, 60, 183
Musk, Elon, 196

Nassetta, Christopher, 141–42
neighbors, 83–85, 109, 118–19, 132–34
network effect, 40–41
New Jersey, 126
New York City, 105–37
  anti-Airbnb alliance, 109
  attorney general's report, 109–110
  Chesky's reaction to, 113
  commercial "multiunit" listings, 110–13,
    115–16
  customer base, 26–28, 106, 119, 126
  future negotiations, 133–37
  objections to short-term rentals, 118–24
  Warren verdict, 108–9
Noirbnb, 102

Oasis, 154, 155–56
Obama, Barack, 18, 28, 92, 161–62, 173–74,
    209
Obama O's, 20–23, 24, 33, 47, 174
Olympics, 156
"one host, one home" policy, 114
onefinestay, 153, 154–55, 158
online travel agencies (OTAs), 148
Open Doors policy, 102
Orbitz, 148
Orlando, 142
Oswald, Lee Harvey, xvi

Packard, Dave, 1
Paltrow, Gwyneth, 59, 60, 191
Panetta, Leon, x
Paris, Airbnb Open, 77–78
parties, 81–90
Patel, Elissa, 159, 209
Patton, George S., 166
payment system, 14, 16, 27, 39–40, 42–43
PayPal, 43
Peak (Conley), 70–71
Penz, Hans, 200
performance metrics, 72–73
photography, xvii, 27, 45, 99, 100–104, 206
Pillow, 75

politics
  Airbnb as force for change, 126–28
  Airbnb guests and, 133
  future negotiations, 133–37
  Lehane and, 125–29
  New York advertising policy, 121–22
  New York short-term rentals, 105–10
pop culture, xv–xvi, 60–61
popular listings, 60
Pressler, Paul, 196
Priceline, 148, 154, 198
pricing, as issue, 27, 99–100
privacy policy, 87, 115
product evolution, 59–60
product/market fit, 34–37
professional operators, Airbnb, 111
profit and earnings, 73, 110, 112–13, 127
property management, 129
Proposition F, 128–29
prototype operations, 177–78

Rabois, Keith, 31
racial discrimination, 99–104
"Ramen profitable," 26, 29
rankings, 16, 72–73, 162
Rasulo, Jay, 196
Rausch Street apartment, 7–8, 14, 25, 36–38,
    179, 183, 208
rebranding, 64–67, 78–79
regulations. *See* legal issues; politics
review system, 16, 72–73, 162
Reykjavik, 131–32, 203–4
Reyneri, Phil, 14
Rhode Island School of Design, 1–4, 42
Riordan, Sheila, 66–67, 132
Roberts, David, 67–68
Room Mate hotels, 158
Roomorama, 154
Rosenberg, Javier, 151
Rosenthal, Helen, 120
Rosenthal, Linda, 120, 121, 123
Royal Caribbean, 152
Rozenblatt, David, 28
Rubell, Steve, 147
Rubey, Kim, 55

Sacca, Chris, 93
safety, 50–55, 92, 97–98, 109, 118, 144

Samara, 178, 205
Samwer brothers, 48–50, 170–71
San Francisco, x, 5–8, 126, 127, 128–29,
    135, 143
Sandberg, Sheryl, 165
Santa Monica, 131
Schneiderman, Eric, 109–10, 120
Schonfeld, Erick, 19
Schrager, Ian, 147–48, 153
Schreiber, Elisa, 58, 79
Seibel, Michael, 14–18, 23, 32, 136–37,
    164
Selden, Gregory, 101, 103
Sequoia, 30–31, 35, 36
sexual assault, 90–93
Shangri-La Hotels and Resorts, 152
Shapiro, Nick, 89–90, 92, 95, 98
Share Better, 113, 114, 120, 123
sharing economy, xvii, 79, 98–104, 142, 154
Sharing Economy, The (Sundararajan), xvii,
    40
Sharp, Isadore "Issy", xvi
Sharples, Brian, 150
Shatford, Scott, 116, 131
Shaw, George Bernard, 135, 136, 159
Shepherd, Carl, 133, 150
Short, Rochelle, 202
short-term rentals
  advertising ban on, 121
  Airbnb listings, 150–51
  Berlin, 126
  fines and violations, 129
  history of, xvii, 149
  hotels and, 141, 153–54
  intimacy of, 79
  legality of, 106, 125–26
  London, 132
  new industry in, 154–58
  objections to, 118–24
  practice of, 107–8
  safety, 97
  Santa Monica, 131
Silicon Valley
  breakthroughs from, 150
  cell signal, 24
  core values, 36
  diversity in, 187–88
  mentors and advisers of, 164–65

Silicon Valley (*cont.*)
  product/market fit, 34
  workspace, 183
Sinek, Simon, 173
"slumlord law," 112
Snow White (project), 177
"snowflake" model, 127
Sonder, 156
Sorenson, Arne, 62, 157
South by Southwest, 12–14, 39
staff
  Airfamily (Airfam), 184
  communication, 166, 168, 176, 181, 183
  culture, 182
  customer service, 43–44
  diversity in, 187–88
  EJ incident, 93–94
  growth of, 35–36, 55–57
  Paris Airbnb Open, 77–78
Stanberry, Parker, 155, 156, 157
Starwood, 148
Stay Alfred, 154
Stay.com, 153
Stern, Andy, 120
Steyer, Tom, 124
Stone, Zak, 96–97
Stoppelman, Jeremy, 46
Sundararajan, Arun, xvii, 40, 66, 98–99
"Superhost" status, 73, 202
Surve, Amol, 8–10

technology, vs. regulations, 107
Teman, Ari, 81
Tenet, George, 165
Thiel, Peter, 182
"three-click rule," 41–47
3DID, 4, 5
Tier coding system, 94
time-share industry, 147
"Toshi," 111
Tosi, Laurence, 197
tourism, 112–13, 191–96
transparency, 173, 186, 197
travelers. *See* guest arrivals

Travelocity, 148
treehouses, xvii, 32, 60, 150
Tribe (Junger), 208
Trips, 191–96, 202–5
Tru, 152
trust, 99
Trust and Safety Operations, 89, 94
24/7 hotline, 92

Uber, 40–41, 152, 157, 158
Ulukaya, Hamdi, 174
Unbound Collection, 152
Urban Land Institute (ULI), 139–40
user experience, 41–47

vacation rentals, 149–50
Valdez, Jean Manuel, 84, 85
values. *See* core values; mission statement
venture capital funding. *See* investors
verification, of guests, 86
Verified ID, 83, 89, 90, 95
Vib, 152
VRBO.com, xi, xvii, 41, 87, 106, 149–50

Walt Elias Disney Enterprises (WED), 195–96
Warren, Nigel, 108–9
Washington, D.C., 28
weddings, 146
Weiner, Jeff, 165
Williams, Jumaane, 122
Wilson, Fred, 29, 32
Wilson, Kemmons, 138–39
Wimdu, 48–50
Wolff, Max, 199
Wylde, Kathy, 134

Y Combinator, 15, 23–26, 30, 34, 177
Yoshino Cedar House, 178
Youniversity Ventures, 31

Zadeh, Joe, 37, 77, 184, 186
Zimmer, John, 165
Zuckerberg, Mark, 14, 22, 49, 165, 166, 173